READERS' GUIDES TO ESSENTIAL CRITICISM

CONSULTANT EDITOR: NICOLAS TREDELL

Published

i

Jago Morrison	The Fiction of Chinua Achebe
Carl Plasa	Tony Morrison: *Beloved*
Carl Plasa	Jean Rhys: *Wide Sargasso Sea*
Nicholas Potter	Shakespeare: *Antony and Cleopatra*
Nicholas Potter	Shakespeare: *Othello*
Nicholas Potter	Shakespeare's Late Plays: *Pericles, Cymbeline, The Winter's Tale, The Tempest*
Steven Price	The Plays, Screenplays and Films of David Mamet
Andrew Radford	Victorian Sensation Fiction
Berthold Schoene–Harwood	Mary Shelley: *Frankenstein*
Nick Selby	T. S. Eliot: *The Waste Land*
Nick Selby	Herman Melville: *Moby Dick*
Nick Selby	The Poetry of Walt Whitman
David Smale	Salman Rushdie: *Midnight's Children – The Satanic Verses*
Patsy Stoneman	Emily Brontë: *Wuthering Heights*
Susie Thomas	Hanif Kureishi
Nicolas Tredell	F. Scott Fitzgerald: *The Great Gatsby*
Nicolas Tredell	Joseph Conrad: *Heart of Darkness*
Nicolas Tredell	Charles Dickens: *Great Expectations*
Nicolas Tredell	William Faulkner: *The Sound and the Fury – As I Lay Dying*
Nicolas Tredell	Shakespeare: *Macbeth*
Nicolas Tredell	The Fiction of Martin Amis
Matthew Woodcock	Shakespeare: *Henry V*
Angela Wright	Gothic Fiction

Forthcoming

Thomas Adler	Tennessee Williams: *A Streetcar Named Desire – Cat on a Hot Tin Roof*
Brian Baker	Science Fiction
Pascale Aebischer	Jacobean Drama
Annika Bautz	Jane Austen: *Sense and Sensibility – Pride and Prejudice – Emma*
Matthew Beedham	The Novels of Kazuo Ishiguro
Stephen Burn	Postmodern American Fiction
Jodi–Anne George	*Beowulf*
Sarah Haggarty & Jon Mee	William Blake: *Songs of Innocence and Experience*
Mardi Stewart	Victorian Women's Poetry
Michael Whitworth	Virginia Woolf: *Mrs Dalloway*
Gina Wisker	The Fiction of Margaret Atwood

Readers' Guides to Essential Criticism
Series Standing Order ISBN 1–4039–0108–2
(outside North America only)

You can receive future titles in this series as they are published by placing a standing order. Please contact your bookseller or, in the case of difficulty, write to us at the address below with your name and address, the title of the series and the ISBN quoted above.

Customer Services Department, Macmillan Distribution Ltd
Houndmills, Basingstoke, Hampshire RG21 6XS, England

Shakespeare's Late Plays
Pericles, Cymbeline, The Winter's Tale, The Tempest

NICHOLAS POTTER

Consultant editor: Nicolas Tredell

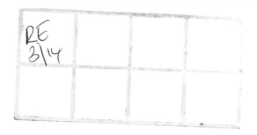

RE
3/14

palgrave
macmillan

First published 2009 by
PALGRAVE MACMILLAN

Palgrave Macmillan in the UK is an imprint of Macmillan Publishers Limited, registered in England, company number 785998, of Houndmills, Basingstoke, Hampshire RG21 6XS.

Palgrave Macmillan in the US is a division of St Martin's Press LLC, 175 Fifth Avenue, New York, NY 10010.

Palgrave Macmillan is the global academic imprint of the above companies and has companies and representatives throughout the world.

Palgrave® and Macmillan® are registered trademarks in the United States, the United Kingdom, Europe and other countries.

ISBN: 978–0–230–20049–4 hardback
ISBN: 978–0–230–20050–0 paperback

This book is printed on paper suitable for recycling and made from fully managed and sustained forest sources. Logging, pulping and manufacturing processes are expected to conform to the environmental regulations of the country of origin.

A catalogue record for this book is available from the British Library.

A catalog record for this book is available from the Library of Congress.

10 9 8 7 6 5 4 3 2 1
18 17 16 15 14 13 12 11 10 09

Printed and bound in China

To Ninon

Contents

play is discussed and that is followed by a consideration of Coppélia Kahn's remarks on the play.

CHAPTER FIVE   59

The Winter's Tale: Early Moderns

The fifth chapter is the first of three chapters on *The Winter's Tale*. The chapter opens with a discussion of comments from *Shakespeare's Last Plays* by E M W Tillyard and moves on to discuss the views of S L Bethell, F R Leavis and G Wilson Knight on the play.

CHAPTER SIX   74

The Winter's Tale: Later Moderns

The sixth chapter opens with Ernest Schanzer's reply to E M W Tillyard and then moves on to discuss Inga-Stina Ewbank's views and those of Northrop Frye, Nevill Coghill and M M Mahood.

CHAPTER SEVEN   96

The Winter's Tale: Post-moderns

The last chapter to be concerned with *The Winter's Tale* opens with Stanley Cavell's treatment of the play and moves on to Valerie Traub's remarks. Finally an essay by Graham Holderness is discussed.

CHAPTER EIGHT   113

The Tempest: Moderns

The concluding two chapters on *The Tempest* contrast a range of 'traditional' and 'modernist' accounts of the play with distinctly 'postmodern' approaches. Chapter 8 returns to F R Leavis's comments on the late plays and then considers E M W Tillyard's treatment of the play before moving on to G Wilson Knight's vision of the play. The chapter concludes with Jan Kott's comments.

CHAPTER NINE   123

The Tempest: Post-moderns

The final chapter concentrates on the closer inspection of some critical accounts informed by 'critical theory'. The chapter opens with a discussion of the essay by Francis Barker and Peter Hulme and moves on to consider Paul Brown's comments, concluding with Meredith Skura's essay.

CONCLUSION: FUTURE DIRECTIONS   145

The Conclusion contrasts the more traditional critical
approaches with the contemporary emphases and suggests
some possible lines of development for future criticism.

Note on the Text

Dates of writers, critics and other significant figures have been given in the Guide wherever possible, but in some cases these are unavailable.

Introduction

When John Heminges (died 1630) and Henry Condell (died 1627) assembled the first Folio edition of Shakespeare's dramatic works for publication in 1623 they arranged them into three sections, Comedies, Histories and Tragedies, in that order, and they placed *The Tempest* in the first section. By doing so they made a contribution to a significant tendency that they may even have begun: the tendency, that is, to see this late play as the culmination of Shakespeare's life's work in the theatre. This tendency begets another (that may have started at the same time): the tendency to regard other plays, seen as similar, as precursor works. These plays together, *Pericles* (c. 1608), *Cymbeline* (c. 1610–11), *The Winter's Tale* (c. 1611) and *The Tempest* (1611), form a loose grouping because they are not like the great comedies of the middle period (*Much Ado About Nothing* (c. 1598–9), *Twelfth Night* (c. 1601), *As You Like It* (c. 1600)) nor are they quite like the 'problem plays' (*Troilus and Cressida* (c. 1601–2), *Measure for Measure* (1604), *The Merchant of Venice* (c. 1596–7)[1]) and, though they have tragic trajectories to start with, they are unlike the great tragedies. Indeed *The Tempest* buries its tragic part entirely in a long retrospective narrative and is not properly speaking even a 'tragicomedy'.

Heminges and Condell were not particularly skilled in, or interested in, generic distinctions. Dr Samuel Johnson (1709–84) condescendingly remarks that the editors of the first Folio, who 'divided our author's works into comedies, histories and tragedies, seem not to have distinguished the three kinds by any exact or definite ideas'.[2] Later generations of editors and critics have been much more careful. The four plays addressed in this Guide are so often regarded together or in relation to one another that it is profitable to address them together and to see what such later generations of editors and critics have made of them.

THE QUESTION OF GENRE

If Heminges and Condell are to be taken to task at all, however, it is perhaps or the account that their distinctions were too few and too general. Their inclusion, for example, of *Measure for Measure* and *The Winter's Tale* in the same category, 'Comedies', as *A Midsummer Night's*

1

Dream and *Love's Labours Lost* seemed to later scholarship to be stretching the boundaries of the category to too great an extent, and to risk, thereby, losing its meaning. After all, a category so broad as to accept into itself all manner of things is of no use analytically. That perhaps is the point: to what use will these categories be put? Why need we know whether a play is a 'tragedy' or a 'comedy'?

Categories are constructed on the basis of similarities and dissimilarities between things such that things that are similar are gathered together under the rubric of a summary of, or a definition of, their similarities, and their dissimilarities are set aside as of little or no significance. Once the balance of similarity and dissimilarity starts to tip in favour of dissimilarity then a new category is required. Such is the case with those 'Comedies' (as Heminges and Condell styled them) *The Winter's Tale* and *The Tempest*: there are simply too many aspects of those plays that set them apart from plays such as *A Midsummer Night's Dream*, or *Love's Labours Lost* to allow readers, audiences and scholars to continue to regard them as comedies. The case of *Cymbeline* is even more curious: Heminges and Condell set that play amongst the 'Tragedies' and *Pericles* is in no case at all as Heminges and Condell did not include it in their First Folio edition of the plays.

In what do the significant differences consist? First it may be said that the tragic part of three of the plays is much more extended than is usual in comedies. That there is a tragic part is not unusual: the plight of the lovers in *A Midsummer's Night's Dream* could easily be drawn out to a tragic conclusion. However, the tragic part in, say, *The Winter's Tale* is drawn out throughout the first part of the play to the end of Act 3 scene 2; the tragic part in *Cymbeline* is so extended that Heminges and Condell's decision to place it amongst the Tragedies may almost be defended. Pericles's sufferings are egregiously extended and Prospero's narrative is of similarly extended suffering. Nor is it only a matter of extension: the intensity of the first part of *The Winter's Tale*, or the intensity of Pericles's suffering, raise serious questions concerning whether any restoration of equilibrium would be sufficient to offset them; to convince an audience that order and well-being had been restored.

A second significant feature of these plays is a much greater dependence on unlikely incident than is usual in plays with a serious intent, such as these plays have for much of the time been taken to be. Comedy may trifle with magic and outrageous coincidence without upsetting their balance but the closer a play approaches to 'real life' the more the illusion it is trying to sustain is endangered by the unlikely. These four plays revel in the unlikely and they do so in the thick of seriousness. Their willingness to exploit the unlikely has led to comparisons with those works usually called 'Romances' in which the magical and the unlikely abound and, indeed, the sources from which it seems Shakespeare is likely to have drawn are themselves, frequently, Romances. Finally, the plays belong to the final period of Shakespeare's creative life. The great tragedies and the great middle period comedies had been written: *Pericles* seems to come just after *Antony and Cleopatra* (1608?); it is followed by *Coriolanus* (1608?) and then by *The Winter's Tale* (1609–10?), *Cymbeline* (1610–11?) and *The Tempest* (1610–11?). After that come *Cardenio*, *All Is True* (*Henry VIII*), and *The Two Noble Kinsmen*. These belong to 1613 and were co-written with John Fletcher (1579–1625); Shakespeare's contribution to the two that have survived has never excited much critical interest. He died, according to his monument, on 23 April 1616 and was buried on 25 April 1616. It is inevitable perhaps that the plays that have excited critical interest, especially *The Winter's Tale* and *The Tempest* should be regarded as 'last' or 'late' plays.

J M Nosworthy's Arden edition of *Cymbeline* takes this idea to a logical conclusion and compares that play with Beethoven's famous 'late' string quartets and piano sonatas. The idea of 'late' works, in which an accomplished and celebrated artist turns in upon himself and reflects upon his art and his success in a mood of introverted self-absorption is a popular notion with Romantic writers and artists, and the figure of Prospero, turning his back on his art having completed a work from which he will personally benefit directly very little, easily becomes a figure of this kind of artistic self-abnegation. We cannot know what Shakespeare would have made of this characterization of his own position, but we can speculate that he found the figure an attractive one as he dramatizes it so effectively. Of course so he does Othello and Macbeth and we are not led to make such speculations in that direction so readily.

A final introductory word must be said in respect of the differences of the plays from one another. Distinguishing each play from the categories into which earlier editors thrust them is only part of the task to be completed: if there are no really significant similarities between them, or if the differences between them outweigh any similarities there may be, then there is no group; only four plays as distinct from each other as they are from other plays that can be grouped together in spite of their differences.

For they really are different, at least on a superficial view. *Pericles* is set in the Ancient world and appears to be an episodic tale of the wanderings of an unlucky man and of members of his family, which, after much anxiety, ends happily. *Cymbeline* is set in Ancient Britain and may, on that account, be compared with *King Lear* (1608?), but any such comparison ends immediately with the recognition that the king in the one has almost no part to play while the king in the other has all to play. *Cymbeline* sets a personal domestic drama against a backdrop of historical political conflict: the course of the relationship, which does not run smooth, between Posthumus and Imogen runs through two countries (three, counting Wales), and, abstracted from the Romano-British conflict against which it is set, could have been set in the same countries as those in which some of the middle comedies are set, say, Illyria or Messina. *The Winter's Tale* is set in Sicily but is so far removed in what may be called its moral world from those plays, that it bears really very little resemblance to any of them, though perhaps a comparison with *The Merchant of Venice* may be sustained for a while, as the theme of vindictiveness is shared by them both. Finally, *The Tempest*, if it is close to any play, reminds one of *A Midsummer Night's Dream* in some respects but not in others, and few plays have such a central figure as Prospero that are not tragedies, commanding, as he does, the whole of the action, quite literally.

What the plays do share is a mood. When Edward Bond (born 1934) wrote that his play *Saved* was 'almost irresponsibly optimistic' he surely knew that eyebrows would be raised.[3] Causing scandal on account of the scene in which a baby in a pram is stoned to death by a group of youths, the play seemed to many to be a picture of a hopeless and degenerate form of human existence. Yet the play's central character, Len, is seen at the end of the play, preoccupied, trying to mend a broken chair. The plays discussed in this Guide share a mood I shall call 'almost irresponsibly optimistic'.

Each play is realistic about sexual desire, realistic to the point of affronting audiences in later times, especially in Victorian times; each play is realistic about politics as well. Each play deals realistically with the terrible disappointment that attends upon our not being able to have what we want or, more dreadfully still, not wanting what we can have. Each play deliberately and extravagantly flaunts the unlikelihood of the events it narrates. In this respect the comparison with *The Merchant of Venice* really is appropriate. At the end of that play, when Antonio has been saved from his fate by the intervention of Portia, the fate that he incurred by making a foolish bargain with Shylock, insuring his ships against a pound of his own flesh, losing the ships one by one and facing his death at last, Portia, when all is at last well, turns to him to give him a letter, in which, she tells him, that he will find that the three ships that he and everyone else had thought lost are in fact now come safely to port:

■ *Portia*: You shall not know by what strange accident
   I chancèd on this letter.
   Antonio: I am dumb! □   (5.1.278–9)

It is not at all necessary that we should have, in addition to the substantial gift of the salvation of Antonio, this additional bonus. The play has already ended very well. Moreover, such an additional bonus runs the risk of stretching the audience's credibility, for all art exists on a cusp between wish-fulfilment and reality and to stray too far towards either end of this continuum is to risk disaster for we do not want an art that merely recapitulates reality and we are too wise not to know wish-fulfilment dreams for what they are and what they do. This, however, is exactly the mood of the plays considered in this Guide. They are realistic to the point of arousing disgust (Leontes's jealousy; the brothel in *Pericles*; Posthumus's infantile maunderings about Imogen; Caliban's enthusiastic endorsement of the charge that he tried to rape Miranda: 'O ho, O ho! Would't had been done! / Thou didst prevent me; I had peopled else / This isle with Calibans.' (1.2.351–3)), and they unashamedly reach out to meet and to embrace our deepest wishes that all would end well after all. If the very greatest art helps us to reconcile ourselves to the way things are, once we have accepted that we cannot change that, this art seems designed to provoke everything we have trained ourselves to put behind us as we grew up and to tell us that we can have what we want.

ART AND CRITICISM

Here we focus on the deepest problem of any literary-historical discussion. It may be clearly stated: what is Art? What is Criticism?

There are many answers and rehearsing them all serves no useful purpose: one has to pick one and take one's stand. This Guide is influenced by the careful remarks of Dr Johnson in his *Preface* to *The Works of William Shakespeare* (1765):

> ■ To works, however, of which the excellence is not absolute and definite, but gradual and comparative; to works not raised upon principles demonstrative and scientific, but appealing wholly to observation and experience, no other test can be applied than length of duration and continuance of esteem. What mankind have long possessed they have often examined and compared, and if they persist to value the possession, it is because frequent comparisons have confirmed opinion in its favour.[4] □

Criticism, in such a view, is not the application of a theory derived from some other discipline or even from the study of critical activity itself but the observation of what 'mankind have long possessed', and the possession of which 'they persist to value', and the conduct of 'frequent comparisons' through which this valuation persists. Criticism, then, is the conduct of comparison. Hence the remarks above in respect of genre will apply to a discussion of criticism: if criticism is comparison then it is the identification of similarities and dissimilarities and the judgement on the ground of these whether a work should be highly regarded or not and to which rank precisely it belongs.

Another view entirely holds that the persistence of the valuation of a work is a phenomenon to be observed and analysed from the vantage point of a theory derived from some other discipline – say, anthropology, sociology or psychology – as though one were observing the doings of men and women in quite another society than one's own. Both of these views will be encountered in the course of an examination of the critical history of these plays.

The question, what is Art, is equally discussed differently from these different positions. The first position is concerned to discover in what the excellence of an excellent work consists: the second is concerned to uncover what underlies the ascription of the value to the work, what are the consequences of the ascription for the arrangements of society, and are they beneficial to some, many or all, or contrary to the interests and aspirations of some, or of many. The first position will hold that this set of accounts will not be criticism at all: the second position will hold that accounts given from the first position are complicit with the consequences of the valuation. As is the case with any hard and fast distinction the reader will find that this useful guidance will hold in some cases and not in others: it is the fate of theories to be true in general and unprovable in particular.

SUBSEQUENT CRITICAL HISTORY

Just as literature has its history so does literary criticism: criticism has its fashions and its changes. We may reasonably say that 'Shakespeare' is always '*our* Shakespeare', or 'Shakespeare for us'. This has become even clearer as the twentieth and twenty-first centuries have seen the difference increase between the critical traditions of the preceding centuries and the critical traditions developing within these later centuries. At the same time, 'Eng. Lit.' has developed further from being 'the literature *of the English*' to becoming 'the literature *in English*'. This 'globalization' has been accompanied by 'decentralization'. Central authorities and over-arching narratives have lost their power to influence. The successes of feminism in challenging patriarchal authority are to be credited amongst several developments that have undermined these central authorities and discredited the larger narratives on which they have depended, as are the later developments such as postcolonialist theoretical positions. The American philosopher Stanley Cavell (born 1926) has identified 'scepticism' as a central theme (associated with the French philosopher René Descartes (1596–1650) especially, but, in

Cavell's analysis, a part of Shakespeare's work) and his discussion of *The Winter's Tale* is duly given prominence in this Guide. Other themes to be noted are the development of critical interest in and, sometimes, respect for plays largely ignored by the eighteenth century (*Pericles* and *Cymbeline*) and the importance of the performance tradition in respect of this development. Indeed, the changing critical appreciation of the performance tradition, moving towards acceptance and, more recently, towards significant respect, is to be noted.

The quality and the quantity of critical attention devoted to each play varies very widely and there is no reason to believe that the play to which most, and the most careful, critical attention has been devoted so far, *The Winter's Tale*, will remain in this prominent position. As scholar-critics devise ever more subtle positions they are able to discover aspects of the plays hitherto unsuspected of existence.

THE STRUCTURE OF THE GUIDE

Chapter 1 discusses eighteenth and nineteenth century criticism of all four plays together while the remainder of the Guide devotes chapters specifically to each play. This is because the significant development in the critical industry is very much a twentieth and twenty-first century phenomenon but also because these centuries have seen the most significant and extended critical attention paid to these plays. The eighteenth century did not think that these plays asked for much in the way of comment compared to the great tragedies, for example. Comments by Dr Johnson, whose opinion of *Cymbeline* in particular was not high but whose estimate of *The Winter's Tale* and *The Tempest* was not very much higher, are included, and the much more favourable views of William Hazlitt (1778–1830) and Samuel Taylor Coleridge (1772–1834). It is too sweeping a generalization to say that the Augustan Dr Johnson disapproves while the Romantics, Hazlitt and Coleridge, approve, but there is some truth in the view. Even so, the level of the comments devoted even by so discerning and imaginative a critic as Coleridge do not reach the heights he reached when considering the tragedies and even some of the lesser plays. The chapter concludes with two Victorians and a Modern: Edward Dowden (1843–1913) whose *Shakspere: His Mind and Art* (1875) was a bestseller in its day and Sir Arthur Quiller-Couch (1863–1944: he wrote popular fiction as 'Q') are the Victorians, and Giles Lytton Strachey (1880–1932: famous for his *Eminent Victorians* (1918), a series of unflattering portraits of such key figures as Florence Nightingale (1820–1910) and General Gordon (1833–85: 'Gordon of Khartoum') in which Strachey shows the feet of clay of which each was possessed) the Modern. Strachey was a founder member of the 'Bloomsbury Group', associated with Leonard Woolf (1880–1969) and Virginia Woolf (1879–1970) and E M Forster (1879–1970) and, therefore, part of the embryonic 'Modernist' movement in the UK at the beginning of the twentieth century.

Chapter 2 devotes its attention exclusively to *Pericles*, a play almost universally believed to be a collaboration in which Shakespeare participated (perhaps the reason Heminges and Condell did not include the play in their 1623 Folio), beginning with Suzanne Gossett's 2004 Arden edition of the play and then considering the 1965 Arden edition of F D Hoeniger (born 1921). Chapters 3 and 4 discuss *Cymbeline*, focusing on Martin Butler's 2005 Cambridge edition of that play and contrasting this edition with J M Nosworthy's 1955 Arden edition. Increasingly, editions of the plays have become important starting points for any critical examination of the reception history of the plays as a review of that history has become a standard feature of the introductions to these editions and those editions have been growing in both length and in the comprehensiveness of their coverage. Neither play has provoked anything significant in critical discussion, though two essays on *Cymbeline* gave rise to some interesting comment by F R Leavis (1895–1978) on the Late Plays, which is introduced in Chapter 4 though that comment primarily concerns *The Winter's Tale* and *The Tempest* and is dealt with at greater length in Chapter 5 and again in Chapter 8. Chapter 4 addresses the Introduction to J M Nosworthy's 1955 Arden edition of *Cymbeline*, and concludes with a discussion of Jodi Mikalachki's essay on 'The Masculine Romance of Roman Britain: *Cymbeline* and Early Modern English Nationalism (1995)' and Coppélia Kahn's remarks on the play in her *Roman Shakespeare: Warriors, Wounds and Women* (1997). Mikalachki and Kahn are 'historicist' critics, interested in exploring the relationship between the works and their context in early modern England, with particular reference to the construction of gender identities.

Chapter 5 considers some early twentieth century critical accounts of *The Winter's Tale*, starting with discussion from *Shakespeare's Last Plays* by E M W Tillyard (1889–1962) and moving on to S L Bethell's ingenious argument that the apparent clumsiness of the dramatic technique of the play is in fact deliberate. G Wilson Knight (1897–1985) offers a highly theorized approach, claiming that 'Shakespeare offers nothing greater in tragic psychology, humour, pastoral, romance'. If anything unites these critics it is an unspoken shared set of assumptions about critical practice: that it depends upon interpretations that the critic can, or at least does, assume will be available to the reader. They do not defend their views as much as present them. Chapter 6 opens with a discussion of Ernest Schanzer's reply to E M W Tillyard and takes into account the interesting discussion by Inga-Stina Ewbank (1932–2004) of the figure of Time in the play and the attempt of Northrop Frye (1912–91) to place the work in a context of Graeco-Roman mythology. Nevill Coghill (1899–1980) draws attention to points of stagecraft and M M Mahood traces some of the key words in the play. In the work of these critics it is already becoming clear that some promotion, if not defence, of one's views, in terms of historical scholarship or theoretical ingenuity, is becoming necessary and the appeal to common 'feeling' is less marked if it is there at all. Indeed, Coghill, to take his essay as an instance, seems at times to be arguing against common assumptions and for common sense. At the same time the ideal reader, the 'common playgoer', as it might be, or the 'common reader', is being displaced by a more erudite figure altogether. The earlier chapters of this Guide have already acknowledged the degree of scholarship that is now displayed in the best editions of the plays: the development visible in this chapter has come to fruition.

Chapter 7 brings the discussion of *The Winter's Tale* up to the end of the twentieth century, looking at Graham Holderness's essay and Stanley Cavell's treatment of the play and finally at Valerie Traub's remarks in her *Desire and Anxiety: Circulations of Sexuality in Shakespearean Drama* (1992). Chapter 8 returns to F R Leavis's comments on the late plays to bring together the key early twentieth century responses to *The Tempest*: Tillyard's and G Wilson Knight's. Jan Kott (1914–2001) in *Shakespeare: Our Contemporary* (1965) offers a nightmare vision of the play that acts as a transition between the early twentieth century and the later twentieth century. Giles Lytton Strachey's comments on the violence and cruelty that can be seen alongside the pastoral tranquillity of the late plays come to mind as Kott lays bare the infrastructure, as he sees it, of these romances. It is not fanciful to say that the development of the twentieth century has been away from visions of tranquillity and towards visions of violence and cruelty. Cavell's identification of scepticism is relevant: it may be that the century has taken its revenge on the confidence in knowledge (especially in scientific and technological developments) that so marks the eighteenth and the nineteenth centuries.

Lastly, Chapter 9 concentrates on the closer inspection of some critical accounts informed by 'critical theory'. Francis Barker (1952–99) and Peter Hulme deconstruct *The Tempest* with the aid of advanced theoretical positions and Paul Brown explores the historical context in detail, again with the aid of some of the theories that have emerged in the last half of the twentieth century, while Meredith Skura's essay rounds off the discussion by taking on both Barker and Hulme and

Paul Brown to offer a psychoanalytical perspective where they have offered a more politically oriented perspective. The Guide concludes with a hope that the ingenuity displayed by critics of various persuasions will not tire and that these plays, that have provoked so much interesting discussion so far, will continue to do so.

CHAPTER ONE

The Late Plays: Critical Opinion in the Eighteenth and Nineteenth Centuries

It is convenient to collect together in this opening chapter some of the key comments made during nearly two centuries of the early reception of the late plays. This is because there is not very much of it that is of sufficient significance to attract notice for this Guide but also because the transition from the nineteenth to the twentieth centuries sees the rapid growth of a veritable industry in literary criticism. It will be useful to recollect some of the comments considered in this opening chapter from time to time, to remind the reader of the whole scope of literary and critical development from Shakespeare's time to our own. The chapter begins with Dr Samuel Johnson and then discusses the views of two Romantic critics, William Hazlitt and Samuel Taylor Coleridge, before moving on to a great Victorian, Edward Dowden and then concluding with Giles Lytton Strachey and Sir Arthur Quiller-Couch. The last two are particularly significant critics: the first a pioneer Modernist and the second a resolute defender of 'traditional' English values, as he saw himself, in literature and in life. Once this background has been firmly established it will be possible to strike out and consider each play individually in subsequent chapters, starting with *Pericles* and considering each in the order in which it first appeared, through *Cymbeline* and *The Winter's Tale* to *The Tempest*.

SAMUEL JOHNSON

Dr Samuel Johnson may be taken as indicative of, if not exactly instrumental in bringing about, a change of considerable significance in the English cultural tradition: the parting of the ways between the theatrical and the critical traditions; the assimilation of Shakespeare's plays to a world of letters. When Johnson stated in his *Preface* to *The Plays of William Shakespeare* (1765) that 'a play read affects the mind like a play acted'[1] he was preparing the way for an approach that would come to see theatrical performance as an option, and an inferior one at that, rather than as the only occasion on which the play's potential could be realized.

Pericles not having yet enjoyed its introduction to the canon by the 1790 edition of Edmond Malone (1741–1812), Johnson's comments are on *The Tempest, The Winter's Tale* and *Cymbeline*. He is unimpressed by *The Tempest*, regarding the regularity of the plot as 'an accidental effect of the story, not intended or regarded by our author'.[2] There is an interesting note on 'the system of enchantment' that he believes that Shakespeare is employing in *The Tempest* and which, he says, 'supplied all the marvellous found in the romances of the Middle Ages'.[3] Johnson explains the relationship of enchanter to the enchanted spirits, which are the spirits of the fallen, some of whom have gone to hell but others of which have been consigned to various locations on, beneath or just above the earth, according to the degree of their guiltiness. Interestingly he comments that the existence of the art of enchantment 'was, I am afraid, believed very seriously',[4] a reminder of just how barbarous Johnson and his age thought that of Shakespeare. He ends this note, 'Of these trifles enough'.[5] His summary observation rather damns with faint praise:

■ But whatever might be Shakespeare's intention in forming or adopting this plot, he has made it instrumental to the production of many characters, diversified with boundless invention, and preserved with profound skill in nature, extensive knowledge of opinions, and accurate observation of life. In a single drama are here exhibited princes, courtiers, and sailors, all speaking in their real characters. There is the agency of airy spirits and of an earthly goblin. The operation of magic, the tumults of a storm, the adventures of a desert island, the native effusion of untaught affection, the punishment of guilt, and the final happiness of their pair for whom our passions and reason are equally interested.[6] □

Of *The Winter's Tale* he has even less to say:

■ This play, as Dr Warburton justly observes, is, with all its absurdities, very entertaining. The character of Autolycus is very naturally conceived and strongly represented.[7] □

Cymbeline attracts a fuller comment only to clarify and deepen what now seems to be a settled distaste for the more fanciful comedies:

■ This play has many just sentiments, some natural dialogues, and some pleasing scenes, but they are obtained at the expense of much incongruity.

To remark the folly of the fiction, the absurdity of the conduct, the confusion of the names and manners of different times, and the impossibility of the events in any system of life, were to waste criticism upon unresisting imbecility, upon faults too evident for detection, and too gross for aggravation.[8] □

WILLIAM HAZLITT

William Hazlitt regarded *Pericles* as a 'Doubtful Play'. He rejects the affirmation of August von Schlegel (1767–1845) (that Schlegel says he got from John Dryden (1631–1700)) that it is Shakespeare's work, rejecting, as he does this, Edmond Malone's conclusion that it was Shakespeare's. Hazlitt gives his reasons for rejecting *Pericles* in a passage in which he explains why he believes that *Titus Andronicus* (1593?) is also not by Shakespeare. His grounds for rejecting *Titus Andronicus* are that 'the grammatical construction is constantly false and mixed up with vulgar abbreviations, a fault that never occurs in any of his genuine plays' and he goes on to say that the same fault 'and the halting measure of the verse' lead him to the conclusion that *Pericles* is not wholly Shakespeare's work either, leaving aside 'the far-fetched and complicated absurdity of the story'. There are hints of Shakespeare to be found and 'The most memorable idea in it is in Marina's speech, where she compares the world to 'a lasting storm, hurrying her from her friends' [Scene 15, 65–72]'.[9]

Of *Cymbeline* he thought very highly: '*Cymbeline* is one of the most delightful of Shakespear's [Hazlitt's preferred spelling] historical plays' He goes on to confuse his opening definition of the play as 'historical', or perhaps to enhance it, by calling it a 'dramatic romance'. Hazlitt is particularly complimentary on the question of plot: 'The most straggling and seemingly casual incidents are contrived in such a manner as to lead at last to the most complete development of the catastrophe'.[10]

Such a view involves a view of the plot of course and for Hazlitt the point of the plot, its climax, is 'the answer of Iachimo to the question of Imogen respecting the obtaining of the ring from Posthumus'.[11] Consequently Imogen is the point of much of Hazlitt's commendation of the play. He allows himself a brief excursion into 'the female character' that strikes the contemporary reader as old-fashioned and seriously undermines the relevance of his remarks for that reader:

■ No one ever hit the true perfection of the female character, the sense of weakness leaning on the strength of its affections for support, so well as Shakespear – no one ever so well painted natural tenderness free from affectation and disguise – no one else ever shewed how delicacy and timidity, when driven to extremity, grow romantic and extravagant; for the romance of his heroines (in which they abound) is only an excess of the habitual prejudices of their sex, scrupulous of being false to their vows, truant to their affections, and taught by the force of feeling when to forego the forms of propriety for the essence of it.[12] □

The stress on 'natural tenderness' in women and the stress on Imogen account perhaps for Hazlitt's view of the pathos of the play: 'A certain tender gloom overspreads the whole'.[13] He returns interestingly to the plot later on. He is talking about character and says 'in the casting of the different parts, and their relation to one another, there is an affinity and harmony, like what we may observe in the gradations of colour in a picture'.[14]

This is an important observation and a useful one. Hazlitt explains further:

■ In *Cymbeline*, for instance, the principal interest arises out of the unalterable fidelity of Imogen to her husband under the most trying circumstances. Now the other parts of the picture are filled up with subordinate examples of the same feeling, variously modified by different situations, and applied to the purposes of virtue or vice. □

He discusses this observation interestingly, introducing another, related metaphor; that of music:

■ The effect of this coincidence is rather felt than observed; and as the impression exists unconsciously in the mind of the reader, so it probably arose in the same manner in the mind of the author, not from design, but from the force of natural association, a particular train of thought suggesting different inflections of the same predominant feeling, melting into, and strengthening one another, like chords in music.[15] □

Imogen disappears from much of the last part of *Cymbeline* and cannot focus the play quite as much as Hazlitt and others wanted her to, but if she is seen as an element in a picture, as he does here, rather than a character in a certain kind of drama, then the part she plays is sufficiently prominent, especially if it is seen as part of a group of characters/ actions displaying a common sentiment in different 'shades', or chords, to use Hazlitt's images.

The main points of interest in his essay on *The Tempest* concern the characters of Caliban and Ariel. Hazlitt describes the character of Caliban thus: 'It is the essence of grossness, but there is not a particle of vulgarity in it'. It is important to Hazlitt to make the distinction between coarseness and vulgarity in respect of the character of

Caliban. Caliban's character is natural, not to be confused with the character of someone formed by complex societies:

■ Vulgarity is not natural coarseness, but conventional coarseness, learnt from others, contrary to, or without an entire conformity of natural power and disposition; as fashion is the common-place affectation of what is elegant and refined without any feeling of the essence of it.[16] □

Ariel is the counterpart to Caliban:

■ Shakespear has, as it were by design, drawn off from Caliban the elements of whatever is ethereal and refined, to compound them in the unearthly mould of Ariel. Nothing was ever more finely conceived than this contrast between the material and the spiritual, the gross and the delicate. Ariel is imaginary power, the swiftness of thought personified.[17] □

He makes the somewhat odd observation that 'The Tempest is a finer play than the Midsummer Night's Dream, which has sometimes been compared with it; but it is not so fine a poem. There are a greater number of beautiful passages in the latter'.[18]

Hazlitt quotes two 'beautiful' passages from The Tempest with very little comment and none of it revealing and he concludes with Gonzalo's speech, in which he says 'Shakespear has anticipated nearly all the arguments on the Utopian schemes of modern philosophy'.[19]

On The Winter's Tale he is perceptive on Shakespeare's skill as a dramatist of tortured expressions of complex feeling. On Leontes he is impressive:

■ Here [1.2.269–80] Leontes is confounded with his passion, and does not know which way to turn himself, to give words to the anguish, rage, and apprehension, which tug at his breast. It is only as he is worked up into a clearer conviction of his wrongs by insisting on the grounds of his unjust suspicion to Camillo, who irritates him by his opposition, that he bursts out into the following vehement strain of bitter indignation: yet even here his passion staggers, and is as it were oppressed with its own intensity [1.2.286–98].[20] □

He judges the play 'one of the best-acting of our author's plays' and recalls a pleasant evening in the theatre watching it.[21] He affects astonishment that Alexander Pope (1688–1744) should have doubted it were Shakespeare's, arguing that the blemishes Pope pointed to 'do not prove it not to be Shakespear's; for he was as likely to fall into them as any body; but we do not know any body but himself who could produce the beauties'.[22] It is a good argument and will do for Pericles if we are as convinced of the beauties of that play as we may be of those of *The Winter's Tale*.

SAMUEL TAYLOR COLERIDGE

Coleridge's observations upon *Pericles* are not extensive, though he claims that Shakespeare's 'alteration' (of a play Coleridge believes was written 'a hundred years earlier') 'may be recognized even to half a line',[23] and his remarks upon *Cymbeline* are not much more extensive, though he makes an interesting distinction between the plays drawing on history in different ways:

> ■ In the purely historical plays, the history *informs* the plot; in the mixed it *directs* it; in the rest, as *Macbeth*, *Hamlet*, *Cymbeline*, *Lear*, it subserves it.[24] □

He contrasts Leonatus from *Cymbeline* and Leontes of *The Winter's Tale* with Othello as part of his proof that Othello has not any jealousy 'properly so called' in his character,[25] though otherwise has little to say about the later play either. His comments on *The Tempest* are much fuller. They appear in a set of notes for a lecture and a report on that lecture and, perhaps typically of Coleridge, are as remarkable for their general observations as for their particular.

His concern in general is to distinguish the idea of a copy from the idea of an imitation, attacking notions of unity of time and place as associated with the French critical and dramatic tradition, and which he characterizes as the belief that 'a perfect delusion is to be aimed at' and which he contrasts with Dr Johnson's insistence, as Coleridge describes it, that 'supposes the auditors throughout as in the full and positive reflective knowledge of the contrary' and he concludes: 'In evincing the impossibility of delusion, he makes no sufficient allowance for an intermediate state, which we distinguish by the term illusion'.[26]

Coleridge appeals to the dreaming state as an illustration. He contrasts the effect of art and the effect of sleep by pointing out that in sleep the images are more vivid as other stimulation is absent; secondly that sensations, 'and with these the emotions and passions which they counterfeit', cause dream-images, 'while in our waking hours our emotions are the effect of the images presented to us', and lastly that in sleep 'we pass at once by a sudden collapse into this suspension of will and the comparative power' whereas by the art 'of the poet and the actors, and with the consent and positive aidance of our own will' we are brought to the point of illusion: 'we *choose* to be deceived'.[27]

Coleridge is opposed to the tendency to 'complicated scenery and decoration of modern times':

■ For the principal and only genuine excitement ought to come from within – from the moved and sympathetic imagination; whereas, where so much is addressed to the external senses of seeing and hearing the spiritual vision is apt to languish, and the attraction from without will withdraw the mind from the proper and legitimate interest which is intended to spring from within.[28] □

Setting large general projects on one side Coleridge spends most of his time considering Miranda, Ariel and Caliban. His praise of Miranda is of the 'simplicity and tenderness of her character'.[29] Coleridge says that Ariel 'has in everything the airy tint which gives the name' and Caliban 'is all earth, all condensed and gross in feelings and images'.[30] Coleridge notes interestingly that Ariel and Miranda never appear together, he surmises, 'lest the natural and human of the one and the supernatural of the other should tend to neutralize each other'.[31] This is perceptive: the two characters are similar enough to weaken each other in each other's presence on stage.

The Shakespearean scholar J P Collier (1789–1883) reported a lecture given at some time in 1811–12 by Coleridge which takes up some of the same themes but develops others more clearly. His discussion of the conversation between the Boatswain and Gonzalo is a masterful example of how Coleridge's theories really did arise from and feed into his critical perceptions. Coleridge distinguishes famously between mechanic and organic regularity, in the former of which the copy matches the mould exactly and in the latter of which 'there is a law which all the parts obey, conforming themselves to the outward symbols and manifestations of the outward principles'.[32] Coleridge says that in the scene he is discussing Shakespeare 'makes men on stage what they are in nature, in a moment transports himself into the very being of each personage and, instead of cutting out artificial puppets, he brings before us the men themselves'.[33] 'The vital writer' is contrasted with 'ordinary dramatists' who 'combine their ideas by association or logical affinity'.[34]

An 'ordinary dramatist' would have Gonzalo react to the Boatswain's lack of respect by 'moralizing or saying something connected with the Boatswain's language' but Shakespeare shows us:

■ The true sailor with his contempt of danger, and the old counsellor with his high feeling, who, instead of condescending to notice the words just addressed to him, turns off, meditating with himself and drawing some comfort to his own mind by trifling with the ill expression of the Boatswain's face, founding upon it a hope of safety.[35] □

It is not an interpretation every reader or actor might choose but it will fit the words and make interesting sense of them and that is all that is required. It is typical of Coleridge to do as a critic what he has said 'the vital writer' does in his plays: to seek out the most interesting sense he can find. This is what good criticism should do.

He proceeds to take the reader through the play's second scene with really insightful comments on how that remarkable scene works, picking up details and showing how with these Shakespeare keeps alive the dramatic interest in what is otherwise a long narrative with little change on stage, the equivalent of what on television is sometimes called 'talking heads'. Coleridge shows how Miranda is revealed to us through this scene in brilliant touches, such as the 'four or five women (1.2.46–7)' she remembers as having attended her:

> ■ This is exquisite! In general, our remembrances of early life arise from vivid colours, especially if we have seen them in motion: for instance, persons when grown up will remember a bright green door seen when they were quite young; but Miranda, who was somewhat older, recollected four or five women who tended her. She might know men from her father, and her remembrance of the past might be worn out by the present object, but women she only knew by herself, by the contemplation of her own figure in the fountain, and she recalled to her mind what had been. It was not that she had seen such and such grandees, or such and such peeresses, but she remembered to have seen something like the reflection of herself: it was not herself, and it brought back to her mind what she had seen most like herself.[36] □

Marvellous speculation in pursuit of his vision of what he believes Shakespeare has created, 'the exquisite feelings of a female brought up in a desert but with all the advantages of education, all that could be communicated by a wise and affectionate father'.[37]

Shakespeare is, in Coleridge's view, possessed of a 'picturesque power' only rivalled by John Milton (1608–74) and Dante Alighieri (1265–1321). What he means by this is the power of creating a picture in the mind, not the power of making a picture for the eye. He calls this elaboration of detailed pictures for the eye 'dutchification', a derogatory aside directed against the Dutch school of realism in painting. Coleridge comments: 'The presence of genius is not shown in elaborating a picture [...] The power of poetry is, by a single word perhaps, to instil that energy into the mind which compels the imagination to produce the picture'.[38] He cites

> ■   One midnight
> Fated to th' purpose, did Antonio open

> The gates of Milan; and, i'th' dead of darkness,
> The ministers for th' purpose hurried thence
> Me, and thy crying self. □   (1.2.128–32)

And he expands: 'by introducing a single happy epithet, "crying", in the last line, a complete picture is presented to the mind, and in the production of such pictures the power of genius consists'.[39]

EDWARD DOWDEN AND LYTTON STRACHEY

Two other powerful opinions must be noted before leaving the nineteenth century: Edward Dowden and Lytton Strachey. This chapter will close with a consideration of Sir Arthur Quiller-Couch's views but before that point is reached a contrast may be drawn between the high Victorianism of Dowden and the proto-Modernism of Strachey to set up a context for Q's ideas, which really do bridge the ages represented so clearly in the contrast between them by Dowden and Strachey. Dowden is the great biographical critic, searching in the work for the man:

■ Serenity Shakspere [Dowden's preferred spelling] did attain. Once again before the end, his mirth is bright and tender. When in some Warwickshire field, one breezy morning, as the daffodil began to peer, the poet conceived his Autolycus, there might seem to be almost a return of the lightheartedness of youth. But the same play that contains Autolycus contains the grave and noble figure of Hermione. From its elevation and calm Shakspere's heart can pass into the simple merriment of rustic festivity; he can enjoy the open-mouthed happiness of country clowns; he is delighted by the gay defiance of order and honesty which Autolycus, most charming of rogues, professes; he is touched and exquisitely thrilled by the pure and vivid joy of Perdita among her flowers. Now that Shakspere is almost a householder he enters most into the pleasures of truantship. And in like manner it is when he is most grave that he can smile most brightly, most tenderly.[40] □

Dowden is telling a life story and sees the last plays as a culminating achievement of personal equanimity after the turbulence of the tragedies and the problem plays. It may be urged that the determination to see the life as an achieved harmony colours excessively the view he takes of the plays. Lytton Strachey is less taken in:

■ Shakespeare, we are confidently told, passed in a moment to tranquillity and joy, to blue skies, to young ladies, and to general forgiveness [...] This is a pretty picture, but is it true? □

'Modern critics', Strachey argues,

> ■ Seem to have entirely forgotten that there is another side to the medal; and they have omitted to point out that these plays contain a series of portraits of peculiar infamy, whose wickedness finds expression in language of extraordinary force. Coming fresh from their pages to the pages of *Cymbeline*, *The Winter's Tale* and *The Tempest*, one is astonished and perplexed. How is it possible to fit into their scheme of roses and maidens that 'Italian fiend', the 'yellow Iachimo', or Cloten, 'that thing too bad for bad report', or the 'crafty devil', his mother, or Leontes, or Caliban, or Trinculo? □

He concludes:

> ■ Nowhere, indeed, is Shakespeare's violence of expression more constantly displayed than in the 'gentle utterances' of his last period.[41] □

This is not just a determination to turn things the seamy side out: Strachey is not wrong about the ferocity of the depiction of violence in these plays: Leontes's brutal fury is only one example. The plays cannot fairly be depicted as a sunny Warwickshire morning in springtime without serious distortion, and this must have a reflection for those determined to look for the life in the art. However what Strachey is overlooking is the final balance achieved by the dramatic action for ultimately it is not the jealous madness that dominates and it is not Iachimo's devilry or Cloten's stupid brutishness, or, more notably still, Antiochus's incestuous passion with which the audience is left, but the strikingly deliberate achievements of reconciliation, reunion, restoration and re-balancing that, though we might question whether they are fully successfully realized, are clearly the intended outcomes of the action. However, just as Dowden had invented a plot for Shakespeare's life realized through his drama, so does Strachey, seeing a growing disgust, exemplified by *Timon of Athens*, punctuated by 'visions of beauty and loveliness' but nonetheless revealing a man whose powers are visibly declining. Strachey contrasts the characters of *Measure for Measure* and *Antony and Cleopatra* with those of the late romances, asking 'but who, one would like to know, has ever met Miranda, or become acquainted with Prince Florizel of Bohemia?'[42] He makes the useful point that the Queen's speech in *Cymbeline* will eventually reach the ears of Octavius:

> ■ It comes with something of a shock to remember that this medley of poetry, bombast, and myth will eventually reach the ears of no other person than the Octavius of *Antony and Cleopatra* and the contrast is the

more remarkable when one recalls the brilliant scene of negotiation and diplomacy in the latter play, which passes between Octavius, Maecenas, and Agrippa on the one side, and Antony and Enobarbus on the other, and results in the reconciliation of the rivals and the marriage of Antony and Octavia.[43] □

He points to the apparent weaknesses of the plays, 'the singular carelessness with which great parts of them were obviously written' and to the lifelessness of some of the characters, saying: 'one is, it cannot be denied, often bored, and occasionally irritated, by Polixenes and Camillo and Sebastian and Gonzalo and Belarius; these personages have not even the life of ghosts; they are hardly more than speaking names',[44] and he concludes:

■ It is difficult to resist the conclusion that he was getting bored himself. Bored with people, bored with real life, bored with drama, bored, in fact, with everything except poetry and poetical dreams. He is no longer interested, one often feels, in what happens, or who says what, so long as he can find place for a faultless lyric, or a new, unimagined rhythmical effect, or a grand and mystic speech. [...] Is it not thus, then, that we should imagine him in the last years of his life? Half enchanted by visions of beauty and loveliness, and half bored to death; on the one side inspired by a soaring fancy to the singing of ethereal songs, and on the other urged by a general disgust to burst occasionally through his torpor into bitter and violent speech?[45] □

SIR ARTHUR QUILLER-COUCH ('Q')

Sir Arthur Quiller-Couch advances a careful argument over several chapters, that Shakespeare may well expose a 'loss of mastery [...] an apparent relaxation of grip on the means to the end' but that this, far from a 'slackening of mental power', may show that 'having triumphed in the possible, this magnificent workman has grown discontented with it and started out to conquer the impossible, or the all but impossible'.[46]

Q draws our attention explicitly to comparisons with earlier triumphs:

■ In taking the theme of *Othello* and altering it into *Cymbeline*, as in taking the theme of *Lear* and altering it into *The Winter's Tale*, he failed, if we will; but he failed by no intellectual decline; rather, in the attempt to achieve something better, certainly more difficult, possibly beyond reach.[47] □

Q's point is that the themes with which Shakespeare is working (the themes transformed of his earlier plays, as Q has just suggested, is the best way to think of this) now demand a new dramatic form:

■ He is occupied with forgiveness, reconciliation, the adjustment, under Heaven, of goodwill among men. But injured women do not forgive in a moment; stubborn enemies are not reconciled in a moment; old wrongs, hates, injuries, jealousies, suspicions are not allayed, redeemed, repented of, forgiven in a moment and made to acquiesce. The process is naturally a slow one: and its perfect success in actual life, if it is to be a durable appeasement and not a flash in the pan, usually depends upon its overmastering a real – often a prolonged and obstinate, but always a real, resistance. To forgive our enemies, to yield to conviction against our will – I put it to the reader as a man of the world that, if their results are to be of any worth, these are *naturally* slow processes. To be sure, the final act of surrender, the stroke of return upon ourselves, may happen in a moment: but the *meaning* lies all in the continued sap and siege.[48] □

But Shakespeare was, had been, a dramatist and the drama is not obviously suited to presenting long drawn-out processes such as Q is describing here. Could it be made so suited? It is Q's contention that this was the challenge Shakespeare set himself. Q attempts no Dowdenesque speculations about why Shakespeare might have turned his attention to this powerful theme but it may be noticed that Q himself adopts an interesting formula, 'the adjustment, under Heaven, of goodwill among men'. If the tragedies contain an element of the drama of offence against Heaven, and not just against men and women, that element is wholly absent from the late plays. The late plays may much more properly be called 'humanist' than the great tragedies and even than the comedies because in the comedies men and women are at their ease whereas in these plays they are not. In this respect they are like the 'problem plays', like *Measure for Measure*, or *Troilus and Cressida*, but whereas the actions of those plays do not take time, the actions of these do. The form that will lend itself most readily to what Shakespeare attempts here (if Q is right) is the novel. Q gives the theme a special flavour:

■ Throughout his last years it would seem that Shakespeare's mind brooded over one hope, now playing with it and anon fiercely asserting it – 'The sins of the fathers shall *not* be visited on the children!' Perdita shall be happy with Florizel, Miranda with Ferdinand [...] Imogen shall be clasped by her lord and her brothers inherit a kingdom. She shall have her happy hour with her father, as Marina with Pericles, as Cordelia with Lear – and not die of it, as poor Cordelia died.[49] □

The popular success of *Pericles* invites us to consider another factor: the public's demand for novelty. Q concedes that the impulse to create anew might not only have been Shakespeare's ambition but also a necessity imposed upon him, and successfully addressed, as the great popularity of *Pericles* would seem to confirm. In his defence of *Cymbeline* Q advances an argument much hedged about with quotation that is worth summarizing. There are truths, he says, of fact, of emotion and of imagination. They are separate but often found together. Addressing Johnson's condemnation of 'the folly of the fiction' Q asks himself, as he owns he can read *Cymbeline* with delight, whether he is 'a very great fool (a point I reserve) or Shakespeare is a magical workman so to charm me into forgetting faults so flagrant'.[50] Note 'forgetting': not failing altogether to be aware of them.

Q's theory is both generous and persuasive. It is generous because it looks for more creditable reasons for a change of direction than does Lytton Strachey's theory and it is persuasive because it is not only hopefully looking but also successfully finding evidence that, when pieced together, both explains the apparent reduction in the skills of stagecraft and offers a view of a changed outlook, or a change of emphasis within the outlook, that makes the experimentation more than just experiment for experiment's sake. If Q is right then these plays look again at reconciliation and renewal as the middle period comedies (*Twelfth Night*, *As You Like It*) had done but with the extended experience of the tragedies behind them. That makes them more fanciful but, paradoxically enough, more realistic as well. What Lytton Strachey sees as their violence becomes, in the light of Q's theory, their realism.

The next chapter will open the consideration of the plays individually, with a discussion of the critical history of the play Ben Jonson called 'mouldy', perhaps because it was so strikingly successful and had put his own efforts in the shade: *Pericles*.

CHAPTER TWO

Pericles

The student of *Pericles* may be forgiven if he or she becomes confused. Before any question of judgement can arise the question is thrust forward, did Shakespeare write all of it? Quickly following upon the heels of that question is another: if he did not, then who wrote the rest? Here we are into the territory admirably mapped out for us by Suzanne Gossett in her 2004 Arden edition of the play. However we must beware from the beginning: scholarship is not united on the initial question. Doreen DelVecchio and Antony Hammond in their 1998 Cambridge edition claim that the play is all Shakespeare's, while Gary Taylor and Stanley Wells much earlier, in the Oxford edition of 1984, accept the view that it is a collaboration and set out briefly and clearly their reasons for believing that it is. Suzanne Gossett spells out these reasons in more detail.

SUZANNE GOSSETT

After we have attended to all these discussions we are left with something that is not any other work from which it has been claimed the play has been derived, to which it shows some resemblance, or which has exerted some influence over its composition, nor is it no more than a collection of parts of some or any of these things: it is *Pericles*, and it was very probably a collaborative effort between George Wilkins (died 1618) and William Shakespeare and it has been (as Suzanne Gossett insists) popular in its own time, enthusiastically revived at the Restoration (as part of a general revival of English theatre at that time), and, though it was neglected theatrically from 1660 (perhaps 1661) until the quite heavily cut Sadler's Wells production of Samuel Phelps (1804–78) in 1854, more recently revived again. Suzanne Gossett notes that Nugent Monck (1877–1958) produced the play at Norwich in 1929 and revived that production at Stratford in 1947. Tony Richardson (1928–91) produced it at Stratford again in 1958 and thereafter it was produced at Stratford with some regularity: in 1969 by Terry Hands (born 1941); in 1979 by Ron

Daniels (born 1942); in 1989 by David Thacker (born 1950). During the eighteenth century editorial interest gave the work currency at least in scholarly discussions. Suzanne Gossett's claim that the lack of critical interest is 'based less on thoughtful aesthetic judgement than on immutable textual conditions'[1] is the point: the producers she cites managed to put on something they thought would do and editors at least since Malone have managed to cobble something together for readers to read but the poor quality of the text means that much has to be emended and supplied. The dangers of this are obvious. Gossett cites Valerie Wayne's approval of the Oxford edition's inclusion of a passage from the novella by George Wilkins on which it is argued that the play was at least partly based that strengthens Marina's character and comments:

> ■ Certainly the text can be improved; rejecting the entire tradition of editorial clarification will appear perverse. However, editors' commitments, including their sexual politics, have varied radically over the centuries and need not reflect those of the authors.[2] □

She continues:

> ■ Since these commitments have potentially differing textual consequences and, in a postmodern age of fragmentation, any all-encompassing hegemonic explanation for the state of the text will be greeted with scepticism, more limited intervention seems appropriate and is followed in this edition.[3] □

Her position is a reasonable one. There must be some intervention or else the text makes little sense: intervention, however, will import the views of those intervening. We may choose to rewrite the play to suit our views, in which case we must be always aware that that is what we are considering: we may leave the play to speak for itself and find that it is almost inarticulate. It certainly cannot be performed without intervention so what we may more or less safely regard as its primary function, as a script for performance, cannot be discharged unless it is emended and added to: that leaves its consideration as a work that may be read, on which the business of criticism must concentrate. Gossett goes further than this, though, describing the situation in which she finds herself as a 'postmodern age of fragmentation', in which 'any all-encompassing hegemonic explanation for the state of the text will be greeted with scepticism'. This needs some comment. The term 'postmodern' has had much currency though its meaning has not always been unambiguous and its history not always undisputed. The *Oxford English Dictionary* currently, and helpfully, defines the word as meaning 'subsequent to, or coming later than, that which is modern', which has the dubious advantage of referring the inquirer back to the also difficult word 'modern'. That this is an advantage is clear upon the reflection that there is no need immediately to find a core definition for 'postmodern': anything that succeeds what can be defined as 'modern' comes under its rubric. This is important because many who march under the banner of the postmodern deny that any core definition of anything is possible without distortion, without importing ideas that are ungrounded, without deceit and illusion. Gossett glances in passing but the significance of the glance should not escape the reader: the postmodern condition is one in which attempts to offer general theories of any kind are regarded with suspicion. Jean-Francois Lyotard's essay, *The Postmodern Condition: A Report on Knowledge* (Manchester: Manchester University Press, 1984) contains the famous remark: 'simplifying to the extreme I define postmodern as incredulity towards metanarratives (p. xxiv)'. A 'metanarrative' is anything that attempts to gather together into larger bundles the little stories, the narratives, we ordinarily work with as accounts of our lives. It may be argued that it is primarily theories of history, such as Marxism, against which Lyotard has a particular animus but the view has encouraged a widespread sceptical attitude towards explanations of all kinds. It should not be imagined that the narrative is held up as epistemologically more reliable than the metanarrative though: the exposure of the metanarrative undermines the narrative as well. There is no element that has resulted from the process of fragmentation that has survived, epistemologically speaking. From the point of view of the study of Shakespeare, and, in particular, of *Pericles*, it must be said that there is little to be certain about right from the outset. Both as text and in performance *Pericles* has manifested itself in very widely varied forms.

The productions that Gossett describes appear to be designed to appeal to a range of appetites. Tony Richardson's 1958 production took place entirely on a ship and was marked by an insistent metatheatricality [a form of theatre in which the audience is constantly reminded that it is the audience in a theatre watching a play], the sailors, for example, calling out 'Come on Gower' until he made his appearance, and, where Monck had toned down some of the play's aspects, Richardson expurgated little. More radically still, Toby Robertson's 1973 Prospect Theatre production in Edinburgh was set in a transvestite brothel. Exactly what draws postmodern attention to the play is what makes its most elusive quality vulnerable to postmodern practice. Gossett quotes Alexis Greene reviewing Brian Kulick's 1998 New York Shakespeare Festival production:

■ All at once there is a king, Pericles, who suffers like Lear, and a recognition scene between father and daughter that rivals the intensity of

Lear and Cordelia. But emotion and poetry go begging, for the director has prepared neither actors nor audience for their appearance.[4] □

This is crucial, for what is at stake in the full critical consideration of any work is not what it means but how successfully it has brought off what we say it is trying to bring off. Greene here believes that *Pericles* is trying to bring off what *King Lear* brings off and he further believes that the play's attempts to do so have been thwarted by the director in this case. However what Greene says about Kulick's production could be said, and has been said, about the last plays in general. What is developed in the great works is sketched and presented in the last plays. This of course is particularly tricky in the case of *Pericles* as the text is so unreliable but the point in principle is just the same: could any amount of work we might imagine Shakespeare doing redeem a play so packed with various incident and bewildering changes of locale, each with a highly specialized set of political or social considerations or even both?

G. Wilson Knight's interpretation of all four romances is that they are spiritual myths, opening with tempests or other emblems of the bewildered state of human existence, moving through adventures to restoration and reunion. Northrop Frye referred to them as 'secular scriptures', parallel to the Christian story. Hoeniger argued that the changes Shakespeare made to his sources (especially to the Apollonius story) were informed by the 'traditional Christian view of the sufferings man must undergo before he can penetrate to a full vision of God's goodness and purpose for him'.[5] He refers to Gower's promise to show that 'those in trouble's reign, / Losing a mite, a mountain gain (Scene 5, 7–8)' and points out that his explanation of the play's purpose, 'The purchase is to make men glorious (Scene 1, 9)' calls to mind 'the basic aim of the Legends of the Saints and of the miracle plays derived from them'.[6] Robert Miola argues that Miranda's protection of herself in the brothel scenes is a 'miniature Christian miracle play'.[7] There are elements in the play that can be assimilated to Christian typology (and it is worth pointing out that Christian thinking frequently interpreted the Old Testament scriptures in Christian terms, as showing prototypes of what was to come and arguing therefore that what had come fulfilled the prophecies contained within the prototypes). Suzanne Gossett points out that the play's locations are associated with the early church (Ephesus, Tarsus, Antioch) and indeed it may be that the association with St Paul (Tarsus) is meant to recall the Damascene journey and the powerful image of conversion that offers. Richard Halpern suggests that the play is 'heavy with futurity, specifically with the arrival of a messiah who will convert its decadent cities into the landscape of redemption'.[8] Maurice Hunt invokes the Acts of the Apostles as an 'intertext' for the play, with Pericles 'both the donor and recipient of proto-Christian virtues so that his divine election for a secularly redemptive dream vision seems appropriate'.[9]

However other critics, favouring a different context, see things differently. Jonathan Bate (born 1958) sees Marina as Proserpina, carried off into an underworld to emerge as 'a bringer of new life, regenerating her father and eliciting a language of fertility'.[10] Suzanne Gossett holds that 'Diana is the presiding deity of *Pericles*',[11] pointing out that, apart from several references to her, 'the wondrous climax of the play occurs in Diana's temple, one of the wonders of the ancient world'.[12] Citing Caroline Bicks,[13] Gossett argues that 'focusing on Diana alters the male-centred Christian reading of *Pericles*'.[14] She reminds us that St Paul was given a hostile reception by adherents of Diana at Ephesus but she acknowledges that this story has a happy Christian ending as his conversion of Ephesus was one of the great triumphs of the early church. Gossett suggests that:

■ These discrepant, conflicting associations of Diana – chastity and fertility, Marian submissiveness and Amazonian independence, restrained virgin and wild 'great mother' – are played out in the religious implications and the complex sexuality that run throughout *Pericles*.[15] □

Thaisa's decision to enter the service of Diana has been subjected to close analysis. Gossett sees it as a metaphor for the purification or 'churching' of women after childbirth that derived from Judaism, that had been preserved in Catholic tradition, and that was transformed by Protestantism, she claims, into 'a "celebration", which removed power from the priesthood and transferred it to the mother and her midwife, "gossips" and supporters'. She refers to Janet Adelman's contention that, psychoanalytically speaking, Pericles is freed from contamination by women's sexuality to restore family and state, and to Caroline Bicks's view that the complex derivation of the ritual churching of women, and its association with Ephesus by the play, makes the whole matter ambiguous, and Thaisa's return 'both authorized and illicit'.[16] F Elizabeth Hart sees the matter as one of legitimization by the maternal body of the body politic.[17] As the action may be so variously interpreted it is difficult to conclude whether any interpretation commands assent more readily than any other. Gossett's summary of the play's satisfactions attempts to find some unifying principle and finds it in paradox. The play begins with incest and ends with either extreme sexual inactivity (Thaisa is a celibate servant of Diana and Pericles is sexually abstinent) or 'unsanctioned sexual availability', figured in the brothel scenes. The play 'can only conclude when in effect it begins over again, with a father sustained emotionally rather than sexually by his daughter'. Gossett suggests that the paradoxes both of

Christianity and of Diana somehow authorize this 'chaste fertility' and she concludes that the play has a satisfying ending because everything can be 'accounted for within the different ideological systems the play incorporates – secular romance, religious providentialism, even the arbitrary variations of Fortune'.[18] Not every set of incompatible ideas is strictly speaking paradoxical and there may be some doubt here whether Gossett has entirely managed to bring under one rule all the different views to which she refers. Moving on, Gossett considers political readings of the play, making an astute point: 'both *Henry V* and *Pericles* are about the formation of a monarch'.[19] Simon Palfrey has argued that the hero's name would have evoked, at least for the educated audience member, the Athenian statesman [c. 495–429 bc] renowned for 'public speeches about patriotism and the civic life', and that the play directs attention towards 'the fundamental cruces of humanist political enquiry'.[20] Richard Halpern suggests that the fishermen's complaints may allude to the 'spate of enclosures in Warwickshire that led to the Midlands Uprising [1607–8]'.[21] Gossett points out that the brothel scenes had topical relevance, especially as the 'stews' were just outside the Globe.[22] Steven Mullaney believes that the play is an attempt to make of drama 'a purely aesthetic phenomenon, free from history and from historical determination' in its suppression of some of the more realistic elements in the narrative on which it draws, such as Apollonius's keeping up his life as a merchant rather than withdrawing as Pericles does, and Tharsia's telling stories in the brothel, rather than 'preaching' as Marina does.[23] However, as Gossett has already pointed out, there are contemporary allusions in the play (or there may be) and as she further points out: '*Cymbeline, The Winter's Tale* and *The Tempest*, are all concerned with the nature of royal authority and with the future of the state; all conclude with careful arrangements for political alliances'.[24] Gossett enters a word of warning after noting David Bergeron's contention that the family in the late plays is the family of King James (1566–1625; King of England, 1603–25), on the grounds that there are certain similarities: 'It is unclear how much more contemporary resonance we may legitimately find in the play's intermittent political events and conversations'.[25] Having warned, Gossett speculates. The plot line (2.4), which is taken up by *The Tempest* incidentally, of a palace revolution threatened and a substitute's growing power, all because of an absent monarch, is undeveloped and this 'may result from damage during the play's transmission, but it could be the product of contemporary discretion'.[26] James's absences from court and his favouring young men were being remarked upon by 1608; 'if anything in the play were marked for removal by the Master of Revels or self-censored in anticipation of objections, such material would be high on the list'.[27] Constance Jordan and Simon Palfrey see reflections of debates concerning the King's prerogative: Jordan argues that the plays demonstrate 'the precarious state of rulers who by their absence invite anarchy or by their presumption threaten tyranny' but this is not a truly distinctive theme, and her suggestion that Pericles's career parallels James's even to the creation of Great Britain is fanciful.[28] Gossett makes the important point that attempts to tease out the political implications of the play tend to find justification from incidents and speeches from the later plays, such as *the Tempest* or *Cymbeline*, and she agrees with Palfrey's conclusion that 'romance's engagement with history is too much taken with things primal and irrational to be contained by either the end or the eloquence [...] of a "vir civilis" ['good citizen']'.[29] Philip Edwards suggested that Pericles's voyages are metaphorical but Richard Halpern argues that the locations represent current concerns, a 'decaying Hellenistic world' revealed as Pericles travels round the Mediterranean.[30] Linda McJannet points out that these travels occur at the time of the 'late Hellenistic kingdoms that governed and fought over Alexander's empire'.[31] Difficulties with precise location (including a puzzle over 'Pentapolis') can be solved at least to partial satisfaction, she holds. Constance Relihan believes that the play's scenes are set in locations associated with 'liminal' cultures and are 'part of an ambiguously imagined Asia Minor which resonates with Turkish and "reprobate" cultures as well as with Christian and classical traditions', arguing that *Pericles* collapses history in a sense, confusing contemporary responses to a Mediterranean dominated by the Ottoman empire with historical associations reaching back through Christianization to a 'classical' world (itself as complicated as the world it became, as Palfrey and McJannet have shown).[32]

Psychological, or psychoanalytical, readings abound: not surprisingly perhaps in a play that starts with incest. Barber contrasts the late with the early comedies, arguing that as the latter dealt with 'freeing sexuality from the ties of family' the late romances 'deal with freeing family ties from the threat of sexual degradation'.[33] The first of these statements is questionable: the comedies end with marriages after a dangerous confusion of desires and fruitless stalemates. The power of desire is certainly a theme in three of the late romances though its place in *Pericles* is less prominent in fact than it is in *The Winter's Tale* or in *The Tempest*. Ruth Nevo boldly suggests that 'the progress of the play is the haunting of Pericles by the Antiochus in himself, the incest fear which he must repress and from which he must flee',[34] though the evidence for this view is hard to find. Gossett reminds us that:

■ The play's obsession with kinship relations should, however, be read not only through a universalizing, transhistorical psychoanalytic lens but also within the specifically early modern cultural construction of the family. In a time of high mortality and rapid remarriage, similar words may describe or suggest incestuous relationships and those created by multiple matrimonies between those of varying ages and marital histories.[35] □

Obsession is perhaps a bit overly emphatic and there is no ambiguity about Antiochus and his daughter, though Hamlet's misgivings may come to mind, as well as the union of Henry VIII [1491–1547; King of England 1509–47] with his deceased brother Arthur's wife, Catherine of Aragon [1485–1536]. Gossett later states: 'Fear of incest broods over *Pericles*',[36] echoing Ruth Nevo. Gossett's evidence is that the words spoken by Pericles when he encounters Marina recall his love for Thaisa. It is, however, by no means a given thing that Pericles' words suggest that he is attracted to Marina. In fact an equally reasonable approach would be to say that he is expressing a wistful sense of the irony of a situation in which he finds himself reminded of someone to whom he was very much attracted by someone to whom he is not attracted at all. The two riddles, again ironically, mirror each another: the one vicious, the other virtuous, the echo of Dante's 'figlia del tuo figlio [daughter of your son]' and other pious acts of recognition of the same fundamental Christian truth being available to audiences at the time and afterwards.

This is not to say that we should not look for the patterns we hope to find and argue for them when we think we have found them: that is exactly what we must do and Gossett's arguments are not weak or wrong-headed but they are not exclusive of other interpretations. To speak, as she does, of 'the play's obsession with violated family relationships'[37] is to over-egg the pudding, though it is true that there are many damaged family relationships in the play, as there are in others as well, nor is it the play's only concern, nor is incest really reducible to the category 'violated family relationships' if it is to share that category with Dionyza's 'murderous favouritism for her child' that really does not 'parallel incest' as Gossett says it does. The effort to find an informing general category is tortuous.

■ Dionyza's accusation – 'you not your child well loving' – charges her husband with the reverse of preference, failure to love or to love enough. Her phrase comprehensively summarizes the form family failure takes in *Pericles*. Not loving a child, whether foster or natural, is the unforgivable action on which the play is built and to which it repeatedly returns. Seen in this light, incest is the extreme variant, the point at which loving too well is the same as not loving well enough. The issue unites both halves of the play and is handled by both authors.[38] □

Gossett lists images of parents and children, drawing together, oddly, the image of mothers ready to eat their children in famished Tarsus with

Bolt's telling his employers that 'the younger sort' listened to his extolling Marina's charms 'as they would have hearkened to their fathers' testament [Scene 16, 94–5]'. There is surely a gap between Bolt's cynical ironic identification of himself as 'father' to potential paying clients and Cleon's, possibly rhetorical, insistence that mothers were ready to eat their 'those little darlings whom they loved [Scene 4, 44]'. 'But their accumulated coldness and hostility characterize the world of *Pericles'*.[39] It is tempting to say that they simply do not, any more than images of warmth and propriety between parents and children do. There simply is no clear preponderance. A final 'thematic focus' considered in Gossett's long introductory essay is 'appropriate exchange and gift giving'. The terminology that appears in this study of 'exchange' in the play effectively de-familiarizes the 'early modern' world. From the beginning:

■ Moral and political worth is symbolized by and measured through generosity. Gift giving is inflected by gender and class but, in the ethical and allegorical registers that tend to predominate in romance, it is always a sign of virtue.[40] □

Stripped of its specialist terminology the point does not surprise and its summary version is only striking because it is not: 'In *Pericles* the good are the generous'.[41] Anthropology earns our interest because it shows us that what we thought different is similar and what we thought similar is different. To show us that what we thought similar is similar raises no eyebrows. If we de-familiarize the early modern world in order to re-familiarize it we are going around the houses and we do not need to. Another piece of assimilation takes place when it is asserted that:

■ The extreme of evil, taking from children, is carried to the furthest point in the incipient cannibalism of the Tarsian mothers. The incest in which Antiochus consumes his daughter is metaphorically another form of cannibalism.[42] □

The riddle in fact says 'I am no viper, yet I feed / On mother's flesh which did me breed [Scene 1, 107–8]', not on children's, and it is not spoken by Antiochus but by his daughter (so it is supposed by the form of the riddle). We cannot simply reduce one thing to another in this manner: we must discriminate or we shall lose our way. Cannibalism is not incest is not taking from children. They are three wicked things, not one, unless one wants to or is prepared to reduce everything to 'evil' in which case one play is much like another. The case is clarified by a later remark:

■ Throughout *Pericles* the blurring of gifts and trade is particularly evident where women are involved. The fishermen joke that 'what a man cannot get [Oxford adds: 'himself,'] he may lawfully deal for with his wife's soul [Scene 5, 155–7]'.[43] □

But the 'joke' depends on a scrupulously maintained set of distinctions or there would be no joke at all. It is not a 'blurring' but a sharpening of distinction that happens throughout the play as similar things are sharply defined against one another, such as the relationship between Pericles and Marina and Thaisa and that between Antiochus and his daughter and that between Cleon, Dionyza and their daughter. Finally Gossett adumbrates a 'biographical' approach. Quoting Simon Palfrey's view that though romance is a 'politically restless genre' the plays themselves end in 'a courtly and royalist haven'.[44] Gossett states: 'the end of *Pericles* is experienced as a fantasy of wish-fulfilment, a promise of impossible restoration'.[45] This is surely right. Having invoked Coppélia Kahn's view that Pericles 'becomes a father anew, accepting his fatherhood as his identity, and stops trying vainly to deny his mortality'[46] and Ruth Nevo's assertion that he seeks 'a symbolic personage representing the mother, lost and forbidden'[47] as well as C L Barber's view that by the end of the play the characters have become 'virtually sacred figures',[48] she recalls Richard Wheeler's insistence that Shakespeare's own 'life record' should contribute to our discussions.[49] Gossett concludes 'It is hard not to see the long mourning embodied in Pericles' almost catatonic withdrawal after his second blow, the loss of Marina, as a projection of Shakespeare's own feelings and experiences'.[50] However it is only 'hard not to see' what we have come to accept: if one is disinclined to see these things they are not there to see.

F D HOENIGER

F D Hoeniger's Arden (1965) comes to similar conclusions as regards the play's composition, indebtedness to and relationships with other texts. On the play's early history he remarks:

■ Jonson's bitter comment, 'a mouldy play', merely betrays the enthusiastic reception *Pericles* received on the Jacobean and early Caroline public stage. But during the ensuing centuries criticism with few exceptions was either negative or confined itself to the non-aesthetic problems of the play. And just as recent decades have witnessed a remarkable revival of interest in the play on the stage, so literary critics have suddenly begun to proclaim its artistic power. I shall follow the trend in this introduction, though perhaps the play's neglect by so many previous generations should put us on our guard, lest it be only the preoccupations and tastes peculiar to our own time, and not any broader, more objective literary judgement, that attracts us to *Pericles*.[51] □

This is just, and an important reminder. We should not conclude that literary judgement can be nothing but 'subjective' merely because we know that it cannot be 'objective'. Hoeniger quotes the Shakespearean scholar George Steevens (1736–1800) writing to Edmond Malone:

■ *Pericles*, in short, is little more than a string of adventures so numerous, so inartificially [with so little art] crouded together, and so far removed from probability, that, in my private judgement, I must acquit even the irregular and lawless Shakespeare of having constructed the fabrick of the drama, though he has certainly bestowed some decoration on its parts.[52] □

Steevens's view arises from his distinction between 'decoration' (he says earlier, and reasonably, that 'a few flowery lines may here and there be strewn on the surface of a dramatick piece; but these have little power to impregnate the general mass') and 'character' (he says that 'Character, on the contrary, must be designed at the author's outset'). Pope, Johnson and the Shakespearean scholar Edward Capell (1713–81) omitted *Pericles* from the canon; Malone established its place (it had not been included by Heminges and Condell though later folios had included it) and nineteenth-century editors followed Malone's lead. Victorian moral views made the brothel-scenes and, to that extent, Marina, a difficulty for them; the views of the first Professor of English Literature at Oxford, Sir Walter Raleigh (1861–1922) in his book for the English Men of Letters series, *Shakespeare* (1907), were an advance:

■ *Measure for Measure* and the fourth act of *Pericles* (which no pen but his could have written), prove Shakespeare's acquaintance with the darker side of the life of the town, as it might be seen in Pickt-hatch or the Bankside. He does not fear to expose the purest of his heroines to the breath of this infection; their virtue is not ignorance; 'It is in the grain: [Oxford has: 'Tis in the grain, sir,'] 'twill endure wind and weather [*Twelfth Night*, 1.5.227]'. In nothing is he more himself than in the little care he takes to provide shelter for the most delicate characters of English fiction.[53] □

J G McManaway describes the mood of the play particularly well, referring to 'a semi-hypnotic state in which everything is experienced as in a dream'[54] and J Arthos has argued that the play's structural unity is more extensive than had previously been allowed.[55] J M S Tomkins and M D H Parker maintained that the play has profound underlying themes.[56] Hoeniger contends that *Pericles* anticipates the other Romances as he calls them, distinguishing them from the romantic comedies:

> ■ They share with them romantic plots with happy endings and certain similar conventions, but there the likeness ends. What sets the last plays apart from Shakespeare's romantic comedies is primarily their kind of action, or rather actions. *Pericles, Cymbeline*, and *The Winter's Tale* are characterized by a peculiar kind of double plot which is found nowhere else in Shakespeare, and hardly anywhere else in Elizabethan drama. Two actions are intertwined, the protagonists of which are a king or a duke and his daughter or, as in *Cymbeline*, his several children and son-in-law. While the relative weight given to these two actions and to the dangers, struggles, and misfortunes sustained by their protagonists differs appreciably among the three plays, in each the fortunes of a king take a sudden happy turn near the end, as a result of some action of the children which brings about, though without their foreknowledge, their recognition and restoration to their father. In none of these plays, therefore, does a love-action, as so often in Shakespeare's earlier comedies, constitute the main issue.[57] □

Following from this the emphasis, Hoeniger says, is on family rather than love-relationship and the handling of time is much freer. Interestingly, Hoeniger classes *The Merchant of Venice* with the 'romantic comedies' as he has called them, which I should not do, and this reveals the risks of categorization (which are that not everyone will agree that the plays are rightly placed in the categories, let alone whether they have agreed to those categories in the first place). By stressing the distinction, secondly, Hoeniger risks losing the sense of connectedness, the sense in which both sets of plays are about restoration, about the correction of imbalance arising due to impetuous or otherwise mistaken action on somebody's part, ranging from Antonio's impetuousness in taking up Shylock's offer to Orsino's insistence (in *Twelfth Night*) that he is in love with Olivia. Hoeniger points to the sense in some at least of these plays 'of man as the plaything of Fortune or of the gods'.[58] Hoeniger rightly says that the 'realistic spirit' of the romantic comedies is replaced by an appeal to 'our sense of wonder'.[59] A useful section on the problem of construction (pp. lxxiv–lxxix) focuses on the undramatic nature of the story compared with those plays (*Othello* is a prime example) that have a central conflict as a focus and sustain the tension of that conflict over the course of the play. The manner of characterization he describes as 'romantic biography', presenting characters over a period of years rather than revealed through the unfolding of a central action. This brings us face-to-face with the key problem of *Pericles*: its central character is a man of blameless, even unimpeachable, moral worth. He will not, therefore, fit into the pattern of fall and redemption into which, for example, G Wilson Knight attempts to fit him.[60] Kenneth Muir's argument that Thaisa breaks a vow to Diana by marrying Pericles[61] is likewise dismissed as foreign to the spirit of the play which Hoeniger, sharply I think, likens to the mood of the Book of Job. We must recognize that we are watching the sufferings of an innocent man, which of course Aristotle had dismissed as a ground for tragedy, arguing that it led us only to dismay. Hoeniger points to a different path, referring us to Wilson Knight's commentary on Thaisa's beautiful characterization of Pericles at Scene 21, 126–8:

■ Yet thou dost look
Like Patience gazing on kings' graves, and smiling
Extremity out of act. □

Wilson Knight describes this as:

■ A serene assurance corresponding to St Paul's certainty in 'O death, where is thy sting?'[62] □

Hoeniger's comment is wisely restrained:

■ When Wilson Knight relates Pericles' words to those of St Paul, he points, I believe, to a very real analogy. For while the series of Pericles' adventures is not to be regarded as a deliberate allegory of the life of the good Christian, it can hardly help reminding us of it.[63] □

Of course the reader will observe that, on the contrary, it cannot be credited with reminding us of anything: we may be reminded by it but in that case we are the active party and, if we choose not to be reminded or are in fact not reminded, that is an end of the matter. Hoeniger's closing remarks are stimulating. He suggests that the play 'is curiously, and I think significantly, like the vernacular religious drama in its later, more developed, and less rigid forms, especially the Saint's play'.[64]

Much of what he has to say about construction is rehearsed here and is indeed one of two main planks of the platform he is building, the other being the character of Pericles. The play is indeed built up 'out of a large number of loosely related episodes', and the play is treated more 'as a "pageant" [...] than a work of highly concentrated action around a central conflict' and of course the idea of 'romantic biography' as the mode of presentation of character as against action building up an unfolding character fits with the manner of the Saint's play very well.[65] Structural parallels apart, the Legends of the Saints are explicit in their intent and Gower does indeed say at the outset that his intent is to 'sing a song' that has often been sung before, of which 'The purchase is to make men glorious'. An interesting reflection is that one line of descent, that usually insisted upon, for the 'tragi-comedy' is the Italianate pastoral play and its popularity on the continent. Hoeniger's argument points to an English line of descent and that will consort nicely with the subject matter of Shakespeare's next attempt in the vein, *Cymbeline* and it is to that play that the next two chapters are devoted: firstly, to the change in temperament between the Victorians and the Moderns and then to a further change in temperament, or at least in critical perspective, between the Moderns and the Postmoderns.

CHAPTER THREE

Cymbeline (1)

Cymbeline has had its supporters, as has been noticed in Chapter 1. Hazlitt, as we have seen, thought it 'one of the most delightful of Shakespear's historical plays',[1] and Sir Arthur Quiller-Couch felt able to like the play in spite of what Dr Johnson called 'the folly of the fiction', though he went on to say that he thought that this proved that 'Shakespeare is a magical workman so to charm me into forgetting faults so flagrant'.[2] Algernon Charles Swinburne (1837–1909), never a great critic it must be said, but a Victorian, stated: 'The play of plays, which is *Cymbeline*, remains alone to receive the last salute of all my love. I think, as far as I can tell, I may say I have always loved this one beyond all other children of Shakespeare'.[3] There is little evidence in these remarks that the Victorians thought Shakespeare's powers were failing in *Cymbeline*. Lytton Strachey did think that of course but he was a self-consciously Modern figure.

F R LEAVIS

F R Leavis comments in a careful though brief discussion of *Cymbeline* and *The Winter's Tale* on what he calls 'the Bradley-Archer' assumptions he detects in Strachey's essay.[4] 'Bradley' is A C Bradley (1851–1935), whose account of *Othello* Leavis attacked in 'Diabolic Intellect and the Noble Hero, Or, The Sentimentalist's *Othello*' (Leavis (1984), pp. 136–59) and 'Archer' is William Archer (1856–1924), whose *The Old Drama and the New* (1923) was reviewed by T S Eliot in 'Four Elizabethan Dramatists', reprinted in *Selected Essays* (1932 and 1951). Eliot and Leavis thought that Archer and Bradley had an old-fashioned view of poetic drama as 'drama in verse', and that they were blind to the 'development of theme by imagery and symbolism', as Leavis puts it in the essay under present consideration.[5] In this essay Leavis is commenting on critics who have written positively of *Cymbeline* and whose high estimate of that play he wishes to dispute. He argues that they have over-estimated the play because they have gone too far in their reaction against the 'Bradley-Archer' school of critical approach to drama and have looked for, and found, a significance in *Cymbeline* that he believes is not there to be found.

Leavis contrasts *Cymbeline* and *The Winter's Tale* to the detriment of the earlier play. *Cymbeline*, he argues, 'contains a great variety of life and interest', and 'out of the interplay of contrasting themes and modes we have an effect as (to fall back on the usefully corrective analogy) of an odd and distinctive music'.[6] However, the play, regarded as a composition, a work comprising elements organized according to certain principles, lacks what he calls a 'commanding significance' according to which every element of the play is chosen and disposed. He speaks of this principle of organization coming from 'a deep centre' and he concludes: '*Cymbeline* is not a great work of art of the order of *The Winter's Tale*'.[7]

The problem that many later commentators have with this language is what seems to them to be its portentousness and its vagueness. It is possible to put the ideas in other language but there is a loss. To speak of 'meaning' rather than 'significance' is to invite a kind of interpretation akin to translation – working out the meaning; to speak of the centre of a pattern or even of the work is to invite the misunderstanding that a spatial metaphor is being invoked. To say that the centre is 'deep' is to suggest that it is not to be found by formal analysis; to talk of 'significance' is to avoid attempted definition. The problem is that such critical formulations run the risk of appearing to be being deliberately evasive, speaking a language restricted to disciples. This is unfair to Leavis but arises from an understandable frustration.

His analysis of the weaknesses of the play in the respect he has pointed to elaborates to some useful extent the full meaning of the phrases he employs:

> ■ The romantic theme remains merely romantic. The reunions, resurrections and reconciliations of the close belong to the order of imagination in which 'they all lived happily ever after'. Cloten and the Queen are the wicked characters, stepmother and son, of the fairy-tale: they don't strike us as the expression of an adult intuition of evil. Posthumus's jealousy, on the other hand [...], is real enough in its nastiness, but has no significance in relation to any radical theme, or total effect, of the play.[8] □

These elements, striking enough in themselves, are not organized in relationship to one another or to any organizing principle that would change their significance. He does understand, however, how it is that the critics whose work he is discussing come to over-value the play:

> ■ In the case of *Cymbeline* the assumption that a profound intended significance must be discovered in explanation of the peculiarities of the

play is fostered by the presence of varied and impressive evidence of the Shakespearean genius.[9] □

Leavis cites two speeches of Posthumus to show where such evidence is to be found: the first at 5.5.43–6:

■ And now our [Leavis has 'the'] cowards,
  Like fragments in hard voyages, became
  The life o' th' need. Having [Leavis has 'of the need: having'] found
    the back-door open
  Of the unguarded hearts, heavens, how they wound! □

He comments:

■ It is a remarkable piece of vigorous dramatic felicity. The precisely right tone, a blend of breathless excitement, the professional soldier's dryness, and contempt (towards the Lord addressed), is perfectly got.[10] □

And the other is at 5.5.97–102:

■ Most welcome, bondage, for thou art a way,
  I think, to liberty. Yet am I better
  Than one that's sick o'th'gout, since he had rather
  Groan so in perpetuity than be cured
  By th'sure physician, death, who is the key
  T'unbar these locks. □

On which he comments:

■ This does not belong to 'romantic comedy', nor does the dialogue with the gaoler at the end of the scene.[11] □

Nonetheless, these and other pieces of 'varied and impressive evidence of the Shakespearean genius' do not amount, in his view, to 'a profound intended significance'. Leavis's comments suggest that we should be looking for a 'significance' that is really there, 'in' the work. How is it possible to talk in this way? Surely significance, like beauty, is in the eye of the beholder? We should not be misled by 'intended': that is not the point, at least at the moment.

When Leavis says 'Cymbeline is not a great work of art of the order of The Winter's Tale' he means (to recall his words from the earlier discussion in this Guide of Cymbeline) a work in which all elements are organized in accordance with a 'commanding significance', arising from a 'deep centre'. There is nothing mystical here: this is a description of a mode of organization and could be applied to anything that can be described as organized, from a flower head to a trade union, from an atomic structure to a mode of government. What distinguishes the first of these pairs from the second is that in the first case the organization occurred by itself, as it were, naturally while in the second – and of course, and crucially, in the case of a work of art – it was intended.

MARTIN BUTLER

Johnson's comment on *Cymbeline* must focus any mind concerned with the late romances:

■ This play has many just sentiments, some natural dialogues, and some pleasing scenes, but they are obtained at the expense of much incongruity. To remark the folly of the fiction, the absurdity of the conduct, the confusion of the names and manners of different times, and the impossibility of the events in any system of life, were to waste criticism upon unresisting imbecility, upon faults too evident for detection, and too gross for aggravation.[12] □

Martin Butler's New Cambridge edition boldly seizes this point and reverses its judgement:

■ Despite [the play's] astonishing variety, its narrative grips and compels, rising inexorably from a naïve tale of sundered lovers to a peripeteia [a sudden or dramatic change; a crisis] of dazzling artfulness. The Victorian critics who supposed the ageing Shakespeare was writing in a mood of philosophic calm or catatonic boredom could scarcely have been more mistaken. *Cymbeline* was produced by a dramatist working at the height of his powers.[13] □

Butler concedes, however, that the taste of our own time is not the same as that of Dr Johnson's time:

■ *Cymbeline*'s pleasures differ from those anticipated by readers trained to admire singularity of effect [...] Modern readers and directors have shown more relish than did Dr Johnson for the play's outrageous crossovers between ancient Rome and modern Italy, its ostentatious disguises, confusions and chances. Such fractures appeal to post-modern tastes for fictions that reveal their engineering and question the terms of their own mimesis.[14] □

The taste of our own time is informed by 'modern anthropological and psychological criticism', which Butler invokes to make the important point that fairy tale narratives, understood by such approaches, 'stage collective desires and anxieties, and frequently invoke the politics of family life: the traumas of growing up, the difficult transition from childhood to adulthood, and the realization of self as entirely separate from the family'.[15]

Turning to the question of genre Butler discusses the echoes of *Othello* in the plot and refers the reader to several recent studies.[16] These studies are interested in what the play has in common with those plays that can be grouped around *The Faithful Shepherd* (1602), the version by Edward Dymock of *Il Pastor Fido* (1590) by the Italian dramatist and poet Giambattista Guarini (1538–1612). Butler reminds us that some have argued that the acquisition of the Blackfriars Theatre, which was an indoor theatre and which, after 1609, the company operated in tandem with the Globe, influenced the development of tragic-comic material.[17] Butler argues that *Cymbeline* at least, to achieve its full potential, needed the open theatre with its more extensive capacity for spectacle: 'it was the open-air playhouses that provided most scope for stunning visual effects'.[18] However the court masques were characterized by elaborate stage machinery and effects and the argument is not overwhelming.

Some interesting pages analysing one or two speeches and echoing Anne Barton's perplexity concerning some of the language of the play[19] suggest a link to tragicomic stereotyping but are equally open to the reflection that the play does not show an overmastering grasp but frequently loses control of its material. A possibility is available to some critics, notably Leavis and Johnson, that the play has been preposterously contrived to meet some end about which it may be interesting but ultimately unprofitable to speculate. Yet Q liked it and so did Hazlitt.

This is the cardinal difficulty of critical judgement: to make up one's mind about moments that are certainly ambiguous. Butler discusses the moment when Imogen[20] awakens beside the headless body and reminds us that R A Foakes, for example, has seen the moment as 'a sort of Jacobean theatre of the absurd'[21] and comments:

■ *Cymbeline* foregrounds the provisionality of its own art more ostentatiously than any other play in the canon.[22] □

Butler points out that the overall disposition of events in the play is set against various characters' differing attitudes to 'fate': whether that is Posthumus's language of sin and redemption or Belarius and the princes's 'pagan naturalism' which 'though pious, is far from encouraging'.[23] Their dirge for Fidele is 'chillingly materialist and offers no consolation for death beyond the grim idea that in returning to dust the body is at last insensible to pain'. Jupiter seems to support the idea that there is a governing power but his account of his justice is 'less than satisfactory'.

When Butler, talking of the soothsayer's deployment of 'ingenious but far-fetched puns to "prove" that the oracle has been fulfilled', says 'the play intrudes a scepticism about the providential ordering that, in other respects, the ending seems to affirm',[24] and when he cites Stephen Orgel's remark that 'the point about tragicomedy is not that it is both tragic and comic, but that it is neither: the comedy undercuts the tragedy, the tragedy subverts the restorations and reconciliations',[25] the suspicion might arise that this is the intrusion of a contemporary attitude. *Cymbeline* invokes a pre-Christian world; is it not just as likely that the implausible and strained resolution of this play is an image of the truth of the Incarnation in a world to which it has not yet been revealed, as that it is a sophisticated piece of aesthetic contrivance? We must be careful to distinguish between what we believe is there to be seen and what is there if we see it because we shall need to think about what we are saying: are we crediting the author or the interpreter? This is not to say that it is not there if it is only there if we see it: it is only to try to be clear about what significance we are arguing for. Orgel may be right about the 'point about tragicomedy' for a contemporary audience but it is to be questioned whether his description will really fit *The Faithful Shepherd*.

Turning to the part played by Imogen, Butler points out that while the early comedies took marriage as a goal towards which their action moved, *Cymbeline*, taking marriage as the starting point 'deconstructs assumptions that the earlier plays leave intact, calling into question the privileged status that, in them, marriage commands'.[26] The Victorian Imogen 'downplayed the negative aspects of her portrayal, and ignored the dysfunctional nature of her partnership with Posthumus'.[27]

Butler links the problematization of marriage in the play to a thematic image in Jacobean political discourse of the nation under King James as a family. This is contrasted with Elizabethan rhetoric in which the Queen's 'virgin immunity to the desires to which everyone else was subject'[28] was emphasized. James's political authority mirrored his sexual authority and right order in the kingdom was mirrored by right order in the family. Butler argues that this emphasis 'bred a correspondingly intense anxiety about male insufficiency, the consequences of impotence, betrayal or loss of sexual control'.[29]

Butler shows how the events may be interpreted to reveal this tension:

■ Since his value resides not in himself but in his ability to command another, his story dramatizes the fragile sexual foundations of early modern masculinity. When his belief in Innogen collapses, so will his belief in himself.[30] □

This is interestingly close to the account Coleridge gives of Othello's passionate disappointment in Desdemona as he becomes convinced that she is not worth his love and, more recently, Stanley Cavell's account of investment of belief in the other in his discussion of the same play.[31] Butler links the two plays explicitly as showing the change in focus from marriage as goal to marriage as problem in Shakespeare's work.

The departure to Rome takes Butler into the territory explored by Coppélia Kahn in her discussion of the Roman plays that will be considered later and Butler is led into a further dimension at this point, the parallel of the market economy. The link is Imogen's 'value'. He cites James R Siemon's interesting essay ' "Perplex'd beyond self-explication": *Cymbeline* and early / postmodern Europe' (1994) in which Siemon distinguishes Iachimo from the other rivals because he alone does not argue in nationalistic terms:

> ■ He alone among the disputants offers a challenge ultimately tied neither to identities of nationality nor to those of individuality. The others champion 'our country mistresses', and even Posthumus is said to articulate praises of the superlatively individual Imogen against such nationally-defined claims of 'any the rarest of our ladies in France (1.4.60)'. But Iachimo scarcely even posits the positive virtues of 'ours of Italy', let alone praising any individual excellence among women. Instead, he challenges any and all values of nation or individual in the name of an imaginary market space that is presented as overwhelming the claim of any actual instance in its capacity for open-ended possibility: 'I have not seen the most precious diamond that is, nor you the lady (1.4.73–4)'.[32] □

Ingeniously, Butler argues that the wager has its roots in the construction of Jacobean masculinity, 'arising remorselessly out of the assumptions about competitive masculinity that possession of her serves'.[33] Because he is only a man in so far as he controls Imogen, and as Iachimo has suggested that he does not control her, Posthumus is bound to stake himself on her chastity or risk losing his confidence in himself as man, and thus to risk losing himself.

Imogen's choosing Posthumus against her father's wishes raises the spectre of female desire, much as Desdemona's choice of Othello against Brabantio's wishes had done: 'Inevitably, the play's praise of her fidelity will be shadowed by anxieties about the wilfully desiring female'.[34] Butler discusses the bedroom, invoking Patricia Parker and Catherine Belsey[35] discussing the contradictory iconography of her décor: from 'Diana on the fireplace and cherubs on the ceiling' that signify the chaste wife to 'blind Cupids in the fireplace' and a tapestry showing 'Cleopatra meeting Mark Antony on the proudly swelling Nile',[36] signifying 'disruptively active female desire'.

Turning to the play's historical dimensions Butler comments:

■ Modern political readings of *Cymbeline* have seen the play as allegorizing James's new state, harking back to a mythical time when the island had been unified, a unity now remade in the Jacobean present.[37] □

James's 'Britain' was never more than an ideal though and Butler points out that the play itself does not make any effort to invoke a union of the three 'nations' under one monarch.

Butler suggests that the Queen's resistance to the Romans echoes Elizabethan rather than Jacobean England and he points out the parallel between Iachimo's invasion of Imogen's bedchamber and the Roman incursion into British territory, setting out the play's vision of a Britain civilized by the Romans but having developed its own identity and firmly insisting upon that identity in the face of the threat of pollution by invading forces. The princes stand for the natives originally civilized, whose fortitude is attractive, but whose propensity for unreflecting savage violence is alarming. The ending 'puts relations with Rome on a new footing, making Britain more a competitor than a colony',[38] and 'suggests a new account of nationhood, a myth of origin that locates Britain in a chain of political paternity descending to Cymbeline from Augustus and Jupiter'.[39]

The point is that Cymbeline's victory establishes his right to independence while his accession to Rome's requirements is a realistic recognition of Britain's place in a larger world order. Further, 'this reconstituted nation is emphatically male-centred'.[40] Butler invokes Janet Adelman's description of Cymbeline's 'Oh, what am I? / A mother to the birth of three? (5.6.369–70)' as a 'parthenogenesis fantasy',[41] a dream of reproduction without sexual intercourse, without women. Butler comments on 'the two Romes':[42] the Rome of Iachimo and the Rome of Augustus and suggests that the contrast between the two 'stages an Oedipal scenario'. Caesar and Iachimo serve as a focus for the anger of the child against the political father and, once they are defeated, 'friendship with the father is renewed'.[43]

Butler refers to Woodbridge,[44] and Coppélia Kahn's *Roman Shakespeare*, on the tendency to map the personal onto the political and the political onto the personal via an alertness to imagery sharpened by familiarity with psychoanalytical processes. Butler's analysis of the 'erotic geography' of the key battle ground, 'a symbolic spot, a "strait lane" that is vulnerable to Roman penetration and intensely fought over by the men who crowd there'[45] must plead guilty a little at least to pre-digestion; 'penetration' is not an unjustified importation but it is an importation and the symbolism of the place is undeniable but the precise reading of it is not a given. Butler wants to interpret it in this way, however, to make the link with the potential violation of Imogen's body, as Woodbridge does. It must be said that the parallel does not really need to be chased into these more *recherché* hiding-places though it all adds to conviction.

A further refinement is the suggestiveness that leads towards the adjective 'homosocial':

> ■ The boys are 'striplings', with skins as delicate as a woman's and more suited to childish games, but so thrilling are their looks that they would turn 'a distaff to a lance' (5.5.34). Inspiring their fellows to 'stand' (5.5.31), they beat the Roman eagles into chickens and inflict 'back door' wounds on them (5.5.45) – alluding to the shame of being hurt in flight, but perhaps suggesting a taint of effeminacy.[46] □

This leads directly into the discussion of the site of battle quoted above, introduced by the word 'Moreover' that implies that the site of battle is a further contribution to a gathering symbolism.

The problem is that such interpretation runs the risk of finding *double entendre* where it certainly can be found if it is looked for but looking for it comes to seem at least over-fastidious. The entire point of the scene in which Posthumus narrates the battle is in his interlocutor's wondering:

> ■ This was strange chance:
> A narrow lane, an old man, and two boys □   (5.5.51–2).

'An old man and two boys' could not be expected to have won such a decisive victory in an open field and to stress the significance of the 'two boys' is to overlook the contrasting significance of the 'old man', whose importance to the story of the play is not less than that of the two boys and whose place in this symbolic encounter is exactly to match their youth with his age as a testimony to British masculinity which is already sprung in youth and has yet not faded in age. The symbolism of the encounter must be imported, though of course the language will bear the importation. The geography is not erotic: it may be eroticized. It would be over-zealous to insist on it however and unsubtle too. The 'narrow lane' is surely as much in contrast with the broad highways built by the Romans and therefore evocative of a stubbornly individualistic 'backward' English countryside, as it is suggestive in other ways, as well as, and more obviously, being the only location in which such a small band could have prevailed.

Returning to the more central character, Butler argues that Posthumus's 'trajectory', in this analysis at least, differs from that of the princes 'for the final act relieves him of any public role in the emerging

British state'.[47] His triumphs are personal: 'He defeats the person who cuckolded him, leaving Iachimo "enfeeble[d]" [5.2.4] and mourning his "manhood" [5.2.2]'.

Butler points out that the eighteenth and nineteenth centuries romanticized the story, making it the story of the lovers, but that 'Shakespeare's more politicized version' of the story retains the central focus of Cymbeline himself.

Turning to Imogen, Butler points out how she touches all points in the gathering hybrid identity at some stage in the play's action:

■ She comes from Lud's Town but makes herself at home in Wales, she finds friends among the Romans, and by her marriage she creates a place in her father's circle for Posthumus, the alienated insider. Thus, 'Cymbeline may be King of Britain, but this realm is more than England writ large'.[48] □

Such a view is interesting, and far from indefensible, but it does not displace other views: it sits alongside them. Quite apart from critical accounts, theatrical presentations interpret the play and the next chapter will glance at the play's production history before considering J M Nosworthy's introductory essay to his 1955 Arden edition. It will then move on to consider two studies inflected both towards historicism and feminism: Jodi Mikalachki's 'The Masculine Romance of Roman Britain' and Coppélia Kahn's comments on *Cymbeline* in her *Roman Shakespeare*.

CHAPTER FOUR

Cymbeline (2)

In 1682 Thomas D'Urfey (1653–1723) adapted *Cymbeline*, changing the names and the action, re-titling the play *The Injured Princess* and in general making the play a more sensationalized and much coarser work,[1] but it was the 1761 version of David Garrick (1717–79) that became a theatrical success, surviving for generations, taken over by John Philip Kemble (1757–1823) and lastly by Samuel Phelps. This Garrick-Kemble version was last produced by Phelps in 1864.[2] The essay by Helen Faucit (1814–98) on her experience of playing Imogen is a fair testimony to Victorian theatrical tastes, echoed by the account by Anna Jameson (1794–1860) of Imogen in her *Shakespeare's Heroines* (1846).[3] The play fell out of favour in the 1860s and really is in eclipse in the theatre until Peter Hall (born 1930) revived it in 1957 at Stratford, followed by William Gaskill (born 1930) in 1962 and, amongst others, Bill Alexander in 1987.[4] Stephen Orgel's entertaining review of Danny Sheie's 2000 production, '*Cymbeline* at Santa Cruz' displays a postmodern mélange out of which the strongest impression to survive seems to be the impossibility of believing in any of the constituent elements out of which *Cymbeline* appears to have been made, whether those are taken to be romantic love, a myth of the formation of a political entity (Britain), beliefs about kingship or the stability of sexual identity (tested, as it is in the comedies, only to be confirmed).

Ironically perhaps, incapacity to believe in such things may be a necessary precondition for understanding the play in the way in which critics in the latter part of the twentieth century and the opening years of the twenty-first century have tended to understand it: as a collection of myths, of ideologically-shaped fantasies about men and women that, to our advanced eyes at least, can seem only quaint. What is still true, however, is that none of these accounts has addressed, still less answered, Leavis's complaint that there was no 'controlling centre' to the work. In fact Danny Scheie's celebration of an unfocused decentred *Cymbeline* may only put forward as a strength what Leavis had deplored as a weakness. This may mean that we are able to see value where he could not or it may only mean that our standards are not as high. Stephen Orgel believes that:

■ *Cymbeline* is very difficult to take seriously. If it isn't funny, much of it is loony, or idiotic, or baffling; and in that case – for a modern theater, at least – it had better be funny.[5] □

In his conclusion he says of Scheie's production that:

■ Nobody has ever made *Cymbeline* funny in this way, because nobody has been willing to acknowledge the genuine craziness of Shakespeare's conception, to do the play and remain true to its manic energy.[6] □

The phrase 'the genuine craziness of Shakespeare's conception' is difficult to make out. It could be a compliment to the audacious inventiveness he showed in a later phase of experimentation; recognition that, in this case, experimentation had overreached itself and fallen short of achievement; reluctant acknowledgement that the author had lost his way, through failing interest or ability. J M Nosworthy makes a case for a serious and unified conception of the play.

J M NOSWORTHY

In his Introduction to the 1955 Arden edition of *Cymbeline* J M Nosworthy set out a claim for the play that put its achievement at a much higher level than many had been prepared to:

■ The charge that *The Winter's Tale* and *The Tempest* are the work of a man half bored to death seems to me only to require a categorical denial, and the detailed analysis of *Cymbeline* which the present edition has imposed has convinced me that it is the creation of a man perpetually fascinated by his dramatic experiment, surprised and exhilarated by the new sensations and discoveries which the elaboration of his unfamiliar material has yielded.[7] □

Nosworthy discusses the interpretations of Tillyard and Wilson Knight especially, focusing on the former's delineation of a pattern of regeneration arising from and completing the pattern pursued in the earlier tragedies, and on the latter's drawing out the significance of the myth of national identity, contrasting Rome and Britain with corrupt and decadent Renaissance Italy:

■ The national pattern, which Wilson Knight isolates, assumes at times a rich significance. There are those moments which catch at the imagination and remind us, as they reminded Shakespeare's first audiences, that behind both Britain and Rome there lies a traditional vision for the preservation of which men have fought and died, a thing which the Sicily, Bohemia, and Naples of the later romances fail to convey. Nevertheless, this national ethos seems to me to have no more real prominence than that of regeneration. If Shakespeare intended either theme to be central, his method of presentation, with its witch-like Queen, its poisons, its caves, flowers and music, can only be regarded as ludicrous. If he conceived of these rambling fancies as a vital extension of his tragic experience, or envisaged Cymbeline, Imogen, and Posthumus as regenerate or regenerative successors to Lear, Othello, and Cordelia, or purposed that a rather sordid little squabble over unpaid tribute, with its stylized battle, should reinforce the moral patriotism of *Henry V* or *Julius Caesar*, he was surely guilty of something for which the Johnsonian 'unresisting imbecility' is far too mild a term.[8] □

Of F C Tinkler and Fr A A Stephenson, and of Leavis's commentary on them which has already been discussed, Nosworthy says:

■ Both seem to be theorizing at some considerable distance from the play itself, and Leavis applies a useful corrective by insisting on the specifically romantic character of *Cymbeline*, though there is a sad lack of critical perceptiveness in his repudiation of a deeper significance.[9] □

Nosworthy advances an interesting argument. He argues that *Cymbeline* has suffered the same critical fate as Beethoven's late sonatas and quartets in that those works, to Beethoven's earliest critics, appeared 'so dispersed, so spasmodic' as to suggest weakening powers in their composer, whereas later criticism came to recognize that the apparent lack of artistry was in fact artistry of the highest kind. Nosworthy claims that *Cymbeline* 'finally expresses something which Shakespeare never quite achieves elsewhere, and that, when all the still valid objections have been taken into account, it must yet be reckoned among his supreme utterances'.[10]

He further argues that a characteristic of Shakespeare's work is that it recognizes that life is 'a confused series of experiences'[11] rather than forming a pattern of any kind, whether comic or tragic, and further:

■ Behind the images of within and without lies the notion of body and mind, which are nominally distinct, being one, and the images of yoking and compounding point to a preoccupation with unity in many forms, in fact to the poet's conscious attempt to unify experience as a whole. Such imagery is in complete harmony with the play's full purpose. In *Cymbeline* what seems a hopelessly varied multiplicity moves towards a great act of union, and two further images are especially relevant. The inseparable union of husband and wife is symbolized in Posthumus':

> Hang there like fruit, my soul,
> Till the tree die. □   (5.6.263–4)

and both national and international unity are powerfully figured in:

■ The lofty cedar, royal Cymbeline,
Personates thee: [Oxford has 'thee:'] and thy lopp'd [Oxford has 'lopped'] branches point
Thy two sons forth: [Oxford has 'forth,'] who, by Belarius stolen [Oxford has 'stol'n'],
For many years thought dead, are now revived
To the majestic cedar join'd: [Oxford has 'joined,'] whose issue
Promises Britain peace and plenty.   (5.6.454–9)
These really amount to clear statements that certain unions have been achieved. At first there are several of them: Posthumus and Imogen; Imogen and Cymbeline; Imogen and the Princes; Cymbline and the Princes; Cymbeline and Belarius; Britain and Rome. The fantastic promiscuity of the earlier acts has now been reduced and simplified, and that, we may suppose, is enough. But Shakespeare is not satisfied until he has subsumed all these independent unions under one union, until he has presented his most complete and triumphant *vision* of unity. The moment that the family relationship is established, the whole concept of such relationship is broken down into something more absolute.[12] □

The careful analysis of the imagery of the play that has preceded this discussion is brought to bear on an ambitious claim that imagery of birds and the cedar with which Cymbeline is compared converges with the Phoenix (Imogen). Nosworthy himself admits that the interpretation of the meaning of the Phoenix tree is by no means established, and refers the reader to Roger L. Green's essay, 'The Phoenix and the Tree' (1948)[13] as well as to 'Shakespeare's great metaphysical epithalamium [a poem celebrating a wedding], *The Phoenix and the Turtle*'[14] though he admits again that 'that poem is open to so many interpretations that its clarifying force is dubious'. Amongst his concluding remarks one is worth singling out:

■ In *Measure for Measure* the Duke tells Claudio that it is death which makes these odds all even. But *Cymbeline* resolves the issue, and it is Shakespeare himself who suggests that a resolution of the Many into the One can be accomplished within the pattern of life itself.[15] □

Those critics who concentrate on what Lena Cowen Orlin has called 'the kinds of work literature does in culture'[16] may well insist that such analysis supports their view that the play is celebrating James's vision of Britain, or they will point out what 'work' the play does defining gender identities and roles. They will not have done what Nosworthy attempts to do, however, and that is to answer Leavis's objection that there is no 'commanding significance' to the organization of the play. Whatever it is taken to refer to, the material organized into *Cymbeline* must be judged as an organization, and Nosworthy has attempted to show how that may be done. He cannot resist 'interpretation' at the end, and the notion that 'a resolution of the Many into the One can be accomplished within the pattern of life itself' is itself an attempt to identify the 'work literature does in culture'. What he does, though, is to show how the play does this as a whole, having shown us, or tried to show us, that it is one.

The difference between Nosworthy and Leavis on the one hand and Butler and, say, Gossett on the other, is that Nosworthy and Leavis are interested in 'significance' and Butler and Gossett are only interested in 'meaning', in 'the kinds of work literature does in culture'. What is at stake here is what kind of explanation is appropriate in criticism. Crudely – and at some risk – we may say that explanations that are not given in terms of 'the work itself' (whatever that may be) are explanations of *something else*. This is not to say that they are mistaken; it is only to say, perhaps, that they are not critical explanations. If this is the case then 'what some have described as a "revolution" in literary criticism'[17] is not so much a revolution *in* literary criticism as a turn away from it altogether. Jodi Mikalachki's essay, considered next, offers an opportunity to compare the strengths and weaknesses of the approach.

JODI MIKALACHKI

Jodi Mikalachki's essay, 'The Masculine Romance of Roman Britain: *Cymbeline* and Early Modern English Nationalism', is interested in the relationship between history and drama and sees *Cymbeline* as a sort of nationalist pageant, playing out a myth designed to harmonize incompatible ends:

■ The tensions of this sixteenth-century project of recovery – its drive, on one hand, to establish historical precedent and continuity and, on the other, to exorcise a primitive savagery it wished to declare obsolete – inform virtually all expressions of early modern English nationalism. These tensions derive from the period's broader social tensions about order, manifested most acutely in anxiety over the nature of familial relations and the status of the family as a model for the order of the state.[18] □

Such a perspective is grounded in a theory:

■ Recent work on the mutually informing constructs of nationalism and sexuality has defined the former as a virile fraternity perpetuated by its rejection of overt male homosexuality and its relegation of women to a position of marginalized respectability. I would argue that this gendering and sexualizing of the nation, generally presented as having emerged in the eighteenth century, had become current by the early seventeenth century in England and involved both an exclusion of originary female savagery and a masculine embrace of the civility of empire.[19] □

Such comments are not meant as definitions of nationalism (nationalism is concerned with more than setting up a 'virile fraternity', though the setting up of a virile fraternity may well be an important part of it) but describe some aspects of the ideology and the cultural activity bound up with it, especially as it is related to that other area, so contested at the time, of the proper behaviour of men and women. That other area is an important part of *Cymbeline* in its own right but appears closely integrated with nationalist sentiment, especially in the Queen's great speech at 3.1.16–33, which, Mikalachki says, has 'long been a stumbling block in interpretations of *Cymbeline*'. She describes it as a compound of 'appeals to native topography, history, and legendary origins', claiming that 'it recalls the highest moments of Elizabethan nationalism'.

Mikalachki comments:

■ The Queen's opening command to remember invokes the restitutive drive of early modern English nationalism. The nation's glorious past – its resistance to the great Julius Caesar, its ancient line of kings, and the antiquity of its capital – depends paratactically[20] on this command, emerging in the incantatory power of names like 'Lud's town' and Cassibelan and in the powerful icon of native topography. Moved by this nationalist appeal, Cymbeline refuses to pay the tribute demanded by the Roman emissaries, thus setting Britain and Rome at war.[21] □

Mikalachki notes that G Wilson Knight puts this speech together with Hastings's reference to the impregnable isle in Act 4 of *3 Henry VI* (1590–1?), John of Gaunt's speech in Act 2 of *Richard II* (1595?), and Austria's description of the kingdom he promises to the young Lewis of France in Act 2 of *King John* (1595–6?).[22] Wilson Knight speaks of 'Elizabethan post-Armada sentiment', which must of course carry over into the rule of her successor for the notion to apply to *Cymbeline*. What neither Mikalachki nor Wilson Knight pays sufficient attention to, however, is that the first importance of these speeches is not historiographical or historical but dramatic. We must ask first what it means for our sense of the Queen and of the play that she should say these things, just as we should ask what it means for our sense of John of Gaunt and of the play as a whole that he should say what he says in that play. The Queen is someone who will exploit the best sentiments of which she knows people are capable in the service of her own ends. It would be naïve to imagine that she meant what she said and that she could be taken as a figure of the feeling she seems to be expressing. John of Gaunt means it, but in a different way, in the service of quite another character. It is a mistake to read history straight from speeches in a play. Of course the significance of the speech for our understanding of the Queen would be much diminished if there were no 'Elizabethan post-Armada sentiment' which carried over into the rule of her successor: that is the contribution historical studies may make to the work of criticism. The 'contradiction', if there is one, concerns the place of the Queen's speech in a play that leads towards a breach with Rome only to end with reconciliation with Rome. Mikalachki concludes:

■ A fear of originary female savagery consistently drove early modern historians and dramatists of ancient Britain to find refuge in the Roman embrace. [...] British origins in all these works emerge as unavoidably feminine, either in the savagery of a wicked queen or in the feminized domesticity and submission of the British male to the Roman embrace. I take the violence with which early modern dramatists and historians rejected the figure of the ancient British queen as an indication of how thoroughly their failure to transform the femininity of national origins disturbed them. Their attempts to avoid this originary femininity led them ultimately to embrace a subordinate status in the Roman empire. While this new status also consigned Britain to a feminized role, it avoided the savagery of the purely British nationalism articulated by ancient queens. It also allowed for a historical afterlife for Britain. In contrast to the ancient queen's savage refusal of empire, the masculine embrace of Roman Britain became the truly generative interaction, producing a civil masculine foundation for early modern English nationalism.[23] □

This is plausible, if 'the violence with which early modern dramatists and historians rejected the figure of the ancient British queen' is meant to imply something about Shakespeare's creative activity in respect of *Cymbeline*, but, like many plausible propositions, it is difficult to prove. It is equally persuasive to see *Cymbeline* as a last British play as well as a last Roman play. A *generic* concern might want to consider the play as an address to both the modes of History from which Shakespeare had profited, artistically as well as financially, over many years. Biographically, it might be added that this might be seen as a farewell to both modes. Coppélia Kahn's essay *Roman Shakespeare* concludes with a brief note on *Cymbeline* regarding it as a Roman play hybridized with a Romance.

COPPÉLIA KAHN

As *Cymbeline* is not a full Roman play Kahn cannot treat it as part of the main body of her argument but nonetheless suggests that it is sufficiently Roman for her to treat it as coming under the remit of that argument. That argument takes the form of an exploration of the plays under the sign, as it were, of gender construction. I say 'under the sign' to indicate a practice increasingly common these days of gathering associated material rather than attempting to establish other kinds of relationship amongst the gathered material. I should say immediately that Kahn's argument requires no other demonstration: no other point needs to be established than that there is a growing body of evidence that ideas of masculinity and femininity are not derived from nature but acquired because repeated throughout culture and associated in their specific forms with specific cultural moments. The contribution to Shakespeare studies of such work is much less certain as it remains only an interpretation amongst other interpretations which can only be preferred on the basis of a sympathy with the project overall or else a demonstration that this interpretation makes more sense of more of the plays as they are seen than any other interpretation.

Kahn's argument is that Roman 'virtue' was a heavily masculinized concept and its use by the Renaissance allows the researcher to explore the connections between aspects of Renaissance English life to reveal the process by which masculinity and femininity come to be defined and assigned to particular persons at particular points in their lives. Kahn believes that masculinity and femininity, like other related concepts, are mutually defining and thus in danger of contaminating each other through imperfect definition, much as Friedrich Engels (1820–95) argued (after G W F Hegel (1770–1831)) that opposites interpenetrated.[24]

Kahn notes that Robert Miola defines *Cymbeline* as a Roman play:

■ Robert Miola puts it decisively under a Roman rubric by tracing its many echoes of theme and incident in Shakespeare's other Roman works, its allusions to Latin texts and its concern with *pietas* [the respect due to an ancestor, country or institution].[25] □

Kahn continues:

■ For my purposes, it belongs with the Roman works because like them it grapples with *virtus* [strength of character, especially associated with masculine character; excellence, worth] as a vexed configuration of warriors, wounds, and women.[26] □

It is the strongly gendered nature of the British nationalism with which the play is concerned that provides Kahn with the link she requires. Kahn acknowledges the persuasiveness of Meredith Skura's idea that 'Cymbeline must finally pay "tribute" to the Rome that generated him and his ideals'[27] and goes on to suggest that:

> ■ Perhaps we can also read his gesture metadramatically: in this play Shakespeare pays tribute to Rome as a cultural model for Britain and specifically, as source and inspiration for his own Roman works – acknowledging his own form of emulation. □

She refers to the imaginative vision that Francis Yates (1899–1981) has of *Cymbeline* as a version of the figure of *translatio imperii,* the movement of the Empire westward from Troy.[28] Patricia Parker notes the same figure.[29] Kahn pertinently remarks that the terms in which British national independence is often described in the play owe much to Roman sources and examples and argues that:

> ■ Rome persists as the emulous reference point for configuring Britain and its men, impelling Britons to surpass Rome in order to found themselves as Britons. In *Cymbeline*, as Jodi Mikalachki argues, 'British national identity is formed from the interaction of the Roman invaders with the native land'.[30] □

Kahn focuses on the 'narrow lane' seeing this as the pre-eminently significant site for the interaction Mikalachki describes and linking it with:

> ■ The sites of emulation projected so vividly in *Julius Caesar* ('young ambition's ladder', [2.1.22]), *Troilus and Cressida* (the steps marking 'the envious fever / Of pale and bloodless emulation', [1.3.133–4]) and *Timon of Athens* [1604?] ('Fortune's high and pleasant hill', [1.1.64]) [...] in these tight spaces jammed with men, each one struggling to get ahead of the others and come out on top, Shakespeare expresses the intense anxiety of institutionalized competition in the Roman ethos. The imagery of the Britons 'hurt behind' evokes a primitive dread of bodily exposure associated with the shame of failure that looms as the alternative to achieving manly virtue. Those who are valiant will face the enemy and 'Stand', the repeated rallying cry of Belarius (5.5.25, 28, 31).[31] □

The old man and the two boys 'comprise a kind of all-male martial family' and are:

> ■ An extension of the pastoral family of Belarius and his two kidnapped sons, which is echoed in the dream vision of the Leonati (in which the mother's role is firmly subdued to the father's, sons and father forming

a martial triad), and finally realized in the reunion of Cymbeline with his sons after his Queen's death. □

Kahn recalls Adelman's view that this all-male family 'constitutes the play's central fantasy of "pure male family from which women can be wholly excluded" which provides "a secure basis for masculine identity"'.[32] This is to sideline Imogen, however, and it may not be impertinent to suggest that Shakespeare and his audience might have been aware that this fantasy could only be a fantasy and could treat it with indulgent irony. Kahn herself reminds us that if Imogen's name is meant to recall the name of the wife of Brute then she will be, as Imogen was, the mother of a nation.

Kahn recalls the famous story of Horatio on the bridge, immortalized in the sequence of poems, *The Lays of Ancient Rome* (1842) by the historian Thomas Babington Macaulay (1800–59) and also describes the 'narrow lane' as 'sexual terrain':

■ As Linda Woodbridge argues, the lane suggests the highly defended site of Imogen's chastity, the narrow entrance to her womb. The Roman invasion of Britain at this distinctive site parallels Iachimo's invasion of her bedchamber and Cloten's parallel 'siege' for her hand; thus 'Imogen's perils are Britain's'.[33] □

The wound that Posthumus says that Imogen's (supposed) infidelity has inflicted on him, 'the testimonies whereof lie bleeding in me' (3.4.22–3) is, Kahn argues, 'healed' by risking other wounds at the site of the 'narrow lane' and Kahn concludes that *Cymbeline* departs strikingly from the Roman model in Posthumus's reconciliation of the conflict in his own mind with Imogen. He has nothing to forgive her for, of course:

■ But Posthumus's forgiveness of Imogen is nonetheless a striking departure not only from the intransigence of Claudio, Leontes, and Othello, but from the Roman pattern of placing women in a separate domain while pairing heroes most importantly with their emulous male rivals rather than with women.[34] □

This is no resolution however, but the influence of the romance genre:

■ Insofar as *Cymbeline* is romance as much as Roman, we shouldn't wonder at this: forgiveness runs strong in Shakespeare's romances.[35] □

The dilemma remains:

■ In the Roman works, the wound that signifies *virtus* remains an open wound in the sense of a persistent but unsuccessful attempt to fix, stabilize, delimit masculinity as a self-consistent autonomy free from the stigma of the feminine.[36] □

Critical and interpretative ingenuity notwithstanding, *Pericles* and *Cymbeline* are perhaps better regarded in any sustained study of Shakespeare's work as a prelude to two plays, however different they are from each other, that are unquestionably the greatest of the movement in Shakespeare's imaginative interests that led to the great experiment of these last plays, *The Winter's Tale* and *The Tempest*, and it is to the first of these that this Guide now turns its attention.

CHAPTER FIVE

The Winter's Tale: Early Moderns

T he twentieth century views *The Winter's Tale* very differently from the nineteenth century. While Sir Arthur Quiller-Couch, for example, who liked *Cymbeline* so much, had no high opinion of *The Winter's Tale*, critics of the early twentieth century, E M W Tillyard, S L Bethell, F R Leavis and G Wilson Knight, regard *The Winter's Tale* as a work of high art.

In Q's view the work did not cohere: 'the play never lodges in our minds as a whole'[1] and 'It leaves no single impression'.[2] An interesting contrast can be drawn with E M W Tillyard's 1938 essay on the play.

E M W TILLYARD

Q says that Shakespeare 'bungled' the question of Leontes's jealousy but Tillyard describes the manner in which Leontes is seized by obsessive jealousy as 'terrifying in its intensity'. He claims that it is unlike any of the states of mind of Shakespeare's other tragic heroes, resembling rather 'the god-sent lunacies of Greek drama, the lunacies of Ajax and Heracles'. Tillyard describes these as 'scantily motivated' and insists that 'we should refrain from demanding any motive'.[3]

Quite why we should 'refrain' is not enlarged upon though the implication is, I think, that as we do not demand realistic motivation in the cases of Ajax and Heracles then we should not, and for the same reasons, in the case of Leontes, and that is because the requirements of realism are inappropriate to the kind of play we are dealing with, and not because we must momentarily believe in the gods of ancient Olympus or some other kind of deity in the case of *The Winter's Tale*. Tillyard sees the play as an advance on *Cymbeline* in the same line as that earlier work.

Tillyard claims that Shakespeare avoided confusing the play with 'all the irrelevancies that had clotted *Cymbeline*', and argues that he is thus able to present what he calls 'the whole tragic pattern' in *The Winter's Tale*. This 'whole tragic pattern', in Tillyard's view, leads from 'prosperity to destruction [to] regeneration, and still fairer prosperity'.[4] This can only be done in a play for the stage by abandoning any notion of what neo-classical critics called 'the unity of time' as the narrative necessitates a much longer reach of time than can be accommodated on the stage without jumping over large stretches of time, such as that necessitated by Perdita's growing to maturity, for example. It is worth briefly noting that the notion of 'unities' was largely an invention of Renaissance critics and translators of Aristotle who took them to be entailed by what Aristotle had said in his *Poetics*. The unity of time was a rule that held that the action of a play should take no longer than a single day and that the narrative should not be interrupted so as to compress events within this narrow compass (what we might call 'real time' narrative). Shakespeare observes this rule in *The Tempest* and it may be imagined that he did so with an ironic consciousness of its importance to other dramatists. Tillyard's view of tragedy is itself innovative, holding that the reversal of good fortune with which Shakespeare's own tragic plays usually end is not the full 'tragic pattern'. That full pattern includes a restoration of good fortune, even to a higher degree, and it is Tillyard's argument that it is only in these later plays that Shakespeare is able to present the full pattern.

He compares Hermione as a characterization favourably with Imogen: 'There is nothing strained or hectic about her love for her husband: it is rooted in habit'.[5]

This helps to underline the fundamentally realistic mode of the first part of the play:

> ■ In sum, the first half of the play renders worthily, in the main through a realistic method, the destructive portion of the tragic pattern.[6] □

'In the main', because Leontes's jealousy, as Tillyard has already established, is not, and should not be regarded as, realistically founded. This is not a contradiction: the play as a whole is not realistic. Tillyard's argument depends upon the view that Shakespeare is attempting to find a dramatic method for realizing what Tillyard regards as the full tragic pattern which the tragedies themselves (which are realistic 'in the main', only much more so) have only partially developed. The 'second half' as it were, of this pattern, is repentance and restitution.

Importantly, the final part of the tragic pattern, the stage of regeneration, is not, in Tillyard's view, represented by Leontes and Hermione: 'At the best they mend the broken vessel of their fortunes with glue or seccotine [fish glue]; and our imaginations are not in the least stirred by any future life that we can conceive the pair enjoying together'. On the contrary, 'it is Florizel and Perdita and the countryside where they meet which make the new life'.[7]

He must argue for the fourth act and this is an uphill struggle because 'convincing pictures of joy and virtue are extremely rare'[8] but he is convinced that 'Shakespeare never did anything finer, more serious, more evocative of his full powers, than his picture of an earthly paradise painted in the form of the English countryside'.[9]

Tillyard argues that 'the old problem of adjusting realism and symbol is so well solved that we are quite unconscious of it. The country life is given the fullest force of actuality'.[10] In this way the 'old problem of adjusting realism and symbol is [...] solved', as the actuality so fully realized has the effect of a symbol, conveys the meaning of regeneration through identification with creative forces and 'Perdita [...] is one of Shakespeare's richest characters'.[11]

Shakespeare pictured what Tillyard calls 'original virtue' in Perdita whom he describes as 'blossoming spontaneously in the simplest of country settings'. She herself does not create anything, though her creativity is 'implied by her sympathy with nature's lavishness in producing flowers' and especially perhaps by 'her own simple and unashamed confession of wholesome sensuality'.[12]

Tillyard comments that references to the classical Pantheon – the gods of ancient Greece and Rome – 'occur very frequently in the last plays of Shakespeare and are certainly more than mere embroidery'.[13] Apollo is, as Tillyard says, 'the dominant god in *The Winter's Tale*', and appears, in Tillyard's view, 'as the bridegroom, whom the pale primroses never know, but who visits the other flowers'. With circumspection, not to say circumlocution, Tillyard comments: 'Not to take the fertility symbolism as intended would be a perverse act of caution'.[14] Of course, if we could demonstrate that it was intended, to refuse to accept it as apparently so well incorporated, would be, indeed, 'perverse'; it is, however, merely reasonable, and not at all perverse, caution not to assume that it was intended in the absence of any proof that it was.

Tillyard is aware of the structural problem of 'centring the creative processes in her and Florizel', which is that 'there is a break in continuity; for though Perdita is born in the first half of the play, as characters the pair are new to the last half. And we have juxtaposition, not organic growth'.[15] However it turns out not to be a problem:

> ■ On the other hand, I find this juxtaposition easy enough to accept; and it is mitigated by Perdita's parentage. She is Hermione's true daughter and prolongs in herself those regenerative processes which in her mother have suffered a temporary eclipse.[16] □

This is a lapse of attention: juxtaposition, however 'easy to accept', is not organic growth and if the lack of organic growth, or the substitution for it of juxtaposition, is a fault then it is a fault in *The Winter's Tale*.

Critical accounts of the late plays must confront the attempts they make to embrace a longer time scale than Shakespeare had attempted before and make the 'two hours' traffic of our stage' (*Romeo and Juliet*, Prologue, l. 12) comprehend a transfer of creative responsibility from generation to generation. S L Bethell sought to claim unity of conception by means of another approach.

S L BETHELL

S L Bethell (1947) poses a severe question: 'Why is his dramatic technique crude and apparently incoherent?'[17] He makes an important point concerning 'that awkward gap of sixteen years between the two parts of the play', which is that 'it must have been deliberate, for *The Tempest* seems deliberately and mockingly to repudiate the suggestion that Shakespeare was incapable of preserving the unities when he wanted to'.[18] He is interesting on the management of business towards the end of 4.4 by a series of asides and direct addresses to the audience: 'surely this is a deliberately comic underlining of a deliberately crude technique'. The stagecraft of modern pantomime comes to mind. Bethell talks of 'a quite conscious return to naïve and outmoded technique, a deliberate creaking of the dramatic machinery'.[19] Of Autolycus he says:

■ From 'my traffic is sheets' the speech [4.3.23–30], in effect, constitutes a 'character of a rogue' in the Theophrastan[20] manner which had become popular, a description of a type in terms of seventeenth-century wit. It is in fact an admirable example of the blend of narrative and the representational, in which the character, as it were, tells his own story to the audience – a convention inherited from the medieval miracle plays.[21] □

Bethell stresses the community of the late plays in terms of this technical oddness:

■ Among a great many other instances we have 'Gower, as Chorus' in *Pericles* and Posthumus' dream in *Cymbeline*, both of which Shakespeare permitted, whether he wrote them himself or not. *The Tempest* presents a different technique but with the same suggestion of inefficiency; we have a positive flaunting of the unities, yet coupled with the mildly comic tedium of Prospero's long narrative to the drowsily obedient Miranda.[22] □

Whether one agrees with Bethell's estimate of 1.2 in *The Tempest* the point may be maintained that it is an unusual departure for a dramatist normally keen to ensure a rapid series of actions on his stage that he should seem so readily to violate one of his own implicit cardinal principles by having the stage dominated for such a long time by such inaction as a narrative as long as Prospero's is, interrupted though it is from time to time by Miranda, especially as it follows such a lively scene of action and exchange and interchange as 1.1.

Bethell suggests that Shakespeare is drawing attention 'to the play as play by obtruding matters of technique upon the audience'.[23] By doing this he 'was able to distance the story and to convey a continual reminder that his play was after all only a play'.[24] Mamillius's own 'winter's tale' ('a sad tale's best for winter', (2.1.27)), that he never finishes,[25] reminds us of the title of the play and of its significance: this is to be a 'sad tale', one fit for winter, though, as it turns out, we shall be pleasantly surprised. Bethell points to the occasions on which characters refer to the notion of 'an old tale' (3rd Gentleman at 5.2.61; Paulina at 5.3.118):

■ Such internal comments upon the nature of a story always remind us of its unreality, breaking through any illusion which may have been created. Thus they combine with the deliberately old-fashioned technique to insist that it is after all only a dramatic performance that the audience have before them.[26] □

Approaching the question of intention Bethell has some useful comments:

■ I do not know what Shakespeare deliberately intended in this play; no one can ever know and the question is not important. What I am attempting to show is what in fact he did and how he did it – the perhaps unconscious reasons which led him to use one type of technique and reject another.[27] □

The material itself, 'an old tale', is served by a mode of presentation that, firstly, resembles the use of archaism to present material in a historical novel, for example; the manner of presentation, secondly, directs the audience towards paying a particular kind of attention: the thrilled absorption characteristic of, say, *Othello* is neither required by nor permitted by *The Winter's Tale*; finally, the mode of presentation 'is also in itself a statement about the nature of reality'.[28] Bethell refers to Tillyard's treatment of the question of what Tillyard calls 'planes of reality' in *The Tempest*. He quotes Tillyard saying of the masque of 4.1 of that play that 'on the actual stage the masque is executed by players pretending to be spirits, pretending to be real actors, pretending to be supposed goddesses and rustics' and he comments that 'Prospero's speech then sees the whole creation as a fading pageant (akin to the dream world – another "plane") and only the eternal remains as the truly real'.[29]

This interpretation is contentious; Prospero makes no mention of 'the eternal' though nothing he says denies it either. In a similar vein, Bethell's brisk run through the play that follows upon his introduction of his theme is as interesting as it is suggestive, and, therefore, convincing or otherwise as one finds it. The unity he identifies in the play is one that fully acknowledges the shifts of tone and focus that are so striking but it is not one that is strictly demonstrable from this play as any work that met the same general description (fragmentary and inconsistent and anti-realist in its mode of presentation) could be interpreted in the same way. Bethell identifies the fragments but has no ultimate organizing principle to refer to beyond the idea that various and sometimes conflicting 'planes of reality' are presented and 'only the eternal remains as the truly real'. Such a principle can lie behind or beyond a great many things without organizing them into anything in particular. It was F R Leavis who most strongly insisted on the centrality of an organizing principle and it is to his comments on the play that we now turn.

F R LEAVIS

Leavis argues that if the play is looked at in what he takes to be the correct manner, then 'what looked like romantic fairy-tale characteristics turn out to be the conditions of a profundity and generality of theme'. He warns us against approaching Shakespearean drama as though the dramatist had taken the same approach in each play. Taking *Othello* as exemplary of one kind of approach to drama Leavis contrasts the treatment of Leontes:

> ■ But if our preconceptions don't prevent our being adverted by imagery, rhythm, and the developing hints of symbolism – by the subtle devices of the poetry and the very absence of 'psychology' – we quickly see that what we have in front of us is nothing in the nature of a novel dramatically transcribed. □

This must not lead the reader to believe that Leavis thought that *Othello* was 'a novel transcribed'. His point is that in comparison with that play Leontes's jealousy will seem 'sudden and unprepared' unless we have been paying attention to the play's peculiar method. The play does not work in the same way in which a novel works. Leavis's view is that in a novel the words are used in such a way as to create character and to move narrated incident forward whereas in *The Winter's Tale*, he argues, 'the treatment of life is too generalizing (we may say, if

we hasten to add "and intensifying")'.[30] While avoiding, perhaps deliberately, a word so potentially misleading as 'poetry', it is towards the
condition of poetry his arguments point the reader, in which effects of
imagery and rhythm, for example, play so large a part and in which,
characteristically, narrative and the creation of character do not, at
least not in such a way as we are likely to associate with the novel.

Leavis's description is of a kind of criticism that is painstaking,
detailed, as suggestive as is Bethell's, but necessarily conducted over a
much larger extent than a short essay such as Bethell's will allow. Also
it must really be conducted in conversation with others, leading them
through conjecture, suggestion, confirmation or rejection: a process of
critical dialogue. It is also of course, every bit as contentious as I have
suggested that Bethell's interpretation of the play is: it is contentious
because the existence of the principle and of the subordination of the
detail to the principle can only be urged, it cannot be demonstrated.
I am only saying that the principle Bethell is urging is too indirectly
related to the details he identifies for the relationship to seem convincing. Bethell is able to itemize the *variety* of detail: the account Leavis
is pointing to will show how every detail leads back to the organizing
vision.

Leavis adduces the pastoral scene as an example of the method,
talking of the 'personal drama' being 'made to move upon a complexity of larger rhythms', a compelling metaphor for a vision of the
play in which poetry sets up currents, as it were, composed of, in the
case of this play, the rhythms of 'Nature' (Leavis cites birth, death,
maturity and the seasonal cycle with which the pattern of individual human growth may be compared and often has been and finds
these in, for example, the Shepherd's oft-quoted remark, 'Thou metst
with things dying, I with things new-born (3.3.110–11)') 'so that the
charming pastoral scene is something very much other than a charming superfluity'.[31]

To take only one remark in this passage, 'the charming pastoral
scene is something very much other than a charming superfluity', is to
reflect at once that it *may* be something more, and certainly *will* be, but
only if one is convinced by an argument such as that of which Leavis
gives the outlines here. The very word he has used earlier, 'generalizing', comes to mind, as does his important qualification, 'if we hasten
to add "and intensifying" '. The difference between the particularity of
realism and the generality of the kind of drama to which *The Winter's
Tale* belongs is that in such cases, the cases in which it is not mere
generalization, the generalities ('birth, maturity, death, birth'; 'Spring,
Summer, Autumn…') are rendered concrete, precise, vividly realized
particularities themselves: not as individual *instances* of the generality
(as is the case with realism) but as particularized presentations *of* the
generality.

It must be noted that Bethell makes an important point: the material from which the play is constructed is various, even heterogeneous. In a brisk summary passage Bethell starkly exposes this heterogeneity:

> ■ The sheep-shearing feast is followed immediately by theatrical plans for escape and Autolycus' satire on the court. In the fifth act the first scene sustains the serio-comic tension in Paulina and the second recounts at second hand in a burlesque version of court jargon the all-important discovery of Perdita's true identity, her restoration to Leontes and the meeting of the two kings in reconciliation. This not only saves the climax for the last scene but in itself adds another plane of reality: 'news', 'gossip', inevitably distorted in transmission. The last scene, theatrically posed, has the religious tone associated previously with the oracle; now it is carried to new heights in the reunion of Leontes and Hermione.[32] □

We may recall Stephen Orgel's comment:

> ■ *Cymbeline* is very difficult to take seriously. If it isn't funny, much of it is loony, or idiotic, or baffling; and in that case – for a modern theater, at least – it had better be funny.[33] □

Bethell himself has talked of 'a quite conscious return to naïve and outmoded technique, a deliberate creaking of the dramatic machinery'[34] apparently without reflecting that 'creaking of the dramatic machinery', whether deliberate or not, is 'creaking of the dramatic machinery'. Now if this 'creaking of the dramatic machinery' is done deliberately in the service of a purpose that transforms it into something else it is not perceived as 'creaking of the dramatic machinery', and Bethell wants to demonstrate that the higher purpose is to reveal, as Prospero's speech in *The Tempest* reveals, that 'only the eternal remains as the truly real'. However, Bethell himself has also pointed out that it is impossible to discover Shakespeare's intentions.

Unfortunately the principle, in Bethell's presentation at least, remains only an implication of what he has identified rather than something he can identify. G Wilson Knight saw the unity of the play and looks, as Leavis and Bethell both look, to visions of what life amounts to, to find that unity.

G WILSON KNIGHT

G Wilson Knight's 1947 volume *The Crown of Life* adopts a High Theory approach which contrasts with Bethell's approach, which is concerned, at least at first, with theatrical practicalities. Knight avoids what he calls 'the side-issues of Elizabethan and Jacobean manners, politics, patronage, audiences, revolutions and explorations', concentrating on 'the poetic quality and human interest of the plays concerned'.[35]

What to Cultural Studies, History and related approaches are central matters, 'Elizabethan and Jacobean manners, politics, patronage, audiences, revolutions and explorations', the very stuff of contemporary criticism, is relegated by Wilson Knight to the status of 'side-issues'. His phrase 'the significance of the completed work of art' recalls Leavis's comments on *Cymbeline*.[36] Wilson Knight believes, as Leavis does, that *The Winter's Tale* is a great work of art: 'Shakespeare offers nothing greater in tragic psychology, humour, pastoral, romance, and that which tops them all and is, except for *Pericles*, new'.

Knight points out that setting the play in Sicily ought to remind us of the myth of Proserpine (Persephone), the figure of Spring, who in the Greek and Roman tale was carried off into the underworld by its king. While there she ate part of a pomegranate and, having eaten in the underworld, is condemned to return there every year. The figure of Spring, coupled with the interpretation of the figure as rising from the world of the dead, is indeed apposite for *The Winter's Tale*.

Knight acknowledges that 'the more profound passages' are rather obscure for theatre audiences to take them in at once but that may be because the unity of the play is achieved by:

■ A vague, numinous, sense of mighty powers, working through both the natural order and man's religious consciousness, that preserve, in spite of all appearance, the good.[37] □

For Knight the play moves inexorably towards 'the crucial and revealing event to which the whole action moves: the resurrection of Hermione'.[38]

He sketches out the plan of the play: a tragic first section followed by a pastoral second section and concluded by a third that he leaves undefined. In addition, 'there is a strong suggestion throughout of season-myth, with a balance of summer against winter'. Dramatically, 'evil passions, storm, and shipwreck are contrasted with young love and humour' and 'Maturity and death are set against birth and resurrection'. This brief sketch gives a strong sense of the shapeliness of the play, though that key word, again, 'resurrection' seems out of place. Maturity and death and birth are facts of life: resurrection is a matter of faith. Leavis remains safely within the bounds of life: Wilson Knight must transcend those bounds.

He is brisk and sharp on the opening scenes, pointing out that Mamillius is central, 'defined mainly by what is said to, or about him',[39] and that Shakespeare establishes in the opening dialogue a view of youth as 'a golden-age existence free from that "hereditary" taint of fallen humanity which appears with the "stronger blood", or passions, of maturity'.[40]

Wilson Knight quotes the fine comment from *The Allegory of Love* (1936) by C S Lewis (1898–1963), to the effect that, in the Romance tradition, as it develops, 'the romance of marriage' comes to succeed 'the romance of adultery'. He puts forward a compressed, and challenging, theory. The 'happy-ending love-drama' frees theatre from religious domination and gives it a new direction, 'thereby witnessing the unexhausted meaning, social and religious, of this persistent theme'.[41] The argument is complex, compressed and not altogether easy to grasp.

Wilson Knight is attempting to show that the general can be presented by the particular and that a particularity that may at first sight appear unpromising, sexual jealousy, can be the vehicle for far-reaching revelations of the contest between good and evil. The fact that Shakespeare is a particular poet writing at a particular time, shaped by history, does not prevent him from expressing 'the unexhausted meaning' of this particularity, an aspect of a moment in the development of European culture in a particular corner of Europe at a particular time. The argument has a bearing on the play with which *The Winter's Tale* is often associated (as it is here by Wilson Knight), *Othello*. Bradley and others noted with unease that that play had none of the obviously tragic traits of the 'great' tragedies and yet they were uncertain about assigning it a lesser rank. A domestic tragedy, it nevertheless seemed to stir deeper feelings than it should have been able to. The answer is usually to be found in the poetry. Wilson Knight cites a telling moment:

■ *Mamilius*. I am like you, they say.
   Leontes.   Why, that's some comfort. □   (1.2.209)

He comments: 'with no loss of human particularization, Mamilius stands before Leontes as Truth confronting Error'.[42]

Whether one agrees exactly with Wilson Knight's interpretation of the moment, he is surely right about the mechanism. Shakespeare's poetry creates what Wilson Knight calls 'reverberations' (and in the earlier passage, 'radiations') and the effect is to invest such moments with much greater significance than they bear as localized moments in human intercourse, 'domestic' moments, without having to move the action to the blasted heath of *Lear*.

Knight has a clear grasp of the significance of the placing, as it were, of Shakespeare's time. The Elizabethan-Jacobean age lies between a 'middle ages' dominated by the Church and a later age, more easily perceived by our own time as congruent with our own time, in which other ideas, notably rationalist and scientific, became more influential. It is useful sometimes to think of Shakespeare's works as occupying a uniquely privileged middle ground between an 'old world' whose grip was loosening but whose influence was not yet exhausted, and a 'new world' whose influence was just being felt as an exhilarating intuition of possibility rather than as a set of shaped projects. Wilson Knight is being economical with the space available to him, and suggestion is all he can fit in; it needs to be opened out much more than he is able to do. What this Guide has already had to say about postmodernism in relation to Suzanne Gossett's discussion of the editing problem concerning *Pericles* in Chapter 2 will be taken up again in the next chapter on *The Winter's Tale* in a discussion of aspects of M M Mahood's essay on that play and will be the basis of the discussion of Francis Barker and Peter Hulme's essay on *The Tempest* in Chapter 9. It is not to say too much to say that the history of criticism, and in particular the history of criticism of Shakespeare's work, is the history of the changing understanding of the human predicament in Europe and North America from Shakespeare's time to our own.

He picks out all the indications that Act 3 scene 3 is a transition between death and life, making a useful comparison with the role of the fishermen in *Pericles* and he is effective on the 'feel' of the scene. He describes the clown's account of the shipwreck as 'exquisite', saying that the humour has the effect of 'subtly veiling the horror and removing its sting'. He comments on the discovery of the child and the gold as follows:

■ The baby is found with a casket of gold. The Shepherd calls it a 'changeling' and attributes his luck to the 'fairies' [3.3.114]. So the craggy setting is lit by the glow of 'fairy gold' [3.3.119]. We have entered a new, and safer, world.[43] □

The Clown's description of the death of Antigonus and the wreck of the ship that brought him is 'exquisite' not, perhaps, in itself, but in its dramatic function, which it perfectly fulfils, of 'subtly veiling the horror and removing its sting'. The device of the imperfect narrator removes the object described from the mind of the audience, putting between it and the object the opaque medium of the description itself. The beauty of 3.3 is not to be found in its parts but in the perfect meshing of those parts together, though the Shepherd's oft-quoted 'Now bless thyself. Thou metst with things dying, I with things new born' is a small masterpiece of compression and economy of expression. 'Now bless thyself' reminds us of the sacredness of such transitions.

Wilson Knight's discussion may be characterized as an attempt to describe the 'feel' of the scene because the concluding comment itself requires some analysis:

■ So the craggy setting is lit by the glow of 'fairy gold' [3.3.119]. We have entered a new, and safer, world. □

There is in fact little warrant for Wilson Knight's 'craggy'. He earlier describes the setting as 'the wild and rugged Bohemian coast, with threatening storm'[44] and later as a 'fierce and rugged spot'.[45] It is true that Leontes has commanded Antigonus to take the child to 'some remote and desert place [2.3.176]' and that Antigonus speaks of 'the deserts of Bohemia [3.3.2]', but these words only mean 'uninhabited'. The Mariner warns Antigonus not to go too far inland because 'this place is famous for the creatures / Of prey that keep upon't [3.3.11–12]' and the same Mariner has already pointed out that 'the skies look grimly / And threaten present blusters [3.3.3–4]' and these dangers are realized quite soon and fatally. Wilson Knight's colouring is not wide of the mark, however, as these elements, in the audience's mind, evoke a threatening, foreboding atmosphere, as 'craggy' and 'wild and rugged' also do, though these are Wilson Knight's words, not from *The Winter's Tale*. The same sort of comment needs to be made on the other part of this beautiful image, Wilson Knight's assertion that 'the craggy setting' is 'lit by the glow of "fairy gold"'. The elements are there: the 'fairy gold' is there ('This is fairy gold, boy, and 'twill prove so', 3.3.119); its light, however, is imported by Wilson Knight. The question is whether such importation is legitimate.

This sort of objection is often raised against A C Bradley who famously imports into the plays the childhood of the characters and characters who do not appear in the plays at all,[46] but criticism is at least in part the business of evoking for the reader the experience the critic believes is the experience evoked by the work. Wilson Knight's description of the 'feel' of 3.3 is evocative and impressive and, above all, uncovers to clear view the point of the scene: 'We have entered a new, and safer, world'. The comma is expressive: there is just the right emphasis to express a cautious apprehensiveness relieved by a welcome confirmation of hope, and that is the feeling one would expect at the transition point of such a play as Knight is describing. His critical view, in other words, is consistent. If, at the end of his analysis, we wish to weigh what he has said, then the consistency of what he has said will be a significant factor. As a last word on this part of Knight's essay it is well to deter any who would take him to task for making the same mistake when he refers to 'the wild and rugged Bohemian coast', as though Bohemia had a coast, wild and rugged or otherwise, that it is often said that Shakespeare made in the play itself. Stephen Orgel discusses this well in his preface to the Oxford edition of the play (1996, pp. 37–8). He refers to S L Bethell's suggestion in *The Winter's Tale: A Study* (1947) that the coast of Bohemia might well be a popular joke against the ignorant as, in our own times, the Swiss Navy or Wigan Pier have been.[47] To describe the coast of Bohemia as wild and rugged is not necessarily a revelation that Wilson Knight believed that Bohemia did in fact have a coast: the play tells us that there is one, and Wilson Knight tells us that it is 'wild and rugged'. If there were one, it might well be. As there is none, there can be no meaningful dispute about what it looks like.

In the second part of his essay Wilson Knight refers to the Chorus, Time, and Time's description of himself, in which Time says of himself that he 'makes and unfolds error [4.1.2]' to show how Shakespeare in these plays is returning to the world of the comedies in which tragedy is often hinted at in order to do something much more radical than they could, that is, to move events towards the reconciliation and justification that tragedy does not approach. His view of Autolycus is at variance with Q's lack of interest in the character. Q had said:

■ I challenge anyone to read the play through, to seat himself at table, and write down what Autolycus does to further the plot. Let me not deny the knave his place in the picture. That is appropriate enough, and delightful. But as factor in the plot, though from the moment of his appearance he seems to be constantly and elaborately intriguing, in effect he does nothing at all. As a part of the story he is indeed so negligible that Mary Lamb [1764–1847] in the *Tales from Shakespeare* left him out altogether. Yet Autolycus is just the character that Charles [Lamb (1775–1834)] and Mary Lamb delighted in. Again I give you my private opinion: which is that Shakespeare meant to make a great deal of Autolycus, very carefully elaborated him to take a prominent and amusing part in the recognition scene, tired of it all, and suddenly, resolving to scamp the recognition scene, smothered him up along with it.[48] □

Wilson Knight sees in Autolycus the embodiment of Shakespeare's 'positive intuitions', an approach one may characterize as seeking always to see the glass as still half-full rather than as already half-empty, at the risk of trivializing what, for Wilson Knight, is almost a lifeline offering rescue from the intuitions that result in tragedy. There is a considerable price to be paid for these 'positive intuitions', however, for 'richest humour offers a recognition of some happy universal resulting from the carefree stripping away of cherished values'[49] and he cites Falstaff and his own writing on that character as a reference point.[50] He says that 'Falstaff, though utterly unmoral, yet solicits our respect, and in that recognition consists the fun'. It may equally be argued that Falstaff solicits many feelings other than respect and that King Harry's rejection of him at last in *The Second Part of King Henry the Fourth* [1596/7–1600] represents the rejection by maturity of youthful follies, however attractive they may be at certain points in one's life:

■ I know thee not, old man. Fall to thy prayers.
How ill white hairs become a fool and jester!
I have long dreamt of such a kind of man,
So surfeit-swelled, so old, and so profane;
But being awake, I do despise my dream. □ (*2 Henry IV*, 5.5.47–51)

It may well be that if one strips away 'cherished values' then one may enjoy a 'carefree' state, but much of Shakespeare's work is concerned to look carefully, and quizzically, at the 'carefree' state. In *Twelfth Night*, for example, he has Sir Toby say, ominously enough, 'What a plague means my niece to take the death of her brother thus? I am sure care's an enemy to life (1.3.1–2)'. This is not unambiguous because the play shows us that Olivia's manner is indeed morbid but also that it is not unconnected with the unwelcome attentions to her of Count Orsino – this is a Shakespearean comedy after all and not a moral thesis – but it does contrast the two words 'care' and 'life', and it offers an obvious meaning, that being careworn leaves one little room for enjoyment as well as a further meaning, that being uncaring is a pre-condition for enjoying life. To be free from care is not the same as being uncaring: the word carefree is dangerously ambiguous in this respect. Wilson Knight himself argues that the portrayal of Autolycus darkens as a 'court' element enters, through Polixenes, and as Autolycus acquires an interest in 'advancement [4.4.836]'. Wilson Knight notes that the same thing happens to Falstaff in *2 Henry IV*.

However the play may delight in these pastoral scenes there is never any losing sight of what Wilson Knight calls the play's 'high seriousness'.

As he says in the summary, many traditions have been drawn upon: what he calls 'orthodox tradition' (by which he means, surely, orthodox Christianity, in the sense of 'mainstream' Christianity, which, in these islands, usually means the Church of England, and not Orthodox Christianity, with reference to the Eastern Christian tradition) as well as 'pagan naturalism'; the Bible and Graeco-Roman mythology, and he concludes:

■ The greatest influence was Life itself, that creating and protecting deity whose superhuman presence and powers the drama labours to define.[51] □

One might add, but not more so than the critic who labours to define the play's labours to define. Shakespeare was able to draw on a 'gallimaufry of gambols [4.4.326]' to make up materials with which to work up a complex drama, the significance of which has to be recovered by later audiences, often with patient labour. Of the critics considered in this chapter, both Bethell and Wilson Knight have shown sharp insight into the complexity of the play's materials, even to identifying incongruity and inconsistency, and both have hinted at the particular moment of the English Renaissance as a key element in any attempt to explore this difficult work. Leavis has put his confidence in the existence of an organizing principle that he does not feel that he must identify, perhaps wisely, as Wilson Knight's appeal to 'Life' in his closing pages risks the bafflement, sympathetic or otherwise, with which Leavis's own insistence that '"Life" is a Necessary Word' is often met.[52] Ernest Schanzer (1964) answered Tillyard (1938) in 'The Structural Pattern in *The Winter's Tale*',[53] and it is with that essay that the next chapter begins.

CHAPTER SIX

The Winter's Tale: Later Moderns

The change of perspective, or of temperament, that led to the early twentieth century's approach to *The Winter's Tale*, so very different from the views more common in the eighteenth and nineteenth centuries before it, does not change again. There is a remarkable consistency of view, persisting through many differences of opinion, that *The Winter's Tale* is a work of distinctive seriousness. Ernest Schanzer illustrates this point very clearly: he takes issue with E M W Tillyard's account but does not disagree with his fundamental view that the play deserves, even demands, close and attentive critical discussion.

ERNEST SCHANZER

Schanzer (1964) argues that *Pericles* provides the structural model for *The Winter's Tale*. He points out that Tillyard's ingenious model, that Shakespeare compressed into the play the entire structure of Dante's *Divine Comedy*, starting with the *Inferno* of Leontes's jealous madness, leading into the sixteen-year *Purgatorio* of his grief and regret, culminating in the *Paradiso* of the reunion with his wife and daughter, ignores Act IV. This inconvenience is considerable, as Schanzer observes, and he proceeds to show how Shakespeare had not Dante in mind as much as he had his own earlier work.

In both *Pericles* and *The Winter's Tale*, Schanzer points out, the first three acts concentrate on the father who is absent in the fourth and returns in the fifth. Most importantly perhaps, as more precise, is the following observation:

■ In both plays the reunion of father and daughter is the result of mere chance, while that of husband and wife is the result of direction, its agent being in the one play the goddess Diana, in the other Paulina.[1] □

He sets out the structural pattern of the play using its own metaphors:

■ Shakespeare has divided the play into a predominantly destructive first half and a predominantly creative and restorative half; into a winter half, concentrating on the desolation that Leontes spreads at his court, and a spring and summer half, concentrating on the values represented by the mutual love of Florizel and Perdita and the reunions at the finale.[2] □

Then he adds metaphors of his own making:

■ Leontes, like Macbeth, creates a wintry landscape of death and desolation around him, destroying all happiness and good fellowship. But whereas Macbeth, the winter-king, has to be killed before spring and new life – represented by Malcolm – can reign in Scotland, Leontes is made to undergo a long process of purgation.[3] □

More than a hint of *The Golden Bough*[4] hangs round remarks like this and just as that work collapsed entire mythologies into one another on the basis of an imagined structural similarity so this parallel between two very different plays is in danger of ignoring what is distinctive in favour of what may look alike. Malcolm can only be taken to be representative of 'spring and new life' as a contrast to a Macbeth whom we have come unquestioningly to regard as a 'winter-king', and only by way of contrast. Nothing in the play associates him with 'spring and new life'. Equally nothing associates Macbeth, distinctively, with winter. We should be especially aware of the logical connector 'whereas' that, here, links two quite separate statements as though they had something to do with one another. On the one hand 'Macbeth, the winter-king, has to be killed before spring and new life – represented by Malcolm – can reign in Scotland', and, on the other hand, 'Leontes is made to undergo a long process of purgation', and we have to add, 'before spring and new life – represented by Leontes newly re-united with his wife whom he had thought dead, sixteen-years after her supposed death, and the daughter whom he has not seen during those sixteen years – can reign in Bohemia'. To do this is to see how utterly unlike the two situations are in fact, though superficially there is some resemblance.

Schanzer quotes Wilson Knight and Coghill in support of the view that 3.3 is a transitional scene, or 'hinge' (as both Coghill and Wilson Knight call it), as Wilson Knight says, 'not only for the story but also for the life-views it expresses', passing 'from horror to simple, rustic comedy', to 'comedy working in close alliance with birth'.[5] Nevill Coghill says that 'we are passing from tears to laughter, from death to life'.[6] However Schanzer argues that though there are contrasts between the two parts of the play that have been thoroughly rehearsed in the critical literature, the parallels between the two parts of the play have not been considered. He points out that:

■ At the beginning of each half (1.2 and 4.2) stands a brief prose scene of almost identical length, consisting of a dialogue between Camillo and another person: Archidamus in the first half, Polixenes in the second. In this dialogue the conversation partly turns upon a happy and harmonious relationship, which is soon to be violently disrupted, that between Polixenes and Leontes in the first half and that between their children, Florizel and Perdita, in the second. In each half Shakespeare then proceeds to bring before us this relationship as it exists for its violent disruption;[7] □

And that:

■ In both halves Camillo plays the same role, advising the victim of the King's anger and helping him to escape from the realm to a place of safety, a parallel which is made explicit when Florizel calls him 'Preserver of my father, now of me [4.4.586]';[8] □

And, finally, that:

■ At the end of each half stands the scene which provides its climax: the trial-scene in the first half, the statue-scene in the second. In each our attention centres on Hermione [...] The first half culminates in Hermione's death, the second in her 'resurrection'. Structural parallels and thematic contrast are here combined.[9] □

In what might be thought a fanciful parallel Schanzer suggests that the figure of the hour-glass alluded to by Time [4.1.16] suggests parallelism in that 'both parts of the hour-glass look alike'. As he puts it 'it may not be fanciful to think that this fact enhances our sense of the similarity of the shape and structure of the two halves of *The Winter's Tale*'.[10]

When we recall that it is not quite so fanciful to imagine that a prop and a piece of stage-business might accompany Time's 'I turn my glass', the parallelism, not quite so convincing to the reader, becomes more convincing. In a similar manner, imagery of Nature, natural cycles, seasons, growth, common to both halves of the play, Schanzer points out, contributes to a sense of parallelism as well as to a sense of contrast (with the mood of the action of the first half of the play). The function of the parallelism is, according to Schanzer, 'to increase our sense of the fragility, the precariousness of human happiness':

■ As we watch, twice over in the play's symbolic pattern, the progression from summer to winter, with the return of spring and summer at the end, the affinity between human affairs and the cycle of the seasons, which is close to the imaginative core of *The Winter's Tale*, is borne in upon us.[11] □

We might as well, I think, suggest another interpretation: that the parallelism does indeed suggest the cyclical and repetitive, the returning pattern, but that the linear pattern of wrongdoing, suffering, redemption and restoration overrides the seasonal cycle, enduring through it and rescuing us from repetition. Either view will appeal to us not so much as a result of contemplating what evidence the play provides but more as a result of our predilections in other, related matters, much as those determine our view whether the glass is already half empty or still half full. Inga-Stina Ewbank concentrates on the hour-glass in her study.

INGA-STINA EWBANK

Inga-Stina Ewbank in her essay entitled '"The Triumph of Time" in *The Winter's Tale*' (1964) takes the sub-title of *Pandosto* (1588: a prose romance by Robert Greene (*c*. 1558–92)), on which the play is based, 'The Triumph of Time', and seeks to show that, while critics have tended to emphasize the late plays' apparent departure from the time-bound realm of the more realistic plays of his middle period, *The Winter's Tale* is really concerned with a benevolent view of Time as the 'beneficent Revealer', transforming 'what the conventional motto suggests – a simple victory of Time, the Father of Truth – into a dramatic exploration of the manifold meanings of Time'.[12] She makes an important point:

■ The chief evidence of Shakespeare's time-thinking in his middle period lies in the time allusions and time imagery of the plays and sonnets. The chief evidence for assuming a lack of concern with time in the last plays has been, it would seem, their almost total lack of time imagery.[13] □

She acknowledges S L Bethell's argument that deliberate anachronisms help to achieve an effect of timelessness[14] and she makes the same point that Schanzer makes, that 'the most obvious indication of Shakespeare's concern with time is the overall structure of the play',[15] pointing out also that 'through the arrangement of the play into two halves separated by the "wide gap" of sixteen years, past and present can be emphatically juxtaposed'.[16] The play is able to explore 'what time does to man'. The conversation between Archidamus and Camillo she sees as a 'scene of exposition' that 'proceeds via a series of references to time seen as natural growth'.[17] Her analysis of the opening scenes shows how the play presents the time that has passed in the lives of the central characters as associated with loss, with loss of innocence, and youth, and young passion. She points out that it is Leontes's remembrance of his and Hermione's long engagement (three 'crabbed months') that 'triggers off Leontes's first outburst of jealousy'.[18] Leontes, in Ewbank's view, fails to trust time, impatiently jumping to conclusions instead of allowing time to take its course and prove his fears unfounded: 'he goes, as it were, against time and is therefore blind to truth; for time, when not allowed to ripen, can only *make*, not *unfold*, error'.[19] Her analysis points to elements of imagery and syntax that reinforce the impression of Leontes's violation of the natural order of time and this analysis contributes not a little to the view that the play is very carefully organized. In Ewbank's view the time-gap in the play is deliberate and the device of Father Time appropriate as it is in fact time that is the focus of the play's attention. Father Time's appearance provides 'a pivotal image, part verbal, part visual, of the Triumph of Time'.[20]

The figure of Father Time, Ewbank reminds us, would have been familiar to audiences of the period:

■ Needless to say, Shakespeare's audience in 1610–11 would have been familiar with the figure of Father Time, from innumerable verbal and pictorial representations and from pageants and masques. Time as the Father of Truth had appeared in the last three royal entries, and Thomas Middleton [*c.* 1580–1627] was soon going to use him in the 1613 Lord Mayor's show, *The Triumphs of Truth* [1613].[21] □

As Ewbank points out, Time was an ambivalent figure, not only bringing to fruition but also 'mowing mankind down' as he first appears, for example, in the masque *The Triumph of Time* (*c.* 1612), by Francis Beaumont (1584–1616) and John Fletcher (1579–1625):

■ Yet, to the Elizabethan or Jacobean imagination, Time is never for long allowed to remain a purely beneficent figure [...] Those who tried to put Father Time on the stage in his dual significance often found themselves ending up with an unresolved contradiction, as in Middleton's *Triumphs of Truth*, where Time, the agent of good, suddenly and incongruously turns destructive:

TIME, standing up in TRUTH's Chariot, seeming to make an offer with his sithe to cut off the glories of the day, growing neere now to the season of rest and sleepe, his daughter TRUTH thus meekely stays his hand.[22] □

Ewbank's deliberate association of *The Winter's Tale* with elaborate entertainments such as the masque and the Lord Mayor's show and the royal entry is an important reminder that the theatre for which Shakespeare was writing these later plays was not the same as the theatre for which he had written the earlier plays. 'Private' theatres, roofed in and more expensive than the public theatres such as the Globe, and the development of indoor entertainments reliant on elaborate stage machinery, such as the masque, were contributing to the development of a more exclusive theatre audience.[23]

Her discussion of the first scenes of Act 4, especially 4.4, the 'pastoral scene', is detailed, leading to the conclusion that:

> ■ These speeches [of Perdita] are not just decorative or just meant to create atmosphere: they not only establish a contrast between this world and the world of most of the first three Acts, but also define the contrast as being between a world where time is taken for granted and one where time is altogether defied.[24] □

The pastoralism is not timeless: 'the love of Florizel and Perdita in a central passage pits itself against time and change. Florizel's adoration is formulated as a desire to arrest time, to achieve permanence outside the flux of time'.[25] Ewbank quotes:

> ■   When you speak, sweet,
> I'ld have you do it ever; [...]
>   When you do dance, I wish you
> A wave o' th' sea, that you might ever do
> Nothing but that, move still, still so. □   (4.4.136–42)

Ewbank might have added that the duality of time is caught beautifully in a little exchange a few lines earlier. Perdita is wishing for some 'flowers o' th' spring' for Florizel:

> ■   O, these I lack,
> To make you garlands of, and my sweet friend,
> To strew him o'er and o'er. □

And Florizel replies:

> ■ What, like a corpse? □

To which Perdita rejoins:

> ■ No, like a bank, for love to lie and play on,
> Not like a corpse – or if, not to be buried,
> But quick and in mine arms. □   (4.4.127–32)

Ewbank comments:

> ■ Both Florizel and Perdita are aware of the precariousness of their love in relation to the extra-pastoral world, and throughout the scene the audience sees the threat to it literally present, in the shape of the disguised Polixenes.[26] □

Ewbank makes some shrewd points about the 'critics of the myth-making school' who insist on seeing the entry of Florizel and Perdita into Leontes's presence, and his reaction to that entry, 'Welcome hither / As is the spring to the earth', as the first sign of the regeneration of the old king. To generalize in this way, she says, is to miss the significance of Paulina's reminders to everyone that an earlier beauty has passed away and that to celebrate the present, and regeneration, is to neglect a duty to the past, to Hermione: 'Perdita's return, then, becomes the occasion for several and varied insights into what time does to man'.[27]

Of the last scene Ewbank says:

■ The whole scene has about it a sense of the fullness of time – pointed at the climactic moment by Paulina's 'Tis time; descend (5.3.99)' – of stillness and solemnity. Speeches are short, the diction plain, the language almost bare of imagery: as if Shakespeare is anxious not to distract attention from the significance of action and movement. Characters' reactions to the statue are patterned in a fashion which approaches ritual.[28] □

The statue scene brings together the different aspects of time that the play has evoked. Ewbank shows how complex a sense of time this closing ritual has to offer but stresses:

■ It would, needless to say, be wrong to think of *The Winter's Tale* as a treatise on time. The play does not state or prove anything. But through its action, its structure and its poetry, it communicates a constant awareness of the powers of time.[29] □

Northrop Frye's account appeals to formal questions rather than to abstractions such as time or 'Life' and that will be considered next.

NORTHROP FRYE

In his 1963 essay, 'Recognition in *The Winter's Tale*', Northrop Frye fastens on the device of recognition in an attempt to bring the play under a rule of some kind. His discussion concludes with a set of somewhat mystical conundrums as is often the fate of criticism of this play:

■ Much is said about magic in the final scene, but there is no magician, no Prospero, only the sense of a participation in the redeeming and reviving power of a nature identified with art, grace, and love. Hence the final recognition is appropriately that of a frozen statue turning into a living presence, and the appropriate Chorus is Time, the destructive element which is also the only possible representative of the timeless.[30] □

The device of recognition Frye identifies as deriving from two Roman dramatic traditions, both of which, Frye says, originate with the practice of the ancient Greek comic poet and playwright, Menander (c. 342–291 BC):

■ In *The Winter's Tale* Shakespeare has combined two traditions which descended from Menander, pastoral romance and New Comedy, and has consequently come very close to Menandrine formulas as we have them in such a play as *Epitripontes*. But the fact that this conventional recognition scene is only reported indicates that Shakespeare is less interested in it than in the statue scene, which is all his own.[31] □

He is perceptive on the structure of the play, in structure *The Winter's Tale*, like *King Lear*, falls into two main parts separated by a storm:

■ The two parts form a diptych [a painting or writing tablet with two hinged panels or leaves] of parallel and contrasting actions, one dealing with age, winter, and the jealousy of Leontes, the other with youth, summer, and the love of Florizel. The first part follows Greene's *Pandosto* closely; for the second part no major source has been identified.[32] □

Thus the fact that 'the play ends in a double recognition scene' is structurally significant as it echoes the bi-partite structure of the play as a whole. Frye points out that the later plays have what he calls 'an emblematic recognition scene, in which we are shown the power that brings about the comic resolution'.[33] Both *Pericles* and *Cymbeline* have scenes in which the gods appear and *The Tempest* is suffused with 'the power that brings about the comic resolution', but *The Winter's Tale* has only the sheep-shearing scene to offer. This is significant because although Apollo is mentioned, he does not appear, and Frye observes that:

■ In any case the controlling power in the dramatic action of *The Winter's Tale* is something identified both with the will of the gods, especially Apollo, and with the power of nature.[34] □

Frye identifies an opposition between the wrath of Leontes and the 'grace' of Hermione and points out that:

■ Such grace is not Christian or theological grace, which is superior to the order of nature, but a secular analogy of Christian grace which is identical with nature – the grace that [Edmund] Spenser [1552?–99] celebrates in the sixth book of *The Faerie Queene* [1596].[35] □

He makes the important point that:

■ In the romances, and in some of the earlier comedies, we have a sense of an irresistible power, whether of divine or human agency, making for a providential resolution. Whenever we have such a strong sense of such a power, the human beings on whom it operates seem greatly diminished in size. This is a feature of the romances which often disappoints those who wish that Shakespeare had simply kept on writing tragedies.[36] □

There is more in the mix:

■ Hermione, like Thaisa in *Pericles*, is brought to life by the playing of music, and references to the art of magic follow. Art, therefore, seems part of the regenerating power of the play, and the imagination of the poet is to be allied with that of the lover as against that of the lunatic.[37] □

Frye identifies three kinds of art in the play: the art of the gardener, from the discussion between Polixenes and Perdita, which he connects with the account of art given in *An Apology for Poetry* (1595), by Sir Philip Sidney (1554–86), as a golden world contrasted with the brazen world of nature but who also 'speaks of art as a second nature'. Secondly, 'there is the kind of art represented by Julio Romano [...] a mimetic realist who "would beguile Nature of her custom, so perfectly is he her ape [5.2.98–9]"'. However as there is no statue 'the entire reference to Romano seems pointless'. Frye suggests that:

■ Neither he nor the kind of realism he represents seems to be very central to the play itself. The literary equivalent of realism is plausibility, the supplying of adequate causation for events. There is little plausibility in *The Winter's Tale*, and a great deal of what is repeatedly called 'wonder'.[38] □

However as Bethell and Wilson Knight have pointed out there is a considerable emphasis on another kind of realism: the realism of local detail. Wilson Knight wisely says that 'Dis [4.4.118] may be classical, but his "wagon" is as real as a wagon in Hardy'.[39] 'As real as a wagon in Hardy' here refers to the works of the novelist and poet Thomas Hardy (1840–1928). The third kind of art in Frye's scheme is associated with this strain of realism as it is 'the crude popular art of the ballads of Autolycus'. Frye takes the opportunity to moralize on Mopsa's question to Autolycus regarding his ballad of 'how a usurer's wife was brought to bed of twenty money-bags at a burden'; 'Is it true, think you? [4.4.264]' she asks. Frye, like Bethell, says:

■ We notice that Shakespeare seems to be calling our attention to the incredibility of his story and to its ridiculous and outmoded devices when he makes both Paulina and the Gentlemen who report the recognition of Perdita speak of what is happening as 'like an old tale'.[40] □

Frye suggests that 'the kind of art manifested by the play itself is in some respects closer to these "trumpery" ballads than to the sophisticated idealism and realism of Polixenes and Romano'.[41] He says:

■ The fact that Leontes' state of mind is a parody of the imagination of lover and poet alike links *The Winter's Tale* with Shakespeare's 'humour' comedies, which turn on the contrast between fantasy and reality.[42] □

Further, Frye identifies points of contrast that help to unify the play, contributing to the central action of Leontes' redemption from his condition of fantasy by means of the art of the statue-scene, containing the flower-dialogue, Polixenes mirroring Leontes' wrath, and Perdita and Florizel at the heart of the pastoral, both contrasting and complementary. If it seems that the conversation regarding grafting is a model of some kind Frye observes that 'as always in Shakespeare, the structure of society is unchanged by the comic action'. The art of the gardener does not seem to apply:

■ A society which is artificial in a limited sense at the beginning of the play becomes at the end still artificial, but natural as well. Nature provides the means for the regeneration of artifice. But still it is true that 'The art itself is nature', and one wonders why a speech ending with those words should be assigned to Polixenes, the opponent of the festival.[43] □

To make sense of all this Frye appeals to Renaissance cosmology. Renaissance cosmology derives from a Christian world-view predicated upon the idea of a Fall (mythologically presented in the story of the Garden of Eden in the book of Genesis with which the Old Testament begins). In Renaissance cosmological theory there are, Frye explains, two levels of Nature: the fallen state in which human being is conducted and the higher order, glimpsed in its remnants, the starry spheres, to which humanity aspires through civilization. The attributes of civilization, such as art and music, education, law, are means by which humanity tries to reach again the former, pre-lapsarian, state. Frye refers to the structure outlined by Wilson Knight in *The Shakespearean Tempest* (1932) in which 'the tempest symbolizes the destructive elements in the order of nature, and music the permanently constructive elements in it'. Music and its association with the spheres, of which the moon, the closest, is usually the focus, is traced through several plays but a contrast is drawn with *The Winter's Tale*:

■ But in *The Winter's Tale* nature is associated, not with the credible, but with the incredible: nature as an order is subordinated to the nature that yearly confronts us with the impossible miracle of renewed life.[44] □

Thus we are left with a scheme that is subverted by a play that fits no model and transforms the traditions from which it derives. It may be suggested that this is what art does: not to express systems of ideas as those are drawn up by scholars but to give expression to the intuitions that those systems emerge from as a rigid expression of what remains fluid in art, shaped but not fixed. Nevill Coghill addresses more immediate practicalities.

NEVILL COGHILL

Nevill Coghill, in a stimulating piece, takes the editors and critics to task for ignoring the fact that *The Winter's Tale* is a stage play:

■ Shakespeare's stage-craft in this play is as novel, subtle and revolutionary as it had been a few years before in *Antony and Cleopatra*, but in an entirely different way: just as he had then found the technical path to an actual and life-sized world – to the drums and tramplings of the Roman Empire – so, in *The Winter's Tale* he hit upon a means of entry into the fabulous world of a life standing (as Hermione says) in the level of dreams. (3.2.80)[45] □

Coghill starts with the supposed sudden onset of jealousy and points out that the opening dialogue prepares us for a scene we do not in the event meet: a scene of kingly amity. Polixenes and Leontes enter separately, Polixenes standing next to a visibly pregnant Hermione and talking to her. Polixenes' speech makes it clear that he has been staying with Leontes and Hermione for nine months. Coghill suggests that the mere opening would make the audience wonder whether the child were Leontes' or Polixenes'. Coghill contrasts the elaborate speech of Polixenes with the coldly reserved and undecorated speeches of Leontes and concludes that:

■ It is clear that Leontes, as in the source-story which Shakespeare was following, has long since been jealous and is angling now (as he admits later) with his sardonic amphibologies [phrases or sentences that are grammatically ambiguous], to catch Polixenes in the trap of the invitation to prolong his stay, before he can escape to Bohemia and be safe.

All this [...] is easy for an actor to suggest, facially and vocally, and it is the shock we have been prepared to receive by the conversation of Archidamus and Camillo. We have witnessed a little miracle of stage-craft.[46] □

Coghill's approach to the second point of stage-craft, the exit of Antigonus, 'pursued by a bear', is equally ingenious. The moment to be dramatized is 'the moment when the tale, hitherto wholly and deeply tragic, turns suddenly and triumphantly to comedy'[47] and 'to pass from tragedy to comedy, it may not be unskilful to build the bridge out of material that is both tragic and comic at the same time'.[48] The explanation needs to be presented in detail:

■ Now it is terrifying and pitiful to see a bear grapple with and carry off an elderly man to a dreadful death, even on the stage; but (such is human nature) the unexpectedness of an ungainly animal in pursuit of an old gentleman (especially one so tedious as Antigonus) can also seem wildly comic; the terrible and the grotesque come near to each other in a *frisson* of horror instantly succeeded by a shout of laughter; and so this bear, this unique and perfect link between the two halves of the play, slips into place and holds.[49] □

Coghill quotes the Clown's description of Antigonus' death to underline his point and summarizes his view thus:

■ So far from being crude or antiquated, stage-craft such as this is a dazzling piece of *avant-garde* work; no parallel can be found for what, at a stroke, it effects: it is the transformation of tragedy into comedy: it symbolizes the revenge of Nature on the servant of a corrupted court: it is a thundering surprise; and yet those Naturals that are always demanding naturalism cannot complain, for what could be more natural than a bear?[50] □

There is at least a suspicion that Coghill is here exercising his ingenuity with his tongue in his cheek, though that in itself does not mean that he does not intend to be taken seriously. However, tragedy and comedy do naturally sit side by side, and popular comedy is particularly adept at switching rapidly between, if not tragedy then at least pathos, and comedy. The pathos of Antigonus' last speech (that speech is melancholy, ruminative, mournfully reflective even, but it is not tragic) is immediately succeeded by the homely rustic meanderings of the Old Shepherd and then by the gabble of the Clown; the bear has been prepared for by the Mariner's warning to Antigonus not to go too far inland as 'this place is famous for the creatures / Of prey that keep upon't [3.3.11–12]' at least in general, as a 'creature of prey'; bears were far from unknown to Jacobean audiences (Quiller-Couch even suggests that the bear-pit at Southwark may have provided the bear[51]); Louise G Clubb has pointed out that in the European tradition bears are both tragic and comic as a rule and often act as a generic marker for tragicomedy.[52]

On Time as a Chorus Coghill says:

> ■ His function is as follows: he shows us that we are being taken beyond 'realism' into the region of parable and fable, adumbrated in the title of the play. Time stands at the turn of the tide of the mood, from tragedy to comedy, and makes a kind of pause or poise at the play's centre; coming to us from an unexpected supernatural or mythological region, yet he encourages us (in spite of that solemnity) to enter with confidence, by the easy-going familiarity of his direct address, into that mood of comedy initiated by the no less unexpected bear.[53] □

In a final defence of his view of the Chorus, Coghill makes a point he has made before that deserves consideration again: 'He who holds too tenaciously in the study of Shakespeare to "realism" and the Unities, has left the punt and is clinging to the pole'.[54] The lesson of Thomas Rymer (1641–1713) is to the point here but more generally Coghill's warning against expecting 'realism' is valuable, especially as it is put more seriously than it was when put earlier ('and yet those Naturals that are always demanding naturalism cannot complain, for what could be more natural than a bear?').

The complex stage-business towards the end of 4.4 that gets Camillo, Florizel and Perdita off the stage, leaving it to Autolycus, the Old Shepherd and the Clown, is discussed in terms of two important assumptions: that the stage directions (that may confuse) are 'the invention of editors'[55] and that the play must be conceived always as performance and not as reading-matter.[56] The only way to test such passages is to try them out in practice, either literally or in imagination, to see whether they can, or could, be made to work. Coghill believes that they can be. In the same line, his defence of the relating of the recognition by Leontes of Perdita by three gentlemen in Act 5 scene 2 draws attention to the displays of virtuosity in wit, much, as he says, in the 'Metaphysical' manner, and accounts for it thus:

> ■ Never in the memory of court-gossip has there been so joyful and so astounding a piece of news to spread; they are over the edge of tears in the happy excitement and feel a noble, indeed a partly miraculous joy, for the oracle has been fulfilled; so far as they can, they temper their joy with their wit.[57] □

It is important to notice that Coghill's immediate appeal is to the theatre, of which he says that 'Whoever saw the production of it by Peter

Brook [born 1925] at the Phoenix Theatre in 1951–2 will remember the excitement it created'.[58]

Finally, the statue-scene. Coghill's most important point is that he wishes to avoid 'those private, still more those metaphysical interpretations, to which even the best of us are liable'[59] and he points out that Hermione is *believed* dead (by Leontes and the audience) and is restored *to him*, not to life; she is not 'resurrected'. It is interesting to note that for Coghill's view the mention of Giulio Romano is 'a novel trick to borrow a kind of authenticity from the "real" world of the audience, to lend solidity to the imaginary world of the play'[60] where Northrop Frye could find no reason for Romano's being mentioned at all: 'Neither he nor the kind of realism he represents seems to be very central to the play itself'.[61] All becomes clear when it is realized that Frye is voyaging without restraint straight into 'those private, still more those metaphysical interpretations, to which even the best of us are liable'. For the reader concerned with interpretation the practicalities of stage-craft are of a secondary importance whereas for a man who made his living from the stage they were of the utmost importance. This is Coghill's chief point.

It is not a 'knock-down' argument: interpretation is not merely 'private'. There are risks attendant upon it but the picture Leavis draws of the activity of criticism is both reasonable and comprehensive:

■ You cannot point to the poem; it is 'there' only in the re-creative response of individual minds to the black marks on the page. But – a necessary faith – it is something in which minds can meet.[62] □

The poem 'is neither merely private and personal nor public in the sense that it can be brought into the laboratory or pointed to'.[63] This attempted dissolution of the subjective-objective dilemma that bedevils so much thinking is welcome, if not as widely accepted, even within critical discourse, as it should be. It will apply, without adjustment, to the notion of interpretation. However Coghill's reminder is salutary too. We must not desert what may be 'brought into the laboratory or pointed to' for what may, on closer inspection, turn out to be 'merely private and personal', even if it has convinced quite a few of us. When Leavis says 'it is something in which minds can meet' he envisaged the most severely critical encounter as a result of which, and only after initial reluctance even, minds met. We know only too well that minds can meet in the most preposterous opinions with the greatest of ease: that is not much of a standard.

Coghill's final point regarding the statue-scene is that there is still some explaining to be done. Hermione after all remains still for more than eighty lines. His answer to the apparent problem – why? – is that:

■ Those among the audience who may think her a living woman, encouraged by Paulina's promise to 'make the statue move indeed', must be *reconvinced against hope that she is a statue* if the miracle is really to work excitingly for them.[64] □

It may not only be for Leontes' sake that he has Paulina warn him that the colour on it is not yet dry (though that may work both ways of course). Coghill says that Shakespeare 'stretched his art' in this scene: no one who has seen it, and seen it work on stage, will doubt that it was worth the risk. The point is in something that Samuel Johnson realized about theatre: that the audience is not misled into believing that what it sees is reality but that what it sees 'brings realities to mind'.[65] No one in any audience believes that the statue is not an actor but every member of every audience is capable of believing, against what it hopes – and hopes reasonably because it obviously is an actor pretending to be a statue – that it is not a live Hermione restored against all hope and deserving; that Leontes will not after all be granted happiness beyond all hope and deserving but only an all too vivid reminder of what he has lost through his own fault; that we, the audience, will not be allowed to glimpse a miracle through the subtle devising of stage-craft. For even though the statue is obviously an actor pretending to be a statue, the audience does not know that that pretence will be ended before the play has ended. M M Mahood explores the 'psychology' of the play that Leavis had said should not concern us, though she does this through the poetry, which he had said should concern us, and does not treat the play as 'psychologizing' in the manner of the novel, against which Leavis had warned.

M M MAHOOD

M M Mahood contributed, in *Shakespeare's Wordplay* (1957), a densely argued analysis of the poetry of *The Winter's Tale*, too tightly-knit to summarize easily. Some of what she has to say about 'play' will indicate the method, and some significant content, of her essay. Her argument is that the poetry in the last plays cannot be appreciated in the theatre but only reveals its full meaning upon closer examination. Once again the tension between Shakespeare to be read and Shakespeare to be acted has surfaced. We need not assume that the results of the close analysis to which she subjects the poetry escape the audience, however: nor do we need to dip into psychology and bring in theories of 'the unconscious level', unless we mean only that the play will bear repeated attention from audiences, who will find more each time they go to see it. We should not assume that these plays were written as much popular entertainment of our own day is written to be used once and then discarded.

Mahood takes Leontes' bitter remark to Mamillius at 1.2.188–90 as her starting point:

> ■ Go play, boy, play. Thy mother plays, and I
> Play too; but so disgraced a part, whose issue
> Will hiss me to my grave. □

And she comments:

> ■ Only the first *play* is used in a single sense. We might paraphrase Leontes' *double-entendre* thus: 'Go and amuse yourself; you mother is also pretending to play by acting the kind hostess, but I know that she is a real daughter of the game and up to another sport which makes me act the contemptible role of the deceived husband. So for the moment I'm playing her like a fish ("I am angling now [1.2.181]") by giving her line'. This ironic wordplay of Leontes is sustained through *disgraced*, meaning both 'ungraceful' and 'shameful', and *issue* meaning 'exit', 'result' and perhaps also 'Polixenes' bastard child that Hermione now carries. □

Clearly this sort of close attentiveness to language, to following its implications and extrapolating meanings, is not possible in the theatre: the action proceeds whether one has caught on or not. Successive returns to the theatre, armed with the results of careful consideration of the text in the meanwhile, will, however, allow an audience member this rich experience. The reward is to hear, when the actor speaks Leontes's words, these resonances that Mahood picks out for us.

She continues:

> ■ But *play*, *disgraced* and *issue* have other functions besides that of rendering Leontes' paroxysms true to life. Shakespeare counters each of Leontes' puns by further meanings which relate the word to the larger context of the play's thought and action. The meaning 'make-believe' is added in this way to all the senses of *play*. Leontes is play-acting in his outburst; it is characteristic of such obsessions as his that the sufferer is deluded yet half knows he is under a delusion – as when we know we are in a nightmare but cannot wake from it. □

This is a startling analysis: Leontes may, in some way, know that his suspicions are unfounded and his wife and friend innocent; he may be under a spell of some kind, the spell of jealous fantasy that he might have allowed to start growing in his imagination, but that he can no longer control. Mahood argues that the narrative of the play suggests that a radical, paradoxical reversal, through make-believe, will cure Leontes and restore him to reality. Only by the make-believe of the statue-scene becoming the reality of the restored Hermione can this intrusion of make-believe into reality be overcome.

Mahood pursues the meanings of the words 'disgraced' and 'issue' further. Leontes is 'dis-graced', as it were, having forfeited grace through his insistent jealousy; the word (negatively) also hints at Hermione's future role in the play as the vehicle of the return of grace. 'Issue' means 'child' (Mamillius obviously, but also Perdita), but also means 'action' in Shakespeare sometimes, and suggests the 'issue' (outcome) of the trial of Hermione and perhaps of the whole of the action of this first part of the play (and then, perhaps, of the whole of the play?).

Mahood then turns her attention to the word 'grace'. She notes that after Polixenes' speech in which he recalls 'a primeval innocence when he was "Boy eternal" [1.2.66]' that 'the word "grace" is used three times by Hermione, the implication being that she acts the role of regenerative grace to Leontes now he has exchanged Innocence for Experience'.[66] The connection is made with Perdita, who has 'grown in grace', theologically speaking as well as bodily; the resonances of 'grace' throughout the play (the grace of Leontes's repentance; Hermione's 'grace' of love and patience) are focused in Perdita's presentation to Polixenes and Camillo of 'rosemary and rue':

> ■ Grace and remembrance be to you both,
> And welcome to our shearing. □   (4.4.76–7)

However, though *The Winter's Tale* may be seen as a morality play, its morality is 'wider and more humane than that of a Puritan inner drama of sin, guilt and contrition'. Importantly, 'something is omitted in the attempt made here to allegorise the play'.[67] What is left out is the pastoral idyll of the scenes in Bohemia, at the heart of which is Perdita herself. If the drama is an inner drama of contrition, repentance and redemption then what is her role? Why should not Hermione fulfil that role herself?

Mahood's answer is to suggest that in Leontes's dismissal of Mamillius ('Go play, boy, play') 'is revealed Leontes' inability to keep himself young, to become as a child again'. Leontes 'cannot recapture the non-moral vision of childhood, the state of the "Boy eternal" who had not as yet the knowledge of good and evil'.[68] Cleomenes pleads with Leontes to forgive himself (5.1.1–6) 'but this is just what Leontes cannot do until Perdita's return'. Mahood's argument is that, while Hermione represents the forgiveness of Heaven, Perdita 'stands for self-forgiveness, for his recapture of the child's non-moral acceptance of things as they are in Nature'. Mahood describes Leontes's inability to forgive himself as 'moral intransigence' and appeals to the belief of J I M Stewart (1906–94) that there may be guilt in Leontes's outburst at an adolescent relationship with Polixenes.[69] Mahood sees Leontes's intransigence as 'moral rigidity born of moral uncertainty' and says that 'he cannot see Hermione's real need to play, to the extent perhaps of a harmless flirtation with Polixenes':

Unable to play in the sense of refreshing himself from the non-moral and instinctive life of childhood, Leontes begins to play in the sense of constructing an intensely moral drama in which he acts the role of deceived husband.[70]

Mahood compares the two kinds of play in the first scene of Act 2, in which on the one hand Mamillius 'produces make-believe shudders with his ghost story' and on the other hand Leontes' delusion 'communicates a real horror to the audience who are to see him, in the grip of his involuntary make-believe, turn Mamillius' winter's tale into earnest'.[71]

Mahood makes an interesting point, in such a very compressed manner that it is almost a throwaway comment. It deserves to be picked out, especially as this Guide has as a theme the development of ideas concerning human being and the human world. This theme has been referred to explicitly in Chapter 2, in respect of Suzanne Gossett's consideration of the problems facing an editor of that play (or of any other play in fact: her point is that such problems are peculiarly focused by *Pericles*) and returned to in the discussion of G Wilson Knight's essay on *The Winter's Tale* in Chapter 5. There it was suggested that Wilson Knight's ideas needed further development than he was able to give them: Mahood's comments offer an opportunity to take the theme further.

Mahood suggests that there is something that our own age, that she calls the 'post-Freud epoch', has in common with Shakespeare's, or, in her terminology, the 'pre-Locke epoch'. Sigmund Freud (1856–1939) is significant because of his discoveries concerning the structure of the mind, pre-eminently his contention that what we think of as 'ourselves' is only a small part, and is much beleaguered by another part of ourselves, that we do not consciously acknowledge as part of ourselves at all, that is made up of all the primary impulses that we recoiled from in fright in our infancy when we started to realize what might be the consequences for us if these feelings took control of us and we acted in accordance with them. In this epoch we are used to thinking of lives unbalanced by the unbearable pressure of this part of ourselves on the fragile and defensive 'ego' and can, Mahood implies, easily accept Leontes's fit. Similarly, before the ideas of the English philosopher John Locke (1632–1704) took hold, audiences were more ready to accept the unreasonable. Locke's view of the mind is commonly associated with the development of what is sometimes called the 'Age of Reason' or the 'Age of Enlightenment'. Mahood's remark suggests that this 'Age of Reason' came to an end with the discoveries of Sigmund Freud, which is a shorthand way of pointing to a gradual diminution of confidence in the idea of Reason as a sufficient explanation of human being and a sufficient approach to the human predicament. What has been, for convenience, called postmodernism in recent times can best be seen as a reaction against the Enlightenment project. Where the thinkers of the Enlightenment were confident that reason could solve the problems faced by human being postmodernism, at its extreme, seems to flaunt unreason. Less extravagant postmodern thinkers have expressed a lack of conviction in reason and have gone further to question whether what has passed for rational account has always been what it purported to be. Feminist thinkers especially have been able to show that reason was used to justify the oppression of women through the construction of pictures of society and gender that assigned to them a secondary and inferior place. Of course to be able to show that reason has been misused is not to be able to dismiss reason's claims altogether but it does seriously damage those claims when it is not easy to show that they are grounded beyond dispute and, on the other hand, when it is often easy to convince people that those claims are misleading and have been used by the powerful to maintain the powerless in their subservient position. It has already been said in the Introduction to this Guide that there is a gathering tendency not to respect authority in criticism, and, indeed in many other matters besides: it is part of the theme being pursued at the moment that this diminution in respect for authority has much to do with a widespread perception that the respect for authority that people have shown in various circumstances has been abused by those claiming to have it. Whatever causes are assigned to the phenomenon, though, and it must be controversial to assign causes, there will be general agreement that the phenomenon exists. Part of the phenomenon is the willingness to recognize unreason to which Mahood is pointing.

What Mahood points to is a re-discovery of something Shakespeare's world knew, though it may have talked about it differently and drawn different conclusions about its origins and about what would be the proper way of addressing it. Where we may hypothesize the intrusion of unconscious material into a fragile and weakened conscious 'ego', Shakespeare's world may have talked of possession.

This diversion sets her discussion in context. It establishes a readiness to accept that a man may become insanely jealous and that we have ways of understanding how it may happen. There is a danger, however, of rationalizing the play too far. From her suggestion that in Leontes's dismissal of Mamillius (Go play, boy, play) '*is revealed* Leontes' inability to keep himself young [my italics]', through her assertion that 'if Hermione *represents* the grace of heaven towards Leontes, Perdita *stands for* self-forgiveness [my italics]' through to her analysis of Leontes' 'moral intransigence' there runs a set of assumptions.

At the heart of this discussion lies her affirmation of 'Hermione's *real need* to play [my italics]'. She glosses this important proposal: 'to the extent *perhaps* of a *harmless* flirtation with Polixenes [my italics]'. Now it would alter the play very much to imagine that Hermione had in fact flirted with Polixenes, however 'harmless' another viewer might take such an activity to be. Mahood herself has acknowledged that 'It is possible, of course, to read long-standing suspicion into all Leontes' speeches to Polixenes and Hermione'[72] and Coghill's analysis of the opening scene will support such a view very well. However, Mahood goes on to say that 'this impairs the dramatic contrast between the happiness and harmony of the three characters when Polixenes has agreed to stay, and Leontes' subsequent outburst of passion'. A very careful balance needs to be maintained in any consideration of *The Winter's Tale*, and indeed of other late plays as well, between a desire to bring the events into accord with a more realistic view and an acknowledgement of the role played by the arbitrary, or at least seemingly arbitrary, in these plays' dramatic structure. The final view one takes of the plays depends upon it. That final view may not accord with some of our most cherished beliefs but that is not a reason for allowing our most cherished beliefs to influence unduly our view of the plays.

Suzanne Gossett's careful reminder that we must not allow our own views to contaminate our editorial practice comes to mind. There is no evidence, other than our own conviction that it is true of ourselves, that Hermione has 'a real need to play' and there is much confusion to be feared in the identification of a desire with a need, even if we were to agree that Hermione might have it. We should pull ourselves together and remember the strictures of L C Knights (1906–97) against A C Bradley's intemperate evocations of the extra-dramatic: Stewart's speculations concerning Leontes's supposed 'guilt at an adolescent relationship with Polixenes for which he cannot forgive himself' might even exceed Bradley's own limits.

Further than that, however, 'is revealed' (of Leontes' supposed 'inability to keep himself young') suggests that this was there all along and is not a matter of interpretation but of discovery, and Mahood's assertions that Hermione '*represents* the grace of heaven towards Leontes', and that 'Perdita *stands for* self-forgiveness' raise all the questions involved in the assertion of the relationship of representation. We simply cannot make statements of this kind. They appear to be factual and cannot be factual. They are interpretative statements and have only the validity that such statements have. If Leontes were a real person then these statements could be tested against his acceptance of them: if he recognized himself in them then they would be true. We must ask whether the action of the play shows us Leontes forgiving himself as a result of his encounter with Perdita, and whether he accepts that heaven has forgiven him when Hermione is restored to him, not whether in some supposed factual state of affairs these things are so, but whether they are so in the play. I am not saying that Mahood is mistaking states of affairs: only that we must not mistake states of affairs, reading Mahood, and we may, because of what she has written. It may be to misinterpret her to read her so, but if it is possible to misinterpret then a warning against misinterpretation is appropriate. After all, our business is interpretation, or at least part of it is, and we do not put it aside when we come to reading critics.

Finally, Leontes' 'moral intransigence' deserves comment. Leontes' 'moral intransigence' suggests 'the moral rigidity born of a moral uncertainty', particularly, it seems, his inability to appreciate 'Hermione's real need to play, to the extent perhaps of a harmless flirtation with Polixenes'. There is nothing moral about Leontes' jealousy. His intransigence has more to do with the feelings of a possession spoiled for him, just as it does for Othello, than it has to do with a moral view of anyone's behaviour. Not only would the play be different were we to accept 'Hermione's real need to play, to the extent perhaps of a harmless flirtation with Polixenes', it would be very different were we to accept that Leontes's attitude is one of 'moral intransigence'. The play would become the tale of Leontes's moral disapprobation of Hermione's independence, but that story would have no resolution in the play as it stands: Leontes could not be brought to approve of her behaviour or, alternatively, she could not be brought to regret it in the story as it stands. As it stands, a Hermione over whom no shadow of suspicion, rightly or wrongly, might fall, is brutally maligned by a Leontes whose jealous seizure is unexplained, and who is saved from the unbearable recrimination to which he is subject once he has recovered from his fit by the apparently miraculous restoration of her to him. It is important for this scheme that she is utterly misrepresented by Leontes in his fit and perceived by the audience as an almost saintly presence, suffering patiently and quite undeservedly. The scheme is similar to that of *Othello*: it is important to recognize that though Desdemona may appear to flirt she does so as a child dimly glimpsing a power she did not realize she had and not as a woman fully aware of that power and exercising it to whatever end a 'need to play' might point. The miraculous restoration of a figure more at home in another kind of comedy altogether would serve no conceivable artistic purpose in the play as it stands.

Mahood's view of Hermione has some connections with her view of 'nature' in the play:

■ In *The Winter's Tale* [...] Nature is neither morally good nor bad; a bear's appetite and a waiting-gentlewoman's lapse are accepted as the way of the world.[73] □

In the scenes in Bohemia 'the reconciliation of heaven and earth is not theological but natural, the fructification of nature by the sun that shines alike upon the good and the evil'.[74]

This may go some way towards explaining the overt presence of the classical deities in the play; Christianity does not have much room for a cult of Nature along the lines suggested here, especially one that finds equivalences between 'a bear's appetite and a waiting-gentlewoman's lapse'. However Mahood follows Wilson Knight is seeing Autolycus, in particular, as 'non-moral' (to use a term that Knight uses of Autolycus and Mahood uses of Mamillius and the boyhood of Polixenes and Leontes: 'the child's non-moral acceptance of things as they are in Nature'). There is a touch of 'Golden Age-ism' about such remarks and a carelessness about the careful discrimination with which the character of Autolycus is treated in the play that goes along with a readiness to accept, or to suggest, a 'need to play' in Hermione, 'even perhaps to the extent of a harmless flirtation with Polixenes'. In the moral world of *The Winter's Tale* (which is not Leontes's: he is as subject to it as anyone, more so than some) there is not such harmlessness: there is responsible behaviour and irresponsible behaviour, and innocence and guilt. Innocence refers both to an original, pre-lapsarian, state, but also may mean not guilty as charged. Leontes and Polixenes are both guilty, though they can remember being 'innocent': Hermione is innocent of Leontes's charges against her. Perdita is responsible, and not guilty; Mamillius is just a child, not innocent but having done no obvious harm. Bohemia is not Eden: if it is 'Nature' it is not pre-lapsarian. Critics may want it to be, but that is not reflection on the play.

The second half of the twentieth century saw the developing influence of what came to be called 'theory' in literary criticism. The next chapter will consider key accounts of *The Winter's Tale* from this later phase.

CHAPTER SEVEN

The Winter's Tale: Post-moderns

G Wilson Knight's essay on *The Winter's Tale* adopts a clearly-defined methodology that is quite at the opposite end of the spectrum of possible approaches from that characteristically adopted by contemporary criticism. When Wilson spoke dismissively of 'the side-issues of Elizabethan and Jacobean manners, politics, patronage, audiences, revolutions and explorations', saying that he would be concentrating on 'the poetic quality and human interest of the plays concerned',[1] he placed his work firmly in the tradition that leads up to that work and that surrounds it, and he demarcated himself sharply from what was to develop soon afterwards.

Whereas a clear, though informal, distinction has always been maintained between the activity represented by, say, the Oxford Standard Authors, a tradition of scholarly attention to detail and refraining from critical judgement (the series aimed to present editions that would enable judgement, not make judgements), and the tradition in which F R Leavis stands and for which he makes so emphatic a case, a tradition of critical judgement (in which Dr Samuel Johnson and Matthew Arnold [1822–88], most obviously, and most explicitly, stand[2]), what developed in the middle of the twentieth century, and was fuelled to such effective heights of performance by developments in the parallel disciplines of political philosophy, epistemology [the study in philosophy of knowledge] and psychoanalytical theory, is quite different from either. Scholarship in the service of these theoretically informed perspectives has recently addressed itself energetically to Shakespeare's work. From detailed discussions of genre to close analysis of possible historical allusions and associations there has been no sparing of scholarship on this as on many Shakespeare plays.

William Morse opines that the play demonstrates a 'radical political openness', that it 'teeters in the gap between the ideology of absolutism and anti-absolutist elements incompletely contained'[3] and Simon Palfrey suggests that the genre to which the play belongs is 'politically restless' and that it offers a 'robust and often irreverent challenge to providentialist or conservative ideologies'.[4] S. Viswanathan,

James Siemon and Richard Proudfoot have exhaustively explored the play's 'iterative' imagery (continuing and developing the line of critical inquiry to which M M Mahood's *Shakespeare's Wordplay* made such a significant contribution in the matter of drawing attention to detailed wordplay);[5] Leontes' jealousy has been variously discussed:

■ In terms of Oedipal anxieties and repressed homoerotic desires, of culturally constructed gender systems and patriarchal fears of a woman's subversive power; and of the theory of social time of the Russian literary critic Mikhail Bakhtin [1895–1975], according to which Leontes' jealousy 'is a type of spatiotemporal derangement of the ethos of gift, hospitality, and expenditure, mandated by the observances of the Winter Festival or Christmastide'. Cultural materialists look to the foundation of the nuclear family and the attention paid in the early modern period to 'marital jealousy as one of the central dangers of love'.[6] □

If the events of the play were actual events in history such discussion might be more in place: as it is, analogies may be found between theories of the way things are and the events of plays and other fictions but nothing will have been proved thereby about the world. Fictions cannot prove anything about the world. The world, however, can be brought in to prove something about fictions. To attempt to prove something true about the world by showing that it will fit a fiction is hopeful in the extreme: to pretend that something has been proven about the world to illustrate the workings of a fiction is deceitful; to believe that something has been proven about the world and can therefore illustrate a fiction is naïve.

Graham Holderness expresses the dilemma facing the contemporary cultural critic. A literalistic interpretation of Marx and Engels's conception of 'ideology' suggests that literary works and other cultural products and activities are illusory in the sense that they are productions of a view of the world that systematically falsifies and misleads. There is no purpose to be achieved by studying these works: the task is to expose their complicity in the business of ideology. Holderness comments:

■ The debate is in one sense a re-enactment of an earlier intellectual battle fought out within the theoretical problematic of Marxism. When cultural analysis tried to work with a reductive interpretation of Marx's 'base / superstructure' model, the result was always inevitably a de-materialization of culture, which became largely understood as a smoke-screen concealing economic and political realities.[7] □

Karl Marx [political philosopher; 1818–1883] had speculated that the entire world of human culture evolved as a 'superstructure' built on a 'base' made up of the relationships into which people entered in order to carry out productive tasks (from primitive hunting and gathering activities, through the development of agriculture to the forms of social arrangement he designated feudalism and then capitalism). This entailed the further view that 'It is not the consciousness of men that determines their existence, but, on the contrary, their social existence determines their consciousness'.[8] This meant that Marxists tended to believe that nothing was to be found in cultural artefacts but reflections of the values entailed by the dominant pattern of social relationships that was, in turn, set up in accordance with the exigencies of the prevailing mode of production. Marx also once wrote 'The hand mill gives you society with the feudal lord; the steam-mill, society with the industrial capitalist'[9] and this remark has encouraged many Marxists to imagine that a play, for example, is ultimately nothing more than a reflection of the current state of technological development in any age.

Finding this too limiting a view, other Marxists tried to discover a less direct relationship between 'base' and 'superstructure': 'Using the same model, attempts were made to insist that "culture" always had a "relative autonomy" of the economic base'.[10] Proponents of these views argued that the consciousness of men could not be regarded as redundant because consciousness had to interpret its situation and did so in various ways. Consciousness did not merely straightforwardly reflect the current state of relationships of production or the current state of technological development. If this were not so, they argued, then cultures would not differ. However, adventurous though these efforts often were, they enjoyed limited success:

■ In practice that proposed 'relativity' was always likely, in the analysis of particular examples, to collapse back into determinism, or the 'autonomy' to become so relative as to constitute something like complete cultural and artistic independence.[11] □

Holderness argues that the work of social anthropologists, such as Clifford Geertz [1926–2006] and René Girard [born 1923], proved beneficial:

■ Their attractiveness to historicist, post-structuralist and neo-marxist aesthetics lay in their capacity to grasp the totality of a society, simultaneously in both its political and economic structure, and its cultural superstructure – neither of which, in practice, could truly be separated from the other. If the purpose of culture is to 'express' the nature of a society, to embody in myth and ritual its deepest social experience, then detailed readings of such myth and ritual become valid methods of understanding a society.[12] □

The anthropologically-inflected comments of Suzanne Gossett in her introduction to her edition of *Pericles*, discussed above, indicate this influence, as, more widely, do the feminist-historicist analyses to which she refers, or those conducted by Mikalachki, Kahn and Traub and discussed in this Guide. It is worth noting that, for Holderness, the objective in view is 'understanding a society' and this marks a divide between such approaches and those of, for example, Samuel Johnson, Coleridge, Sir Arthur Quiller-Couch, F R Leavis, and many others discussed in this Guide. It may seem that an older 'criticism' has been replaced by a newer 'scholarship', or 'research' and it is true that modes of critical approach do change, and not only between individual critics but also between ages, so that it is possible to talk of, for example, Romantic criticism, or Modernist criticism, with some accuracy. However, the more useful distinction is to be made between what is the object of study in each case as many contemporary critics do in fact address 'society' as an object of study while others really do continue to address the work. On closer inspection of course it turns out that making a hard and fast distinction between work and society is unsustainable and that any work that requires our serious attention will direct that attention at some point towards the society in which it was composed and to which it addressed itself.

The work of the American philosopher Stanley Cavell embodies this view. Uncommitted to any particular theory – not sailing, as it were, under any particular colours – Cavell gives the impression of open-ended inquiry, pursued where it will lead.

STANLEY CAVELL

A philosopher by profession, he has written on film as well as on literature: his essays collected in *Disowning Knowledge* (1987) are a contribution to Shakespeare criticism. He is, from the point of view of criticism, a traditional critic, pursuing the business of interpretation. He is not looking at 'a society', as a Cultural Materialist, New Historicist or Marxist might, he is not looking at Gender, as a Feminist might, or at Text, as a Deconstructionist might. He is not looking at any object that has to be specified by a theory beforehand nor is he looking at an object in order to develop a theory after the event.

His work resembles that of A C Bradley more than that of any other more recent critic, except for Janet Adelman, and this connects him with Dowden as well as with Adelman and it also specifies a 'modern' period in which severely restrictive theories (such as L C Knights's rejection of Bradleyism in 'How Many Children Had Lady Macbeth?', and Leavis's rejection of the 'Bradley-Archer thesis' in his discussion of the late plays) attempted to cordon off 'the work' (as did New Criticism in America at roughly the same time). A 'modern' period, so specified, would include aspects of Deconstruction to the extent that in that approach there was any attempt to limit discussion (by excluding 'liberal humanism', for example). Cavell's approach is that interpretation is free to explore and to experiment with hypotheses as long as the reader is prepared to put up with it.

Cavell describes his project in his Introduction as follows: 'The plays I take up for respective interpretations of scepticism as they yield to interpretation by scepticism'.[13] He later says:

■ The issue posed is no longer, or not alone, as with earlier scepticism, how to conduct oneself best in an uncertain world; the issue suggested is how to live at all in a groundless world.[14] □

Cavell makes a connection with our own time, suggesting that 'our scepticism is a function of our now illimitable desire' whereas for Descartes the ground still existed in God's existence, but if certainty in that were shaken then the entire world shook. The sceptical problematic addressed by Shakespeare, Cavell asserts, is 'the question whether I know with certainty of the existence of the external world and of myself and others in it' and he classes his view of Shakespeare's work deliberately not as a hypothesis (as, for example, a historian of ideas might want to do) but as an intuition, because a hypothesis would require evidence and all Cavell feels that he can offer is all that intuitions require and that is 'let us say, an understanding of a particular sort'. He then quotes the assertion of the American essayist, philosopher and poet Ralph Waldo Emerson (1803–82) that 'Primary wisdom [is] Intuition, whilst all later teachings are tuitions' and interprets this as saying that 'the occurrence to us of intuition places a demand upon us, namely for tuition; call this wording, the willingness to subject oneself to words, to make oneself intelligible. (Tuition so conceived is what I understand criticism to be)'.[15]

His account of the process of criticism is interesting: he sees the process as one of 'experimentation' and he says that if he speaks 'incredibly or outrageously' all that will happen is that the words will not 'go through' as an error in computation, by analogy, will mean that the computation does not work out. The words, in this case, will 'simply drop out as worthless'.[16]

In other words Cavell is not seeking to prove anything by adducing evidence that will compel assent to a certain type of argument (as sources, influences, and so on): he is testing a reading against the willingness of his audience to go along with him.

By means of a series of bold associations Cavell is able to sketch out a view of scepticism that it is not motivated by 'a (misguided) intellectual scrupulousness' so much as 'a (displaced) denial, by a self-consuming disappointment that seeks a world-consuming revenge'.[17] Scepticism itself is, in a sense, tragic. Cavell is able to say that 'Everyone knows that *something* is mad in the sceptic's fantastic quest for certainty'.[18] Understanding knowledge as dominion (after the German philosopher Martin Heidegger (1889–1976)), of grasping a thing, Cavell is able to read Lear and Othello as models of frustrated, sceptical, yearning to possess something and as raging in their disappointed ambitions. He sees a gender dimension to knowing:

■ The violence in masculine knowing, seems to interpret the ambition of knowledge as that of exclusive possession, call it private property.[19] □

Reflecting that this scepticism is not shared by Hermione, and in fact is what isolates Leontes from Hermione most extremely, Cavell is moved to ask 'is scepticism a male business?'[20] Paternity is always less obvious than maternity (women cannot easily doubt that the child is theirs) and Cavell concludes that '*so far as* scepticism is representable as the doubt whether children are yours, scepticism is not a feminine business'.[21] Scepticism as a masculine business and not a feminine business is finally represented, for Cavell, by female satisfaction: 'Is she satisfied and is the satisfaction directed to me?'[22] This question can only be answered by a man in an extreme state of passive receptiveness because it cannot be answered by any effort on the part of the man; on the contrary, his efforts to be answered will only increase his sceptical conviction that the answer is in the negative. It is this requirement of extreme passiveness that undoes Othello, in Cavell's view, and he goes on to outline the origins of his thinking on the whole matter in these two plays.

His view of *Othello* was shaped by a conviction that Othello had sought, unwittingly enough, an alternative answer to the difficulty identified by Descartes, that is, how can I convince myself of the existence of other human beings? He describes the awful daring of Othello's attempt as the play's interpretation of scepticism, which suggests that Shakespeare was, consciously or otherwise, grappling with scepticism as a problem, or as a condition. The next step is bolder still. Cavell convinces himself that Leontes's jealousy is a cover for his doubt whether his children are his, which is itself an expression of a fear that Hermione's satisfaction is not of him and that, in turn, arouses a doubt concerning his own reality. His ruminations along these lines, he tells us, began in his considering psychoanalysis and cinema and his view that both originated in the suffering of women, 'in particular in the form of a conviction of the woman's unknownness, hence in her existence', and that this problem arises with Descartes and Shakespeare.

Before moving on to Cavell's discussion of Descartes it will be worth noting that the discussion of female sexuality that Cavell has entered on here will be taken up (without reference to Cavell I should say) by Valerie Traub, amongst others, and her views will be considered later in this chapter. Traub's argument depends upon the recognition of a culturally-instituted 'fear of female erotic power'[23] and the 'strategies of containment'[24] that societies, and individuals, pursue as a consequence. Cavell's view may be contrasted as compassionate rather than combative but he too acknowledges, as anyone has to acknowledge, that in these plays it may be said that the anxiety provokes the jealousy shown by their central characters but cannot be offered at all in extenuation of the necessary judgement of their conduct.

Cavell points to Descartes's Third Meditation, at the end of which Descartes advances his certainty in his own being as a ground for asserting the existence of God and Cavell's question, with regard to *Othello*, is why did he not attempt to find such a ground in the assertion of the existence of another human being and his conviction that that is what Othello does in that play (for example 'My life upon her faith' (1.3.294), comes to mean, if she is not satisfied of me then I do not exist). This line of thinking supplies the prelude to his consideration of *The Winter's Tale*. What Cavell calls 'wording' is of central importance to any consideration of what he says (he talks also of 'tuition', following Emerson, meaning 'wording'). A view of words is implied and that is that words are not in any case directly related to things (or to ideas) so in no case is a word inappropriate unless it is not accepted. So-called 'direct' reference (indication) is no more appropriate than indirect (say by metaphor, or allusion, or euphemism). What we must pay attention to is what the words are doing in any case and accept them or reject them in the light of that understanding. The signal advantage of Cavell's method is that the reader is not invited to consider additional assumptions or new theories, only to abandon a favourite prejudice, in order to be put in touch with a view of big ideas working through the most intimate connections in our lives, a form, perhaps, of what the French philosopher Michel Foucault [1926–84] has called the 'archaeology of knowledge', though without the necessity of discussing priority or causation.

He starts with the dead boy:

■ Now here at the end of *The Winter's Tale* a dead five- or six-year old boy remains unaccounted for.[25] □

He has already told us that he associates the boy with the *Ode: Intimations of Immortality* by William Wordsworth (1770–1850) and also with an account by Freud of a phobia in a five-year old boy and he summarizes the meaning of the figure for him in the image of 'adult human life struggling toward happiness from within its own "debris" '.[26] Then follows an ingenious passage at the end of which Cavell concludes that Leontes's fear is in fact of being Mamillius's father rather than of the opposite, that Mamillius is Polixenes's son. The reasoning is intricate and depends upon our perception that mother and son are discovered in an intimate position and have got into it 'as a result of mutually seductive gestures', though having allowed the word to slip in, as it were, he compensates by insisting that all is 'well within the bounds, for all we know, of normal mental and sexual growth'.[27] But what do we know of 'normal mental and sexual growth' except what we have heard of by way of rumours of Freud? And what does 'for all we know' hide from us? Cavell's strategy is to imagine what may be imagined and see where it leads. Because we are 'by now so accustomed to understanding insistence or protestation, perhaps in the form of rage, as modes of denial',[28] then 'we will at least consider that the *negation* of this tale [that Mamillius is not Leontes's son] is the object of Leontes' fear, namely the fear that he *is* the father'.[29]

This enables Cavell to ask: 'Why would the father fear being the true father of his children?'

Several reasons are suggested. There might be, Cavell says, 'some problem with the idea' that he (Leontes) has impregnated the son's mother; some concern that the son will displace him in Hermione's affection; that Leontes himself will 'father' that very displacement (in fathering, bringing up, the son); some concern that this displacement will 'ratify' (Cavell's word) the loss of the affection he and Polixenes enjoyed as boys, which he associates with youth and innocence, and which he, and Polixenes, acknowledge was lost when the women who were to become their wives came on the scene. These 'reasons' are all, deliberately it might be suspected, provocative. They are provocative in that they ask us to follow an analytical path into the emotional life of someone who is not a person anyway but only a character in a drama and who, if in reality a person, might fervently deny any such reasoning about his feelings. Psychoanalysis has a habit of responding by saying that of course he would deny it: and that denial is exactly what proves the correctness of the reasoning. Cavell is taking this kind of thinking further and further away from persons in analytical encounters and deeper and deeper into the cultural meshes in which we are all entwined.

Whatever the reason, Cavell continues, this line of thought would make us suspicious of Leontes's jealousy 'not merely because it makes the jealousy empirically baseless' – because he is not afraid that he is not Mamillius's father but that he is – but 'because it makes it psychologically derivative'. That is, it is not a motivation but is itself motivated.

Cavell wants to put to one side the idea that 'jealousy between brothers [is] a rock-bottom level of human motivation'.

Cavell points out that Leontes's 'diseased opinion' vanishes immediately upon hearing of Mamillius's death. He proposes that the scene in which Mamillius whispers in Hermione's ear is 'explicitly one to cause jealousy',[30] and 'hence the son's death reads like a satisfaction of the father's wish'. Apollo is, then, Cavell suggests, not angry because Leontes has paid no attention to his oracle but because Apollo has been outsmarted by Leontes, 'or rather by his theatre of jealousy', and 'tricked into taking his revenge *for* him, as if himself punished for believing that even a god could halt the progress of jealousy by a deliverance of reason'.

Cavell asks of Leontes's speech, 'I have too much believed mine own suspicion [3.2.150]', 'How much would have been just enough?' This is devastating, for it suggests that the suspicion is not gone, only having gone too far Leontes has drawn back. In Cavell's terms the sceptic remains sceptical but has withdrawn from the brink over which he has peered; it is as though the spider he has glimpsed (2.1.41–7) is still there, though he has averted his gaze.

Cavell moves by way of a series of puns through what he calls 'Mamillius's whispering of a tale of generation, namely ideas concerning telling or relating and ideas concerning breeding and issue'.[31] Moving from relating to recounting to counting back to telling (but now with other meanings of 'counting') Cavell introduces a dualistic vision, 'the opposite faces of a world of partings, of parting's dual valence, as suggested in the paired ideas of participation and of parturition, or in other words of the play, ideas of being fellow to and of dissevering'.[32] He speaks of the play being 'engulfed by economic terms' and he enumerates those terms. He associates that language with the language of computation and through that with an idea of language itself as telling. That leads through a digression into the difficulties of knowing anything at all to Descartes's fear that his thoughts might lead him to express ideas that may make others think him a madman. 'Whereas Leontes is, while in doubt, certainly a madman. What is their difference?'[33]

Leontes is allowed to recover, and the rest of the play is the story of this recovery, 'by seeing something, beyond being told something'.[34] The contrast between the manner in which the discovery by Leontes of his daughter is discovered to the audience and the discovery of his wife is discovered becomes for Cavell a competition between narrative romance and theatrical romance, a competition made more than merely artistic rivalry because the contrast is between a daughter empirically lost, in fact, and a wife not lost in fact, but lost to Leontes, Cavell says, 'transcendentally'. He wants us to see Leontes as blind, to

himself and to Hermione because blind to himself, 'as it were concep-
tually unprepared for her'.[35] Cavell links this to the problem of succes-
sion as that is treated in Shakespeare and as it was a concern to his age:
the problem of recognizing the heir.

Perdita was, by contrast, 'in empirical fact lost', and the telling of
her discovery a much simpler matter. This paragraph makes sense of
something Cavell has said earlier, that in the question whether his wife
had been faithful or not, 'her faithfulness would be at least as bad as her
faithlessness would be'.[36] Cavell is placing faith and doubt, or trust and
doubt, in the scales as alternatives equally demanding and equally to
be feared ('at least as bad'). Why? In his essay on *Othello* he has argued
that what he calls 'the stake of the other' is a recognition that one's
existence depends upon the existence of the other as what you know
(in this case) her to be. Othello's knowledge of Desdemona is what
he cannot accept, his having staked himself on the other. Moreover,
another that exists for one as a body.

The line of reasoning here has to do with the significance of 'the
other' in Cavell's thinking. The significance of the other is derived
from an understanding of Descartes's pursuit of certain knowledge
that he is not alone in the world. Cavell considers Descartes's assertion that he could well imagine forming ideas 'which represent men
similar to myself' by combining other ideas he has. In Descartes's reasoning only God can be other in such a way as to enable Descartes to
know beyond doubt that he is not alone in the world. Cavell argues
that Descartes could not in fact easily imagine others because he would
have to be able to have an idea of the body he imagined having 'a
unique relationship to its mind in that special quasi-substantial way
that he asserts is not like the way a ship is related to its pilot'[37] and
Cavell believes that Descartes does not show that he could have such
an idea. He formulates Descartes's difficulties by saying that the idea of
a double nature (of mind and body) is the idea of Christ and the idea
of Christ is in fact the idea of each individual human being so that 'the
human problem in recognising other human beings is the problem of
recognising another to be Christ for oneself'.[38] These things he says
as part of his introduction to his discussion of *Othello* but because he
sees the two plays as so closely to do with each other (even as the later
play revisiting the earlier) they are relevant to a consideration also of
The Winter's Tale. Cavell's proposal concerning Leontes's anxiety about
being Mamillius's father is thus explained: if Hermione is the child's
mother then she is not the union of the dual natures (the idea of Christ
being the idea of God in man) Leontes needs to confirm his own existence. Furthermore, and crucially, if he is the father of her son then
he has himself destroyed her as this union he needs her to be. He has
brought his fate of loneliness upon himself.

In pursuit of his theme of telling and counting, Cavell makes an important observation that, though one can talk of telling a goldfinch from a goldcrest one cannot, at least in the same way, speak of telling a goldfinch from a peacock, 'or either from a telephone, or any from a phone call'.[39] That is, to distinguish something from something that closely resembles it is easier than to say what something is in itself. A goldfinch does not sufficiently resemble a peacock for any really distinguishing contrasts to be drawn, and the same may be said, only more strongly so, where either bird and a telephone or a phone call is in question. This enables him to make a point about narrative and theatre in the play, the point that it is saying something about showing and telling: it is saying something about what knowledge is, or what it has to be. It is not enough to tell Leontes what he has to learn by being shown Hermione apparently coming back to life from death; for it to tell, to count, he must be shown, and the showing is not just illustration of something that exists somewhere else but a revelation or a creation of the knowledge itself: 'To speak is to say what counts'.[40]

At the heart of his concern is what he describes as 'a portrait of the sceptic at the moment of the world's withdrawal from his grasp'.[41] In such a picture the sceptic is an obsessive about knowledge and wilfully rejects faith and trust as modes of being. Thus human being is divided by scepticism into dissatisfaction with itself and in some the reaction to this dissatisfaction is a violent desire for annihilation.

Cavell links the two parts of the play he has identified (two intellectual 'regions') by a series of puns on the word 'part' as we have seen and moves now into the second region, that of 'departure, separating, dividing, branching, grafting, flowering, shearing, issuing, delivering, breeding: parturition'.[42] He fastens on the play's closing words:

> ■ Good Paulina,
> Lead us from hence, where we may leisurely
> Each one demand and answer to his part
> Performed in this wide gap of time since first
> We were dissevered. Hastily lead away. □   (5.3.152–6)

He asks, 'when were we first dissevered? Who is we?' and advances a general thesis that neither plenitude nor nothingness would satisfy Leontes's fanatical desire, a desire expressed in a vision of the whole world itself as sexualized, a 'bawdy planet'. What Cavell calls the 'world economicized' is what confronts this vision, a world of counting and recounting. Both visions involve the dilemma between plenitude and nothingness, neither of which conditions satisfy Leontes's fantasy. Cavell suggests that Leontes wants to get at Time itself, at life itself, 'its issuing, or separating, or replication'.[43] Leontes's jealousy derives from the 'precipitousness' of scepticism, the sense of the brink at which the sceptic finds himself in his obsessional pursuit of certainty. The 'economicization' of which Cavell speaks is neatly focused by him in the Clown's comical computation at 4.3.35–48: here the reminder is that

> ■ All the arithmetical operations – not alone the multiplying, but dividing, adding, and subtracting – are figures for breeding, or for its reciprocal, dying.[44] □

Autolycus of course supplies a figure himself, in his tale of the usurer's wife 'brought to bed of twenty money-bags at a burden [4.4.261–2]'.

Cavell's reading of the bear is typically adventurous: 'nature seems to be reabsorbing a guilty civilisation'.[45] He is right to point to the coordination of the bear dining on the gentleman with the storm devouring the crew of the ship (which it 'swallowed') and he is interesting on the ramifications of Leontes's 'If this be magic, let it be an art / Lawful as eating (5.3.110–11)', connecting it with the bear, and leading into an idea of nature's violence as the beginning of the process of 'redemption, or rescue, from the shipwreck of human violence, with its unpayable debts'.[46] By comparison, Valerie Traub's more 'mainstream' comments on *The Winter's Tale* illustrate what feminist criticism can do with such a work.

VALERIE TRAUB

Valerie Traub sees connections not only with *Othello* but also with *Much Ado About Nothing*, commenting:

> ■ The erotic anxieties of which *Othello* is a particularly vehement testament are to be found throughout the Shakespearean canon. Othello's strategies of containment, for example, form a part of the earlier play, *Much Ado About Nothing* (1598–9). In fact, it is as if the Hero/Claudio plot of *Much Ado About Nothing* were split into two parts, each trajectory followed to a different destination in *Othello* (1604) and *The Winter's Tale* (1610–11). The fraught courtship of Claudio and Hero is replicated in Othello's marriage to Desdemona, whereas Hero's semblance of death for restorative purposes is, even in the failure of its ritual resolution, reproduced in *The Winter's Tale*.[47] □

Traub's footnote to this comment reads:

> ■ The bond between Hermione and Leontes is restored in much the way as is the bond between Hero and Claudio: the woman is hidden away,

presumed to be dead, and then re-offered in a ritual marriage ceremony; in both plays, the attempted rejuvenation of an emotional bond fails. □

Her account of the place of *The Winter's Tale* in the canon is worth noting. She sees *Much Ado About Nothing* as a kind of exemplar: 'The flip side of Claudio's romantic idealism is his misogyny, and both stem from a fear of female erotic power'.[48] *The Winter's Tale* is fitted in as follows:

■ The tragic brutality of *Othello*, however, seems to have operated as a kind of exorcism. Although fear of women's sexual power dominates *King Lear* and *Macbeth* (1606), never again are the strategies employed to combat these fears so vitriolic and vituperative – or so horrifyingly final. Rather, Lear and Macbeth are themselves victimised by the sexual power wielded by commanding and evil women. With *The Winter's Tale*, however, Shakespeare returns to his previous paradigm, as if in an effort to moderate both its ferocity and efficacy.[49] □

Traub acknowledges that the common view of *The Winter's Tale* is that it 'reintroduces the possibility of mutuality in the Shakespearean canon' but she makes the important reservation that the positive elements 'do not resolve the primary conflict posed by the fear of woman's erotic betrayal'.[50]

Traub argues that there is less to be gained by attempting to understand Leontes's jealousy psychoanalytically than there is to be gained by attempting to identify 'what nexus of cultural relations creates the conditions for such a paranoiac reaction'. Traub points to the significatory power possessed by the female body in a masculinist culture: as a reminder of, and a stimulus to, erotic activity, the product of which is visible in Hermione's pregnant body and again in Mamillius, the child whose name, Traub believes, recalls the female breast.[51]

Leontes is acting like Othello:

■ Hermione is an offering made in hopes of reconstituting Leontes' sacred, desexualised feminine ideal.[52] □

Traub asks why there is a need for the 16-year gap and concedes that 'exigencies of plot [...] require that time pass: Perdita and Florizel must meet, woo and marry, and Leontes must demonstrate devotion to his dead wife'.[53] Also 'Hermione's patience must be given dramatic form'.[54] Traub goes further:

■ I would argue that, in addition, Leontes must experience a reprieve from the exigencies of female erotic life before he can re-enter marriage with any degree of psychic comfort; and, most importantly, that

Hermione's 'unmanageable' sexuality must be metaphorically contained and psychically disarmed.[55] ☐

What Traub calls 'the strategy of containment' begun in *Hamlet* and *Much Ado About Nothing* and 'given its most extreme form in *Othello*' is continued in *The Winter's Tale*. Her summary is single-minded but where other critics make allowances for complex interpretation Traub's single-mindedness is a refreshing reminder that the play may be read as an indictment of a relentlessly cruel regime of oppression. For Traub feminist criticism is not merely one mode amongst others. The note of conviction is unmistakeable:

■ Out of cultural anxieties regarding women's erotic power, Leontes fantasises Hermione's adultery, and the projection of those anxieties leads to her metaphorical death. That death is reversed only when another symbolic form of stasis and control is imposed: Hermione's 'dead likeness (5.3.15)' re-presents her living body through the illusion of preserved female integrity. 'Warm' but not hot [5.3.35], Hermione is chastened (made chaste), her erotic power curtailed. Upon her revivification, Hermione is granted one speech of eight lines, and this speech is a maternal blessing and query directed toward her daughter.[56] ☐

What little ambiguity is allowed for cannot work towards ameliorating the harsh verdict Traub pronounces on the play's meaning:

■ [Hermione's] silence toward Leontes bespeaks a submissiveness, or perhaps an emotional distancing, most unlike her previous animation. Rather than a victory for the wronged heroine, the final scene works as a wish-fulfilment for Leontes, who not only regains his virtuous wife and loses his burden of guilt, but also reassumes his kingly command of all social relations, represented by his deft matchmaking and integration of the two remaining isolated figures, Paulina and Camillo.[57] ☐

Traub concedes that 'many feminist critics would argue that Leontes' repentance, Hermione's forgiveness, and Paulina's unifying role illustrate a victory of "feminine" over "masculine" values', citing Juliet Dusinberre, Marilyn French, Irene Dash and Marianne Novy.[58] On the other hand, Coppélia Kahn, Carol Thomas Neely and Marilyn L. Williamson argue that 'such an expression of "feminine" values may perpetuate patriarchal gender distinctions'.[59] Traub cites Carol Cook who argues that 'Alternatives cannot be generated from within the binary structures by which patriarchy figures gender',[60] or, in other words, 'feminineness' is as much a creation of patriarchy as 'masculineness'. Traub comments: 'Within Lacanian terms [the terms of the French psychoanalytic theorist Jacques Lacan (1901–81)], insofar as "feminine values" exist, they are merely the figuration of the reduced other of full, masculine presence'.[61] Traub reminds us that though 'Hermione is reunited with her husband [...] the anxieties that incited the imposition of stasis upon her are still immanent, indeed inherent, in their relationship'.[62]

There is an element that is missing from the description of the play given by Traub that might be described as *education*. That it should be missing is not surprising: Traub is dealing with what is commonly called (though, I believe, mistakenly) the 'political' aspects of the work and 'the anxieties that incited the imposition of stasis upon her are still immanent, indeed inherent, in their relationship'. However this ending is unsatisfactory from a dramatic point of view. What has been achieved? It is enough for Cavell, for example, to accept that the end of the play 'does not work', or for Traub to say that 'Hermione's patience must be given dramatic form'. What we must see, though, if the play is to have dramatic integrity as a work of art, is that, through a process of education, Leontes's repentance is sincere. Graham Holderness's account acknowledges feminist discussions but comes to the conclusion that Traub has dismissed when she has found it in other feminist accounts.

GRAHAM HOLDERNESS

Graham Holderness offers an unambiguous affirmation of the play as a demonstration of the 'power of the female':

■ The powerful men of *The Winter's Tale*, two kings, are here [5.3] firmly constituted as spectators of the enacted performance, as open-mouthed dupes of a female conjurer's legerdemain.[63] □

He contrasts *The Winter's Tale* with *Much Ado About Nothing* where Traub had stressed the similarities. In the earlier play:

■ The fact that the woman herself has been unjustly slandered and maliciously 'framed' is recognized; but the affirmation of her innocence and the denunciation of her wrongers seems less of a priority than the symbolic destruction of this irrevocably contaminated female body. In fact it has been contaminated with nothing but masculine suspicion, jealousy, mistrust and fear: nonetheless only its total ritual destruction can achieve the clearing of Hero's name. She will be restored, not to life, but to her pristine innocence. The image of her corrupted flesh will be replaced in Claudio's imagination by a restoration of that idealized image of courtly adoration which initially attracted him, and which proved so inadequate as a basis for a real sexual relationship.[64] □

The plays are not realist novels and to expect a picture of 'a real sexual relationship' from either *Much Ado About Nothing* or *The Winter's*

Tale may be to look for the wrong thing. Holderness's use of *Much Ado About Nothing* reminds us that we get from it a picture of a true thing – later explored tragically in *Othello* – that a man must be able to believe things about the woman he loves if he is to be able to live out that love with her. If he is to be sincere, and he must be, he must have a picture in his 'imagination's study' in which he can believe. Different plays explore different aspects of this: in *As You Like It*, for example, Orlando must reach the point that he reaches at last at 5.2.48 when he says to Rosalind (whom he believes to be the youth, Ganymede, pretending, for him, to be Rosalind), 'I can live no longer by thinking'. At this point he has recognized that his fantasy of being in love is insufficient, though it is where he started. He has been educated. Claudio must realize what it is like to live without Hero: only in this way will he learn the reality of her. One way of thinking about *The Winter's Tale* is to say that this true thing has been revisited by Shakespeare with a much more realistic, and a much less optimistic, view of it.

It is not the responsibility of the women these men purport to love to change: it is the responsibility of the men who purport to love them to change. It may be that in changing they realise that they do in fact love the women that they say that they love. The uncomfortable fact is that the change that is necessary is not easy to accomplish and Friar Francis's ruse, for example, is, in a play, one way of accomplishing it. The men must be educated: they must endure a process of change that, it seems, can only partially be willed. The earlier plays treat the theme comically, though *Much Ado About Nothing*, at least, suggests the tragic potential that *Othello* is to realize in full later on. *The Winter's Tale* treats the theme with that ambiguity that is characteristic of these late plays. If Claudio realizes what it would have been like to have had to live without Hero and in that way learns his lesson, Leontes learns what it is actually like to live without Hermione and it is not a lesson that teaches him what he would have lost: it is that loss itself.

Holderness is keen to use the contrast between the two plays to point a moral from a feminist perspective. He observes that what he calls a 'conspiracy to construct an illusion of Hero's death and rebirth' has no positive effect on 'the male ideology that created the entire crisis in the first place' but leaves it 'virtually intact'.[65] However, in the later play, 'the same crisis is negotiated entirely by the courage and resourcefulness of a woman'[66] and 'it is by no means an ideological consolidation of existing power'.[67]

Holderness places much interpretative weight on Hermione's silence:

■ When Hermione does speak, she speaks only to her daughter: her silence towards Leontes is remarkable, and she defines the purpose of her preservation as a desire to see 'the issue' of her daughter's loss and recovery. The text continually turns back on its own romance materials, criticizing their implausible dénouements as the creaking machinery of 'an old tale' [5.3.118]; and Leontes' arbitrary assigning of Paulina to Camillo in marriage is machinery of an almost grotesque implausibility.[68] □

It is significant that Hermione's silence towards Leontes should be read so differently by different critics, and that is a reminder that plays must be staged and that much can be done on stage with a silence. If it is true to say that in *The Winter's Tale* Leontes actually loses what Claudio does not actually lose; if it is true to say that the later play shows what does happen where the earlier shows what might have happened, then it might be true to say that Hermione's silence is the theatrical presentation (which is to say that it may be presented theatrically in this way) of that loss. That loss may be compared with the loss of innocence and the fall into experience, as William Blake [poet and engraver; 1757–1827], for example, contrasted those states in his *Songs of Innocence* (1789) and *Songs of Experience* (1794). That is, it is, of all the losses that may befall people, the most profound. If it is true that these late plays address themes of redemption and reconciliation it will be very important not to allow the sentimental desire for a happy ending to obscure the difficult truths that a more subtle interpretation may offer.

The theatricalization of the narrative of accident and misfortune, and of the resilience and patience needed to endure it, that begins with *Pericles* and that is developed in *Cymbeline*, found, for critics of the early twentieth century, its culmination in *The Winter's Tale* and it is just this tone of seriousness that has to be teased out sometimes from both critical accounts and theatrical performances of *The Winter's Tale* in which those critics found that culmination. For some of those critics the play that is most often seen as the finest achievement of the last phase of Shakespeare's career, *The Tempest*, was something of a disappointment, and it is to that play, and to those critics, that the next chapter turns its attention.

CHAPTER EIGHT

The Tempest: Moderns

The last two chapters of this Guide consider critical discussion of the play that acts as a focal point for all discussion of the 'last' or 'late' plays, because it is a play that tempts so many to identify its central character with Shakespeare himself, and Prospero's farewell to his art as Shakespeare's own; because it is a consummate work of art and very beautiful; because its thematic material is so rich and condensed; because Heminges and Condell put it at the front of their Folio edition of Shakespeare's works. The broad distinction already introduced, between Moderns and Postmoderns, will serve here, as elsewhere in this Guide, to indicate broad distinctions of interest: the present chapter discusses some key Moderns; the following chapter some key Postmoderns. F R Leavis's comments on *Cymbeline* and *The Winter's Tale* have already been introduced. Now we turn to his discussion of *The Tempest*.

F R LEAVIS

Leavis claims that *The Tempest* is quite unlike *The Winter's Tale* in that it is 'much closer to the "reality" we commonly expect of the novelist'. This is because the 'unreality', 'instead of penetrating and transmuting everything as in *The Winter's Tale*, is in *The Tempest* confined to Prospero's imagery and its agents'. Apart from Prospero's management of the shipwreck, and of course apart from Ariel and the masque, the characters 'strike us, in their behaviour and conversation, as people of the ordinary everyday world'.[1] The contrast Leavis draws between the two is, perhaps deliberately, paradoxical. There is no unreality of the kind to be found in *The Tempest* to be found in *The Winter's Tale*. Theatrical illusion is strained further than in other of his plays but there is no magic and there are no supernatural beings. There is a marked and clear distinction, on the face of it, between plays that admit the idea of magic and plays that do not. Coincidence and other strains on theatrical illusionism are not to be compared with the invention of a realm

113

of supernatural activity. To describe *The Tempest* as characterized more by reality than *The Winter's Tale* and *The Winter's Tale* more by unreality than *The Tempest* seems bizarre, even outrageous. However, Leavis's point is that, once you have identified the realm of the supernatural, it is severely circumscribed by the play: 'not only does Prospero finally renounce magic, break his staff and drown his book, but the daydream has never been allowed to falsify human and moral realities'.[2] Furthermore, the behaviour of the main characters, once the magic has been set aside, is strikingly realistic in terms of the presentation of the behaviour of characters from similar walks of life in other plays of his and of the period, a point taken up by E M W Tillyard.

E M W TILLYARD

The notion that *The Tempest* was in any sense 'realistic' cuts across the grain of eighteenth- and nineteenth-century views. E M W Tillyard has a different agenda. He claims that the view that *Cymbeline* and *The Winter's Tale* are Shakespeare's first attempts at something that he finally achieves in *The Tempest* is mistaken. He believes that both plays approach the same end by different routes. *The Tempest* does not deal directly with the destructive section of what Tillyard holds is the full tragic pattern but narrates it retrospectively whereas the earlier play presents as a fully realized theatrical experience the destructive part of the pattern. Tillyard acknowledges that some critics have found the juxtaposition of the destructive part of the pattern in the first part of the play with the regenerative experience of the second part an unsettling experience, though he says that he is not one of them:

■ The simple truth is, that if you cram a trilogy into a single play something has to be sacrificed. Shakespeare chose to make a different sacrifice in each of his two successful renderings of the complete tragic pattern: unity in *The Winter's Tale*, present rendering of the destructive part of the tragic pattern in *The Tempest*.'[3] □

Tillyard's 'proof' of his view is an appeal to judgement: 'one has only to look at the total plot to see that in its main lines it closely follows that of *Cymbeline* and *The Winter's Tale*, and that tragedy is an organic part of it'.[4]

Tillyard points out that, except for the fact that Prospero and his infant daughter are cast adrift and not murdered, the story related by Prospero in 1.2 has all the makings of an Elizabethan revenge tragedy: 'Allow Prospero to be put to death, give him a son instead of a daughter to live and to avenge him, and your tragic plot is complete'.[5]

Tillyard comments on the contrast between both *Cymbeline* and *The Winter's Tale* on the one hand and *The Tempest* on the other. Neither Cymbeline nor Leontes are the agents of regeneration: they are beneficiaries rather. Prospero, though, brings about the regeneration that is the answer to the destruction, for his part in which he bears full responsibility. Shakespeare plays down this responsibility though, passing over it by means of retrospective narration so that what the audience sees is regeneration: 'It was by this centring of motives in Prospero as well as by subordinating the theme of destruction that Shakespeare gave *The Tempest* its unified structure'.[6]

The creation of character is one of the play's chief strengths, but, while 'Antonio's transformation from the cynical and lazy badgerer of Gonzalo's loquacity to the brilliantly swift and unscrupulous man of action is a thrilling affair',[7] of Miranda, Tillyard says that, though she is, like Perdita, a symbol of what Tillyard calls 'original virtue' and also of fertility, she is much less satisfactory as a character: 'The touches of ordinary humanity in Miranda – her siding with Ferdinand against a supposedly hostile father, for instance – are too well known to need recalling. They do not amount to a very great deal and leave her vaguer as a human being than as a symbol'.[8]

Tillyard takes Middleton Murry to task, saying that he 'is not at his happiest when he says that "they are so terribly, so agonisingly real, these women of Shakespeare's last imagination"'. He comments: 'as far as Miranda is concerned, any agonising sense of her reality derives from the critic and not from the play'. This is an important distinction to make, and suggests that 'the play' is not just a matter of 'impressions': there is something which makes impressions and critics must get that clear and not run away with their own fantasies.

It is noticeable though that Tillyard shows less enthusiasm for *The Tempest* than he did for *The Winter's Tale* and his discussion of Miranda reveals the same quality. It would be wrong to call it a lack of enthusiasm; it is just that the later play does not call up the same intensity of engagement. Tillyard concludes:

> ■ Not only do Ferdinand and Miranda sustain Prospero in representing a new order of things that has evolved out of destruction; they also vouch for its continuation. At the end of the play Alonso and Prospero are old and worn men. A younger and happier generation is needed to secure the new state to which Prospero has so painfully brought himself, his friends, and all his enemies save Caliban.[9] □

G Wilson Knight looks also for a vision of unity but makes perhaps the boldest claim of any critic to have found that unity in *The Tempest* itself.

G WILSON KNIGHT

G Wilson Knight offers perhaps the most developed of all accounts of *The Tempest* that see it as a 'last' work. Shakespeare invents a story to suit himself, Wilson Knight holds, and the result is that *The Tempest* 'patterned of storm and music' presents a vision of what Wilson Knight argues is 'Shakespeare's world'.[10]

Wilson Knight addresses the entire body of Shakespeare's work and identifies a theme: what he calls 'a recurring sense of desertion, of betrayal' and arising upon this 'a general nausea at human falsity'. He adds: 'This disgust tends to project the action into wild nature, conceived [...] as an improvement on the falsities of civilisation'. He traces the pattern in other plays, suggesting that *The Winter's Tale* shows a movement similar to that in *Two Gentlemen of Verona* (prob. late 1580s), *As You Like It* and *King Lear*, 'from falsehood through rugged nature to an idealised rusticity'. He sees Timon of *Timon of Athens* as the prototype of this movement, a movement taken up again in *The Tempest*. It may be summarized as a withdrawal from civilization into Nature, much as a familiar Romantic stereotype suggests. Knight goes further, linking Timon through Prospero with a series of figures, rulers whose lack of political success triggers insight, such as Hamlet, Brutus, Richard II and Henry VI. He sees Timon as an 'archetypal figure, being a complex of many heroes' and argues that those characters that resemble him share a rejection of their society as corrupt and, though not acting themselves, control other persons in the play, 'half magically, from within'.[11]

An old debate has been named as being between 'lumpers' and 'splitters': those who gather items together, stressing the things they have in common; those who separate things out from one another emphasizing what distinguishes them. Wilson Knight is here lumping with a vengeance. He has forgotten that the movement he describes, 'from falsehood through rugged nature to an idealised rusticity', does not end, at least in all the plays he lumps together, in that happy state of 'idealised rusticity', but in a return to court; even in the case of *King Lear*, in connection with the Third Act of that play, talk of 'idealised rusticity' must seem at least inappropriate. However, 'lumping' has as much to recommend it as has 'splitting', in principle at least. There is nothing to say that things must not be gathered together under the banner of what they have in common rather than being carefully distinguished: in fact one must do both. This is at the heart of the question of genre.

Wilson Knight sees in Prospero the culmination of a process of meditation on and dramatization of the figure of the politically dispossessed prince whose exile or fall from power is accompanied by a gift of insight into things. Prospero represents Shakespeare's final thinking on this figure, seeing him as deliberately cultivating what was imposed on others, using the exile and the insight to positive effect. Prospero is, Wilson Knight argues, not only controlling the action of this play but, as this action is, Wilson Knight asserts, Shakespeare's own life-work in dramatic form, he is controlling 'the Shakespearian world'.[12] In this way he is the person of Shakespeare and even speaks 'with Shakespeare's voice'.

In his discussion of some of the characters Wilson Knight resorts to what is best described as loose associations of characteristics. He describes Ariel as 'mercurial' and the coincidence of sound enables him to link Ariel with Mercutio from *Romeo and Juliet* and that allows him to link Mercutio's description of dreams 'as thin of substance as the air' (1.4.99) with Prospero's description of Ariel at 5.1.21, 'thou, which art but air'. However, it is perhaps unfair to single out any of the associations to which Knight points: they are, in the mass, subtly impressive and his tracing of connections through the Shakespearean *oeuvre* is, if it is not a proof, highly suggestive. What Wilson Knight is after emerges quite slowly and is never fully theorized: that is, his findings are never laid at the door of some description of something else, such as the occult functionings of the mind. The antecedents, or at least contemporaries, of Wilson Knight's thinking come clear in such phrases as 'whittling off the non-essential and leaving the naked truth exposed', 'prototype, or archetype', 'an archetypal figure', 'transcendental speculation' and even 'pattern', used with a certain implied force. This is the language of mythopoeia.

Many critics were enchanted by the prospect of an integrated picture of the cultural activity of Europe and of North America and of the countries and peoples influenced by those cultures. Clearly the direct way to such a picture lay in discovering the foundations of the building, or the structural principles according to which it was constructed, or in a way shown by some other, similar metaphorical pointer. Not everything has a foundation; not every starting point is an origin. Some things grow and change in such a way that it makes no sense to try to find in what their essence lies. Certainly such efforts are out of fashion nowadays. Wilson Knight's linking the sea-voyage of Prospero and Miranda not only to other plays but to 'the Nordic origins of our literature in *The Wanderer* or *The Seafarer*'[13] may be regarded by some as adventurous but will be regarded by others as making at best a tenuous link between two things (three things in fact; the relationship between *The Wanderer* and *The Seafarer* is not as direct as Wilson Knight's lumping them together implies) that really are not connected by any other than the vaguest and most general resemblances. There have been many sea-voyages, in literature and out of literature, and what they share is at least matched by what they do not.

On the other hand it must be said that there are stories that have gathered up into themselves many other stories. Indeed much of cultural activity can be much more profitably regarded as a continuous process of the successive gathering in and refining of pre-existent materials (often other, earlier, works) than as a series of isolated original acts. Shakespeare's work, as Wilson Knight points out, very frequently arises from just such a gathering-in and refining of earlier works. Even so, once one starts talking of 'archetypes' and 'transcendental speculation' and 'whittling off the non-essential and leaving the naked truth exposed' one is in danger of putting aside the only thing that matters about a work, and that is the work itself.

When Wilson Knight comes to address the heart of the play he is really bold: Prospero, Ariel and Caliban are all representatives of aspects of Timon. He discusses the other characters and their affinities with other plays but he is not really engaged by them or detained long by them. When he comes to Ferdinand and Miranda the tone is revealing: they are 'representative of beautiful and virtuous youth' and are thus like many other characters from many other plays, such as Marina from *Pericles*, Guiderius and Arviragus from *Cymbeline*, and Florizel and Perdita from *The Winter's Tale*. The pair in *The Tempest* are 'whittled down' to their virtues of purity and constancy and are less impressive as characters than the other Wilson Knight mentions, in his view. In their characterization 'essences are abstracted and reclothed'.[14]

This is the problem with the method, especially if it is used not merely to judge plays but to write them. If Wilson Knight is correct then the difficulties Tillyard has had in getting up much enthusiasm are easily explained: the characters are 'essences [...] abstracted and reclothed'. 'Essences' are not great characters.

Wilson Knight makes some really grand gestures, such as claiming that Prospero's speech at 5.1.33–57 charts Shakespeare's own progress as a creative artist from tragedy to the mood of reconciliation of the last plays. Further, he claims that Prospero's plot to draw his enemies to the island and there use his power to bring about a grand reconciliatory drama resembles Shakespeare's personal struggle to convert into art a struggle with 'bitterness' and 'rejection' that, Wilson Knight claims, is quite a usual human experience. Shakespeare achieves this end by paradoxical means: 'By destroying his protagonists, he renders them deathless; by expressing evil, in others and in himself, he renders it innocent'. Perhaps most daringly, and interestingly, of all, Wilson Knight claims that at the heart of this frenzied activity a 'centre of faith and love' must be preserved 'from the taint of that rich, wild, earthy, lustful, violent, cursing, slimy yet glittering thing that is creation itself, or Caliban'.[15]

Such a treatment of the play as a myth of creative activity itself, and of creative activity seen as an echo, or repetition, or analogy or even as a continuation of the creative act at the heart of existence itself (if that is what lies behind what Wilson Knight is saying) makes quite a startling and even extravagant claim about it and asks the reader to make some vertiginous connections. It is not without its charm as an account. There are many, especially Romantic, accounts of poetry and of life itself that closely resemble what Wilson Knight is saying and what he says reminds us that behind all critical accounts lies what we think the world and life amount to as a whole. It is impossible, and it would be undesirable, to attempt to detach what we think about life from what we think about plays: life is, after all, what plays refer to. We may think about plays without thinking about life at all only by narrowing our concern about them to those matters which do not, or do not directly, ask us to consider what we think about life. There are ways of thinking about history, about matters to do with textual concerns, with editing and even with composing, that do not directly invoke questions of how we behave or how we should behave. Wilson Knight has dismissed all these matters as 'side-issues'[16] and his doing so asks us implicitly to consider what we believe the criticism of plays is all about.

The method does frequently release insight: his picture of Ariel as Prospero's art and Caliban as the world, locked into a dialectical relationship in Prospero's own activity is challenging and the picture that it implies of what life is like has a horrible charm. It is a picture that will bear comparison with that provided by Jan Kott, later in the century. It is particularly worth noting how the elements of Wilson Knight's picture may be seen in Kott, as having been further drawn out, exaggerated maybe, towards even darker implications.

JAN KOTT

If Knight is idealistic, Jan Kott is realistic to the point of morbidity, though both critics share a desire to look beyond the detail of the work to underlying themes. Kott's essay starts by pointing to a structural feature:

■ *The Tempest* has two endings: a quiet evening on the island, when Prospero forgives his enemies and the story returns to the point of departure; and Prospero's tragic monologue, spoken directly to the audience, a monologue out of time. But *The Tempest* also possesses two prologues. The first of these is the dramatic one; it takes place on the ship, which is set on fire by lightning and tossed on the rocks by the wind. The other prologue consists of Prospero's account of how he had lost his dukedom and came to live on the uninhabited island; it narrates the previous history of the *dramatis personae*.[17] ☐

The function of the first prologue is to provide a real tempest as the setting for a moral tempest but it is also to show something that Kott describes as 'one of the great Shakespearian theses, a violent confrontation of nature with the social order':

■ In the prologue to *The Tempest*, the deprivation of majesty's sacred character – so characteristic of the Renaissance – is realised once more. Faced with the roaring sea, a boatswain means more than a king.[18] ☐

The other prologue takes up another 'of the main, basic – almost obsessional – Shakespearian themes: that of a good and a bad ruler, of the usurper who deprives the legal prince of his throne'.[19] Kott comments: 'This is Shakespeare's view of history, eternal history, its perpetual, unchanging mechanism'.[20]

The story is repeated in the play by the story of Ariel and Caliban and Kott, again, describes what he sees as the typical structure of the Shakespearian drama. It is not unified, in terms of action at least, but composed of multiple, interacting plots that mirror one another:

■ The same theme returns in various keys, in all the registers of Shakespeare's music; it is repeated lyrically and grotesquely, then pathetically and ironically. The same situation will be performed on the Shakespearian stage by kings, then repeated by lovers and aped by clowns. ☐

The essence of Kott's vision of Shakespeare is that 'all the world's a stage' and so the stage is the world:

■ Situations in Shakespeare's theatre are always real, even when interpreted by ghosts and monsters.[21] ☐

Kott has already claimed that the first prologue (as he calls it) 'repeats Panurge's famous invocation from the fourth book of *Gargantua and Pantagruel* [(1532, 1534) by the French satirist François Rabelais (1494?–1553)]',[22] and the picture he provides here of a world turned upside down echoes the reference to that book. The sense of exhaustion that arises from the kind of description that Kott has given cannot be straightforwardly ascribed to Shakespeare's plays, however, without recognizing that the description involves a considerable degree of abstraction, repeatedly performed, to make many things appear more or less exactly similar. Also, the most obvious parallel in Shakespeare's own work to the description offered by Kott is Jacques's speech in *As You Like It*, 'All the world's a stage (2.7.139–66)', and, as has often been pointed out, after this cynical depiction of people playing out fore-ordained roles, a young man enters carrying his worn-out servant, apparently justifying Duke Senior's faith in the human world.

Kott is perhaps no Jacques, but his analysis ruthlessly refuses to distinguish between acts that may be regarded as similar. He points out, for example, that 'Caliban was overthrown by Prospero, just as Prospero had been overthrown by Antonio'[23] and that, therefore:

■ Even before the morality proper is performed, and Prospero's enemies undergo the trial of madness, two acts of feudal history have already been played out on the desert island.[24] □

Kott discusses briefly the attempts of various scholars to locate the island, concluding that the world Shakespeare depicts 'is always the whole world' and that 'It is useless, therefore, to look for the longitude and latitude of Prospero's island'.[25] Later he says 'Prospero's island is either the world, or the stage. To the Elizabethans it was all the same; the stage was the world, and the world was the stage'.[26] Those who see the island as an Arcadia are interpreting the play 'through bad theatre performances; those with a ballet-dancer and a translucent screen'. Kott looks at the poetry:

■ The island has salt and sweet waters, barren and fertile lands, lemon groves and quagmires. It abounds in hazel-nuts, apples are ripe, there are truffles in the forest. The island is inhabited by baboons, hedge-hogs, vipers and toads. Jays have their nests here, sea-gulls perch on the rocks. Berries grow here, there are sea-shells of various kinds; feet are hurt by thorns; one hears mastiffs bark and cocks crow.[27] □

In conclusion, 'the island itself is outside time'.[28]

Kott goes further, spurred perhaps by his reference to Rabelais, introducing as an illustration the paintings of the Netherlandish artist Hieronymus Bosch (*c.* 1450–1516), especially 'The Garden of Earthly Delights' and 'The Temptation of St Anthony'. Kott describes the worlds Bosch paints:

■ They rise out of a grey sea. They are brown or yellow. They take the form of a cone, reminding one of a volcano, with a flat top. On such hills tiny human figures swarm and writhe like ants. The scenes depict the seven deadly sins and the human passions, above all lechery and murder, drunkenness and gluttony. As well as people there are demons with beautiful, slender angelic female bodies and toads' or dogs' heads. Under the tables shaped like big tortoiseshells, old hags with flabby breasts and children's faces lie embracing half-men, half-insects with long hairy spider-like feet. Tables are set for a common feast, but the jugs and plates assume the shape of insects, birds or frogs. This island is a garden of torment, or a picture of mankind's folly. It is even similar in shape to the Elizabethan stage. Boats arrive at a quiet harbour at the foot of the mountain. This is the apron-stage. The main scenes take place in large caves and on terraces of the volcanic cone. The flat top of the mountain is empty. There are no actors on the upper stage. No one gives his blessing or sits in judgement over the follies depicted. The island is the scene of the world's cruel tortures.[29] □

He makes a useful point about grotesque as well:

■ Tragic scenes in Shakespeare often have *buffo* [typical of Italian comic opera], grotesque, or ironic undertones and the *buffo* scenes are often mixed with bitterness, lyricism and cruelty. In his theatre it is the clowns who tell the truth.[30] And not just tell it; they re-enact situations usually reserved for princes. Stephano, the drunkard, and Trinculo, the clown, want power too.[31] □

This vision allows Kott to conclude that 'On the island, which Shakespearian scholars took to be Arcadia, the history of the world has once more been performed and repeated'.[32]

The contrast Kott draws between his vision of the play and that cherished by 'Shakespearian scholars' is in fact exaggerated, if, at least, one chooses one's scholars, or rather, critics, carefully, as this chapter has tried to do. The next chapter moves even further away from the view of *The Tempest* as genial, even delightful, that united critics before the middle of the twentieth century and into the territory commanded by the theoretical rigour that developed in the later twentieth century.

CHAPTER NINE

The Tempest: Post-moderns

*T*he Tempest is the play of all the late or last plays that lends itself most
obviously to postmodern treatment, more so even than *Pericles* and
Cymbeline, plays which have been gleefully exploited in performance
by postmodern directors but which lack the crucial element so clearly
structural to *The Tempest* and so important to postmodern thinking, conscious reflexivity. *The Tempest* is a self-conscious play: a play
about theatre, that enacts a piece of theatre (Prospero's management
of the shipwreck and the conduct of the shipwrecked on his island)
and that contains a masque deliberately interrupted by Prospero who
thus shows that it is his to control. Such a degree of self-consciousness
recommends itself to a culture that values self-consciousness as postmodernism does. Self-consciousness manifests itself paradoxically in
postmodernism, showing extreme self-doubt and uncertainty at the
same time as it enthusiastically embraces fragmentation and inconsistency. Its pursuit of liberation from oppression of all kinds leads it into
complex positions and the central essay to be considered in this chapter is not easy reading. It might be argued on the other hand that the
play that it addresses is not easy reading either: its clarity has proved
deceptive and its apparent willingness to offer itself to a variety of interpretations, let alone uses, is itself instructive, as the following brief
survey, that will act as an introduction to this chapter that ends the
consideration of the last plays of Shakespeare, will show.

The Introduction to the Arden edition of *The Tempest*, third series in their reckoning, edited by Virginia Mason Vaughan and Alden
T Vaughan, whose essay on the character Caliban is indispensable
background reading,[1] is packed with useful detail, from a section on
'Contexts' that summarizes exhaustively the historical relationships
that might bear upon the play, to an equally exhaustive list of uses
to which the play has been put, 'Appropriations' being the word they
use. There is a strong sense in which this word is entirely appropriate
on some occasions: somewhere in the middle of all the industry that
has been brought to bear upon it the play has wandered off. This is not
unusual in contemporary accounts of *The Tempest* as the forthcoming

discussion will show: it is the meanings, the implications, or the uses to which it can be put in pursuit of some other goal on which critics concentrate, a process that can only be said to have begun with *The Enchanted Island* (1667) of John Dryden and Sir William D'Avenant (1606–68) if we are prepared to overlook the use of the play to celebrate the marriage of Prince Frederic (1596–1632; Elector Palatine 1610–20, King of Bohemia 1619–20) to Princess Elizabeth (1596–1662), the eldest daughter of James I, during the winter of 1612–13.

That *The Tempest* has lent itself to variations is part of its critical history, if only indirectly. It has lent itself to so many: to Hollywood science-fiction (*Forbidden Planet*, 1956), in which Fred M Wilcox (1906–64) directing made technology bring forth Freud's 'unconscious' quite literally, the repressed returning to wreak a terrible revenge on the arrogance of those who thought they could evolve into pure mind and leave the body behind them; to Derek Jarman (1942–94) for an imaginative and sexually charged interpretation in his 1979 film version;[2] to the fantastic elaboration of Peter Greenaway (born 1942) (*Prospero's Books*, 1991); to Michael Tippett (1905–98) for his 1970 opera, *The Knot Garden*; to W H Auden (1907–73) who composed the strangely drab 'The Sea and the Mirror' as a sort of commentary on *The Tempest*, between 1942 and 1944; to Aimé Césaire (1913–2008), who in *Une Tempête* (1968) turned the play around to make it Caliban's. All these have avoided the play, as, it might be argued, did its use in pursuit of something else, that is, a royal wedding, very shortly after its first appearance before the king at Whitehall on Hallowmas Eve, 1611. It may be its fate to have gathered around it so many 'contexts' as Virginia Mason Vaughan and Alden T Vaughan's Introduction suggests, to have become the meeting point rather than the focus of these contexts and thus a cross roads from which to depart in many directions rather than as a destination at which to arrive. The 'discursive con-texts' of the play is what Francis Barker and Peter Hulme set out to explore, or perhaps rather to expose, in their ground-breaking essay of 1985.

FRANCIS BARKER AND PETER HULME

The essay pits itself against, in particular, the Arden edition of Frank Kermode (born 1919) (the fifth in their reckoning at the time) of the play, first published in 1954. Barker and Hulme set out their stall boldly, pointing to the packaging of Shakespeare for the tourist industry as an example of the way in which his work is used to construct a version of English history, 'a past which is picturesque, familiar and untroubled'.[3]

They go on to argue that, though modern scholarly editions of the plays have seemed to distance themselves from this sort of simplification by exploiting the work of historical scholarship and setting their own work as editors and critics carefully within that, they are in fact only underlining their concern with values and views conveyed by the text that 'turn out not to be historical at all, but eternal'.[4] The essay promises to challenge such a 'mystificatory' view of the relationship between text and historical context, using, to do so, perspectives deriving from 'newer analyses', which however must themselves be challenged before being put to use. This complex approach is necessary because of the scale of the task: in their view the authors must challenge an entire, entrenched tradition and also take on those attempts that have been made to challenge its claims that have been of limited success.

Barker and Hulme are attempting a revaluation of the critical tradition from a point of view that regards that tradition as implicated in a historical situation in which some groups have systematically oppressed other groups and have sought to justify their behaviour, to themselves, to others, those they oppress, as 'natural' or even as virtuous. Those oppressed groups have developed perspectives, or have been offered perspectives by sympathetic outsiders, from which their oppression can be seen as oppression, and not as a condition deserved by them as the natural consequence of some defect or just punishment on account of some vice. Objecting to oppression does not of itself entail agreement with the perspective that sees all activities as bound up in the act of oppression. The specific power of the idea of ideology is that it promises to pursue oppression into its secret hiding places and to root out its attempts to justify itself. This is especially important when oppression justifies itself by implicit accusations of vice or inferiority on the part of the oppressed. In such a case all survivals of such suspicion must be exposed and dismissed if the grounds of oppression, and thus the threat of the return of oppressive behaviour, are to be finally vanquished.

They begin with a denunciation of what they call the 'autotelic' text, by which they mean a text regarded as having a single fixed meaning. 'Autotelic' may be taken to mean, loosely, 'an end in itself'. By this is meant a work that may be regarded in isolation from, in theory at least, anything else; anything other than itself. Whether much criticism has really had as its object, implicitly or otherwise, such a text is debatable. This 'autotelic' text may be something of a straw man against which attacks are very likely to succeed -but which are not likely to have achieved very much in so doing. 'Structuralist' and 'post-structuralist' criticism (so described by Barker and Hulme) has 'sought to displace radically the primacy of the autotelic text'.[5] It has done this by arguing that a text cannot be restricted to what its author intended it to mean, whether that can ever be determined with any precision or not. The notion that a text 'originates' is replaced by the notion that it is repeatedly 'inscribed'. The authors make the useful point that *The Tempest* as Sir Walter Raleigh wrote about it in 1914 is not the same as *The Tempest* edited by Frank Kermode for consumption in schools and universities. In the one case it is being treated as part of the output of an English national poet (perhaps The National Poet) in a time of national crisis, at the beginning of the First World War; in the second case it is being prepared as an object of study, placed in a historical context and served up almost as a curiosity. Where Sir Walter Raleigh stresses its immediate relevance to the present (the presence, as it were, of the past, *for* the present), Kermode treats it as part of a vanished past with sets of beliefs, habits and customs that separate it off from the present. It may be broadly remarked that the first tendency decreases and the second increases as the twentieth century advances. Q and F R Leavis are separated by much disagreement but united by a shared belief in the relevance to the present of the work they study, even by a sense of the necessity of preserving that work, as a force in the present.

The approaches with which Barker and Hulme want to take immediate issue, the 'newer analyses' of which they have already spoken, depend on 'intertextuality', or the determined practice of establishing links between texts that has, as an ultimate goal, the revelation of the foundational conviction of this approach that there are not texts, there is only text; that is, that each apparently individual text is, upon examination, found to be a fragment of an extending text. Eventually the world itself is revealed as 'textuality', the capacity for transformation into and communication as text. The authors' challenge to this supposedly radical position is an interesting one and, I think, unanswerable. If such a view is carried to its logical conclusion then the use of texts, or of readings of texts, to combat dominant ideologies is impossible as no one interpretation can be established as having more authority than any other.

It may be argued that combating dominant ideologies is not the business of criticism, but the proponents of the 'newer analyses' under consideration do claim to be undertaking the responsibility to do precisely that. Barker and Hulme resist this anarchy of interpretability. The danger they see is that of 'pluralistic incorporation', of 'peaceful co-existence with the dominant readings'. What they want is 'contestation of those readings themselves'. As they put it, 'struggle can only occur if two positions attempt to occupy the same space, to appropriate the "same" text'; otherwise ' "alternative" readings condemn themselves to mere irrelevance'.[6] This is strong stuff: a 'liberal' tradition has merely served to sustain the dominance of dominant readings by setting alongside those readings merely 'alternative' readings: the challenge is to overturn those dominant readings. To do that critics will need to establish a ground upon which unchallengeable counter-readings may be erected as siege towers that will topple the walls of the dominant.

The process Barker and Hulme envisage is one in which new readings, 'especially radical readings aware of their own theoretical and political positioning', engage in 'a *critique* of the dominant readings of a text'.[7] The term 'critique' is used, preferentially, 'in reference to a powerful radical tradition which aims not merely to disagree with its rivals but to *read their readings*: that is, to identify their inadequacies and to explain why such readings come about and what ideological role they play'.[8]

There is a particularly significant point to be made here. Because, so Barker and Hulme claim, capitalist societies[9] insist that the beliefs and practices that sustain them are natural and universal, the only way of challenging them effectively is to use history itself. In pursuit of that view some very elevated language indeed is employed. Making the point that the text must be read through its 'con-texts [their hyphen-ation]' Barker and Hulme claim that literary-critical history is, in effect, the history of a process of 'occlusion', though they are aware of the paradoxical nature of such a claim:

■ This may seem a strange thing to say about the most notoriously bloated of all critical enterprises, but in fact 'Shakespeare' has been force-fed behind a high wall called Literature, built out of the dismantled pieces of other seventeenth-century discourses.[10] □

This is a useful passage to comment upon as two features of the essay as a whole strike the attentive reader. One is the use of relatively erudite terminology ('occlusion' is an example) and the other is the use of elaborate metaphor (the horticultural image of the 'force-feeding' of 'Shakespeare'). Such rhetorical activities are by no means restricted to Barker and Hulme or to proponents of similar views: in fact any critic may resort to them at some point. What is significant is the kind of material put to metaphorical use in such figures and the kind of semi-erudite or unfamiliar terminology employed. It will have already been noticed that there is a marked use of language such as 'struggle', 'con-test', 'dominant', of 'strategies' and 'deployment', a military language in fact, and a metaphorical transformation of the object of the conflict of ideas into a battlefield or 'site' on which these contests and struggles take place. There is a heroic, even a romantic, note in such descriptions. The imagery of force-feeding suggests a prison. Metaphor is powerfully illustrative of course but it is important not be misled by it into thinking that something has been demonstrated where it is has only been illustrated, and that, often, in a highly tendentious manner.

Barker and Hulme identify two examples of 'occlusion' in the work of Frank Kermode. Firstly, Caliban's political claims are occluded, paradoxically, by placing him at the centre of the play. Kermode argues that the play stages a thematic contest between 'Nature' and 'Art' and it is in terms of this conflict that Caliban's role is seen by Kermode as central. However, Barker and Hulme argue that Kermode leaves out 'the historical contextualization that would locate [this thematic contest] among the early universalizing forms of incipient bourgeois hegemony'. The claim to be 'civilizing' the 'savage' that is staged by the play sets forth the common justification by European colonists of their activities. Had this been made clear by Kermode, they argue, then Caliban's claims would not have been 'occluded'. Rather he would have been seen as the wronged in a colonial contest for power. Secondly, they identify Kermode's use of source criticism (his invocation of the Bermuda pamphlets to demonstrate Shakespeare's apparent indebtedness to those accounts when he was putting the play together) as introducing the historical context only to render it ineffectual by treating it only as source material instead of investigating it to use it to show up the internal contradictions of the colonial enterprise of which, these authors believe, *The Tempest* is a part.

Kermode's argument is seen as a de-historicization of the play; an attempt to separate text and context that has the effect of preserving the 'autotelic' text. There is, Barker and Hulme are arguing, an inconsistency in the approach they are dealing with, and in all such approaches. Though critics and editors alike wish to claim for *The Tempest* itself the most complete and comprehensive inclusiveness of the range of meaning embraced by the play, it is almost inevitable that any successful work will refer outside itself, to some other work. Barker and Hulme pick on an instance of this in Kermode's ascription of Prospero's irritability to the descent of the character 'from a bad-tempered giant-magician',[11] that is, from a tradition comprising other works, folk tales and romances and the like. The text is not independent of other texts at all.

Further, as well as denials or concealments of the work's indebtedness to other works, there are attempts to explain away inconvenient aspects of the text. Kermode's explanation of the abrupt conclusion of the masque of Act 4, is highlighted to its disadvantage. Kermode describes this moment (of which Barker and Hulme are preparing to make a great deal) thus: 'a point at which an oddly pedantic concern for classical structure causes it to force its way through the surface of the play'.[12] That is, Kermode's argument is that Shakespeare is here slavishly following classical precedent and ensuring a sudden heightening of tension. For Barker and Hulme this is to explain away anything that might be pursued by critics with different ends in view to produce a different meaning. The text, that is, is being produced. It is not being allowed to stand by itself as it could if it were genuinely independent: its dependence on other texts is being denied or concealed or minimized and any awkward moments are being explained away so as to preserve an illusion of its consistency. Prospero's interrupting his masque is a prime case.

Kermode is taking on the argument of Enid Welsford (1892–1981) that the play should be considered a dramatization of the court masque type of work rather than a working out of a specifically classical type of dramatic production. Kermode argues to the contrary in some detail that the structure is in fact classical, citing the increasing turbulence typical of the *epitasis* – the part of the play in which the plot thickens – as recommended by the theorists of drama at the time and mentioning Prospero's interruption of and cancellation of the masque once he has suddenly and unpleasantly recalled Caliban's plot against him as a further proof of his case, a deliberate, if 'oddly pedantic' determination to point up the disturbance that unsettles this part of the play as the academic theorists held that it should, that must seem threatening in proportion as the resolution is to be found satisfying. For Barker and Hulme this is to sanitize what may be productive, in other hands, of a different meaning, more challenging to dominant ideologies. To show how this might be done they will have to draw on extensive theoretical resources.

'Theory' (from the ancient Greek *theoria*, a view) has come to mean a form of critical approach that denies that any critical discussion may proceed immediately from the text. The text has to be theorized, that is, subjected to a procedure that shows it up in a certain light, before any engagement can be undertaken with it. This is because ideology occludes meanings and naïve, immediate approaches will fail to penetrate ideology's defences and will only reproduce what ideology has set up. Ideology, in this view, is false consciousness: it is a distorted view of things that presents itself as a true view of things. It is, in fact, a theory, but it masquerades as empirical truth. The task of theory is to unmask the imposter ideology and expose the truth. This is not as simple as it may seem because if we have been used to mistake ideology for the truth how shall we know the truth when it is exposed to us? We shall need a touchstone of some kind.

For Marx, and for Marxists for the first generation or so, the touchstone was a conviction that working-class revolutionary seizure of the means of production and of the apparatus of state power and the establishment of socialism was the true aim of history, properly understood, so anything that tended in the direction of the achievement of that aim was more likely to be true than anything that tended away from that direction. Subsequently things became more complicated as Stalinism led to a radical revision of Leninism by the Trotskyist tendencies, as Maoism came to influence European socialist thinking, and as structuralism infiltrated Marxism in Europe and became a fad in the United States. Progressive thinking incorporated psychoanalysis and structuralism and re-read Marxism in the light of the ideas of certain strongly influential French intellectuals. A key concept in these discussions was the concept of discourse.

Barker and Hulme draw heavily on the theoretical work of Michel Foucault and develop their argument by means of an analogy with grammar. The perspective taken at this point is governed by the conception of language associated with the Swiss linguist Ferdinand de Saussure (1857–1913) so we are already in theoretically laden territory and it may seem that we must make up our minds about de Saussure and about Foucault before we can get very far with Barker and Hulme. However it is not always the case that the theoretical underpinnings of the argument in an essay are structurally prior: it is often the case that the essay's conclusions can be tested on a somewhat naïve basis, by asking what sense they make of, in this case, *The Tempest*.

Barker and Hulme argue that, like grammar, which operates at the level of language as a whole, discourse is a sub-grammar of sub-sections of language as a whole. Whereas the concept 'register' is used by those who study language to identify appropriate language-use for particular situations (one does not talk with one's boss in quite the same way one talks with one's children, for example) discourse is interested in particular *subjects* or topics under discussion. The question is whether there is a kind of grammar of, say, class or gender, and whether this kind of grammar changes through time. Discourse is distinct from grammar, however, in that it cannot be codified. Discourse is an unspoken, and unspeakable, grammar. Just as ideology does not visibly shape people's thinking but does so invisibly, so discourse (which is clearly related to ideology though it is a function specifically of language while ideology is more generally prevalent throughout cultures) invisibly shapes what people say and write. In both cases, of ideology and discourse, its operations can be detected from the outside. Outside *The Tempest* is being historically posterior to it.

So discourse is implicated in ideology and its operation is observable only in retrospect. We are considering what people thought and asking ourselves what limited it and postulating that what limited it directed it. Foucault was interested in the idea that all knowledge could be explored as an aspect of the unending struggle for power over others that each of us was engaged in and of the unending pursuit of pleasure that was the purpose of the struggle. The question of truth never arose. The true nature of the process was buried in layers of self-imposed obfuscation designed to conceal from us what we were doing, a habit of self-deception so thoroughly developed that we could not find our way back through it even if we tried. Only the relentlessly sceptical can imagine what the world is like outside this cocoon within which we have trapped ourselves. The picture Barker and Hulme give is of intersecting discourses producing texts precisely as the area of overlap created by the intersection.

Those unsympathetic to the sort of view held by Barker and Hulme will say that the assertion that all the world is a tissue of assumptions and prejudices cannot be made without that assertion itself falling foul of the assertion, and if the assertion that all the world is a tissue of assumptions and prejudices is itself a tissue of assumptions and prejudices then why should we believe it? However something more is going on here than can be dismissed so easily.

The heart of Barker and Hulme's paper is their discussion of Prospero's interruption of the masque he has prepared for Miranda and Ferdinand, Frank Kermode's discussion of which has already been considered:

> ■   I had forgot that foul conspiracy
> Of the beast Caliban and his confederates
> Against my life. The minute of their plot
> Is almost come. □   (4.1.139–42)

After this Prospero dismisses the spirit-actors who are putting on the entertainment, a dismissal that is anticipated in an extraordinary stage direction:

> ■ *Enter certain reapers, properly habited. They join with the nymphs in a graceful dance; towards the end whereof Prospero starts suddenly, and speaks [...] To a strange, hollow, and confused noise, the spirits in the pageant heavily vanish.* (4.1.138) □

'Heavily' means dejectedly or showing discontent or disappointment; the actors have after all turned up 'properly habited' and are enjoying a graceful dance only to be stopped short and sent off with a brisk 'Well done!' Kermode simply comments 'Play-"masques" could never end properly'.[13] This is because the court masque as it had developed into the reign of James I 'ended' with an act of transformation as the actors were revealed, having been concealed 'as the result of adverse spells' then 'freed from enchantment by the beneficent powers of the sovereign' and revealed as members of the Court itself.[14] In the play of course no such 'ending' is possible as the actors 'all are spirits' and there is much to be done before the play can conclude. Such reasoning

appears to Barker and Hulme to be an attempt to explain away something that should be investigated more thoroughly.

Barker and Hulme start by declaring that they intend to take 'the
ensemble of fictional and lived practices, which for convenience we
will simply refer to here as "English colonialism"' and 'the figure of
usurpation as the nodal point of the play's imbrication into this discourse of colonialism'. Much is going on more or less covertly in such
passages: the conflation of 'fictional and lived practices' is in need of
spelling out and quite what a nodal point of imbrication is if it is anything other than what resemblances may be proposed between the
play and other things (fictional or lived practices) is, again, in need of
spelling out.

Barker and Hulme acknowledge that critical accounts of the play
have frequently drawn attention to the theme of usurpation but claim
that the instances of usurpation are not present in the play as a theme
but as 'figural traces of the text's anxiety concerning the very matters of dominance and resistance'. That is, the text is not in control
of the presentation of these instances, but is, to some extent at least,
thrown off balance by them. They take Prospero's narrative of his and
Miranda's arrival on the island as an example, pointing out that first
Ariel is introduced and then Caliban who offer alternative versions
of this event, it might be argued, which have been set aside by critics
assuming that Prospero is the authoritative voice not only by virtue
of his power but by right. Prospero's control of the events of the play
is then something that follows quite naturally, but Barker and Hulme
are surely correct to note that 'Prospero's play and *The Tempest* are not
necessarily the same thing'.[15] That is, there may be a way of looking at
The Tempest that will see Prospero's control of the events he controls as
itself staged by the play and observed and even commented on (metaphorically speaking) by the play.

However, Shakespeare is dramatizing Prospero's story and we do
not really need to imagine pre- or un-conscious influences built into
language in order to explain 'the text's anxiety' if we take this merely
as an impressive metaphor guiding our attention towards Shakespeare's
art. It is difficult to be clear about how a text may display anxiety
anyway, though easy enough to see how a person would do. However
Barker and Hulme want to locate anxiety within discourse itself; not
as something experienced by an individual human being, but as something invading the very culture in which individual human beings
participate. This is to bring psychoanalytical perspectives to bear not
on persons but on culture itself. This in turn may imply that those who
hold such views hold also the view that culture is not an effect of the
interaction of persons but that persons are an effect of the action of
culture. This can only mean that to attempt to insist that either aspect

of a relationship is dominant over the other is to make a mistake in thinking: culture does not create persons any more than persons create culture; culture and persons are both aspects of each other and even of something larger still, the world, or reality perhaps.

To introduce their argument, Barker and Hulme describe Prospero's counter-accusation of attempted rape as a means by which he sweeps aside Caliban's claim and, further, they imply that critics who do not object are complicit with Prospero's act of oppression. Furthermore, they see Prospero's act as typical of European colonists who, they claim, routinely denied that whoever they found in lands they desired to conquer had any right to be there at all.

They bring in Frank Kermode's note to 2.2.147, 'I'll show thee every fertile inch o'th'island' to convict him. Kermode says of Caliban:

■ Twelve years earlier he had shown them to Prospero [1.2.338–40]. The colonists were frequently received with this kindness, though treachery might follow.[16] □

They point out that what might seem to be treachery from the invaders' point of view might seem to be a reasonable response to invasion from the point of view of the invaded, and then, arguing that Prospero is 'forging an equivalence between Antonio's initial *putsch* and Caliban's revolt', they claim that 'this allows Prospero to annul the memory of his failure to prevent his expulsion from the dukedom, by repeating it as a mutiny that he will, this time, forestall'.[17]

This is a complex argument: it asks us to believe that Prospero is staging a reparation, as it were, to himself of what was taken from him by his brother's revolt, and it seems that Barker and Hulme do not want to argue that he knows that this is what he is doing. In that case we may ask whether Shakespeare is doing this deliberately himself, to show up Prospero's unconscious intentions, but this does not seem to be what they mean either. The moment of Prospero's suddenly recalling that revolt and cancelling the masque he has arranged they describe as a moment of 'textual excess' a 'disproportion between apparent cause and effect' and cite Kermode's remarking the 'apparently inadequate motivation' for Prospero being so upset.[18] They suggest a psychoanalytical interpretation and a formal interpretation.

Psychoanalytically, 'Prospero's excessive reaction represents his disquiet at the irruption into consciousness of an unconscious anxiety concerning the grounding of his legitimacy, both as producer of his play and, *a fortiori*, as governor of the island'. Briefly, 'the effort invested in holding Prospero's play together as a unity is laid bare'. Secondly, formally, 'Prospero's difficulties in staging his play are themselves "staged" by the play that we are watching, this moment presenting for the first time the possibility of distinguishing between Prospero's play and *The Tempest* itself'.[19] They make an interesting point:

> ■ One way of distinguishing Prospero's play from *The Tempest* might be to claim that Prospero's carefully established relationship between main and sub-plot is reversed in *The Tempest*, whose *main* plot concerns Prospero's anxiety over his *sub*-plot. A formal analysis would seem to bear this out. The climax of Prospero's play is his revelation to Alonso of Miranda and Ferdinand playing chess. This is certainly a true *anagnorisis* [recognition or discovery] for Alonso, but for us a merely theatrical rather than a truly dramatic moment. *The Tempest*'s dramatic climax, in a way its only dramatic moment at all, is, after all, this sudden and strange disturbance of Prospero.[20] □

This would seem to suggest, or at least allow a reader to suggest, that Shakespeare's artistry in constructing such a drama was indeed considerable and, if Barker and Hulme were judged to be correct in their view by such a reader, justly praised by them. This is not what they mean though. Sensing the danger, they draw back from confirming Shakespeare's subtle art, reminding us that:

> ■ In the end [Prospero's] version of history remains *authoritative*, the larger play acceding as it were to the containment of the conspirators in the safely comic mode, Caliban allowed only his poignant and ultimately vain protests against the venality of his co-conspirators.[21] □

They point out that 'the lengths to which the play has to go to achieve a legitimate ending may then be read as the quelling of a fundamental disquiet concerning its own functions within the project of colonialist discourse'. Describing the reconciliation as the 'patching up of a minor dynastic dispute within the Italian nobility' they are simultaneously ridiculing and underlining the significance of the hardly achieved comic closure.[22]

Perhaps the best way to envisage the implications of such an analysis for Shakespeare as the imagined author of all this is to see him in the mind's eye as grappling confusedly with imagery and action, groping towards some dimly conceived goal, his way alternately lit by intuition and clouded by ideology, both seeing and unseeing at the same time, and *The Tempest* as the result of this struggle. The essay concludes with an earnest (and important) reminder that dramatic work is less susceptible to the kind of analysis to which they have subjected *The Tempest*, creating as it does:

> ■ An effect of distantiation, which exists in a complex relationship with the countervailing (and equally structural) tendency for audiences to identify with characters presented – through the language and

conventions of theatre – as heroes and heroines. Much work remains to be done on the articulation between discursive performance and mode of presentation.[23] □

Paul Brown will take this kind of argument deeper into contextual detail.

PAUL BROWN

Paul Brown's ' "This thing of darkness I acknowledge mine": *The Tempest* and the discourse of colonialism' (1985) is at once less theoretically ambitious than Barker and Hulme and more revealing of interesting parallelisms to be offered. He states his thesis as follows:

■ *The Tempest* is not simply a reflection of colonialist practices but an intervention in an ambivalent and even contradictory discourse. This intervention takes the form of a powerful and pleasurable narrative which seeks at once to harmonise disjunction, to transcend irreconcilable contradictions and to mystify the political conditions which demand colonialist discourse. Yet the narrative ultimately fails to deliver that containment and instead may be seen to foreground precisely those problems which it works to efface or overcome.[24] □

The play is seen as an engagement with a specific historical crisis: 'the struggle to produce a coherent discourse adequate to the complex requirements of British colonialism in its initial phase'.[25] Brown begins with a careful and illuminating analysis of the incident of the letter of John Rolfe (1585–1622) to the Governor of Virginia, seeking his blessing on Rolfe's marriage with Pocahontas (*c.* 1595–1617). The windings of Rolfe's reasonings are patiently laid out and Brown comments:

■ The threats of disruption to Rolfe's servitude to conscience, Governor and God have thus become the site of the affirmation of psychic, social and cosmic order. The encounter with the savage other serves to confirm the civil subject in that self-knowledge which ensures self-mastery.[26] □

Brown points out that the race discourse of 'savagism' and the class discourse of 'masterlessness' contribute to the discourse of colonialism, in the figure of bringing under a rule, and he adds in 'a courtly and politicised discourse of sexuality' so that race, class and gender are all comprehended by the discourse of colonialism and so, we may add, involved in its production and affected by its operations. 'Colonialism' properly understood involves the extension of the boundaries of the known into the unknown and is haunted by the savage, and the wild man, as well as enticed by the exotic – as Rolfe seems to have been by

Pocahontas – and, within, as it extends its reach and runs the risk of distraction from affairs at home, by the masterless man (and, one may add, by domestic disorder). Brown's argument goes further than suggesting encounter, however: in order for colonialist practice to work properly it must *produce* the dangerous other, not merely find it in encounters, 'producing a disruptive other in order to assert the superiority of the coloniser'.[27]

Brown's discussion of *The Tempest* begins with a description of Prospero's 'interpellation' of some of the chief characters in the opening scenes: Prospero 'invites them to recognise themselves as the subjects of his discourse':

> ■ Thus for Miranda he is a strong father who educates and protects her; for Ariel he is a rescuer and taskmaster; for Caliban he is a coloniser whose refused offer of civilisation forces him to strict discipline; for the shipwrecked he is a surrogate providence who corrects errant aristocrats and punishes plebeian revolt. Each of these subject positions confirms Prospero as master.[28] □

The conventions of the masque contain a readiness to recognize such arrangements in the celebration of the just and good monarch who is so often the object of such entertainments and there has never been any serious objection to the claim that the play observes these conventions. Brown himself cites an occasion at Kenilworth in 1575 on which Queen Elizabeth I (1533–1603; reigned 1558–1603) was confronted, late in the evening, on the margins of the grounds of the house, by an 'Hombre Salvagio' whose discovery of speech took the form of a joyful expression of subjection to the monarch.[29]

A strong feature of Brown's own discourse is the insistent coupling of notions of pleasure and power with knowledge, owing much, clearly, to Foucault's concept, 'power-knowledge-pleasure',[30] as well as his use of such notions as 'interpellation', a concept associated with the work of Louis Althusser [French philosopher; 1918–1990] and referring to the way in which society invites an individual person to recognize himself or herself in certain ways, much as – so Althusser argues – if a policeman calls out in the street, 'Hey! You!', whoever turns as though they were the one addressed is recognizing himself or herself as the one addressed. The word '*interpellation*' in French is used to mean 'being taken in for questioning by the police' and can also mean the right of parliament to call ministers to question.[31] This self-recognition lies at the heart of Althusser's description of the operation of ideology and contributes to Barker and Hulme's analysis of *The Tempest* as well as it does to Paul Brown's.

These notions, in Brown, do not, however, add much to an argument that is itself quite sound, that *The Tempest* has much to do with notions of the savage, of masterlessness, of orderly social life, of the extension of the influence of the English monarchy over, first, Wales, and later, Ireland and the New World, none of which has been contested before. The theory must show that it can reveal something hitherto contested or unknown before it can justify itself. The translation of a discussion familiar enough in ordinary language into the more rarefied technical vocabulary of 'theory' does little by itself. However the bent of Brown's discussion is towards an important argument: that power seeks to efface itself as power and to appear as something else. One such thing is aesthetic order. The requirement of social orderliness becomes not a matter of obedience to the dictates of power but an observance of aesthetic considerations. This he calls 'euphemization' after the rhetorical trope euphemism, or the deliberate avoidance of direct reference to something in pursuit of decorum.

These considerations are relevant to Brown's discussion of Caliban's speech at 3.2.138, 'the isle is full of noises', with its moving vision of beauty. Brown points out that Caliban's eloquence is Prospero's, as the language is his and Miranda's 'gift' to Caliban, and argues that 'obviously the play itself, heavily invested in colonialist discourse, can only represent this moment of excess through that very discourse: and so the discourse itself may be said to produce this site of resistance'.[32] This is important because the burden of Brown's argument is that colonialist discourse produces not only the colonizer but also the colonized, and Caliban's vision of beauty seems to point to something outside Prospero's control (this is why Brown terms it a 'moment of excess'). However, if the 'work' of discourse is self-effacement, then here we have its triumph. Caliban, Brown argues:

■ Takes *literally* what the discourse in the hands of a Prospero can only mean *metaphorically*. This is to say, the colonialist project's investment in the processes of euphemisation of what are really powerful relations here has produced a utopian moment where powerlessness represents *a desire for powerlessness*. This is the danger that any metaphorical system faces, that vehicle may be taken for tenor and used against the ostensible meanings intended. The play registers, if only momentarily, a radical ambivalence at the heart of colonialist discourse, revealing that it is a site of *struggle* over meaning.[33] □

This is a complex idea. Caliban's dream of beauty ends with his yearning for surrender (as it might be described): 'I cried to dream again (3.2.146)'. Caliban has taken the notion of surrender (which is what Prospero – in such an interpretation – demands of him) and made it his own, paradoxically enough, by using to express his deepest desire at that point. Brown takes the vocabulary developed by I A Richards

(1893–1979) to describe metaphor: 'tenor' to identify what the metaphor referred to and 'vehicle' to identify the figure by means of which
the metaphor referred to it. For example, when Barker and Hulme speak
of Shakespeare being 'force-fed behind a high wall called Literature'
the 'tenor' is the production, as they see it, of Shakespeare and the
'vehicle' is the force-feeding of prisoners. Caliban takes the system by
which Prospero controls his world ('the isle is full of music') and turns
it into an object of desire. Thus the island becomes a site of struggle:
dreamed of as beautiful by Caliban and ruled over by Prospero who
justifies his rule by means of the very elements of Caliban's dream.
The 'vehicle' by means of which Prospero expresses metaphorically his
right to rule is taken as a 'tenor' by the ruled.

Brown's final trope is Freud's 'dreamwork', with its associated figures of 'condensation', 'displacement' and 'symbolization'. Brown easily shows that these mechanisms are at work in the play (it may be
said that they are at work in any work of art, and routinely) and insists
that the dreamwork model provides a template for the operation of
colonialist discourse. Perhaps most impressive is the point raised by
the phrase Brown uses in the title of his essay: 'This thing of darkness
I / Acknowledge mine [5.1.278–9]'. He has pointed out that the ter-
mination of Prospero's play is his self-extinction as the powerful colonizer, and an implication of that self-extinction (if Brown has been
right about the central thrust of his argument) is the extinction of
the powerless other. In parcelling out the masterless to various owners
Prospero claims Caliban. Brown comments:

■ Even as this powerfully designates the monster as his property, an
object for his own utility, a darkness from which he may rescue self-
knowledge, there is surely an ironic identification *with* the other here as
both become interstitial.[34] □

'Surely' is not an argument but, if taken as guiding a director and
actors, it may be tried out in performance. Certainly 'acknowledge'
does not rule out a degree of reluctance where 'claim' would have
done. 'Interstitial' is an example of an unnecessarily *recherché* notion.

Brown is effective on the endless cycle of resistance and oppression necessary to display the superior power of the colonizer, suitably
effaced, or euphemized; his adducing examples from contemporary
practice is illuminating; his 'repunctuation' of the play, as he styles it,
amounts, however, to little more than a re-telling in terms of the work
of Foucault, Louis Althusser and Freud. What such re-tellings do is to
validate the interpretations they offer by showing the play's capacity to
conform to the theories enlisted: they do not invalidate other readings,
even, and perhaps especially, those convicted of appealing to 'timeless'
ideas. Unless one has become convinced otherwise that such ideas are

invalid, these accounts of *The Tempest* will not achieve what they do not even attempt. To offer a reading is to add to the stock of readings, not to sweep other readings aside. Even if rival readings are mutually incompatible we only have to ask whether both can be accommodated by the play, and not which one must be true, as both can be. Whether we want to try to entertain both is a matter for what we believe about other things. Critiques of those who would critique are the fate they court, and Meredith Skura's essay to be considered next does just that to both Barker and Hulme and Paul Brown.

MEREDITH SKURA

Meredith Skura summarizes the shift in perspective that is represented by Brown and Barker and Hulme (on whose work she draws) by saying:

■ Revisionists [...] emphasize the discursive strategies that the play shares with all colonial discourse, and the ways in which *The Tempest* itself not only displays prejudice but fosters and even 'enacts' colonialism by mystifying or justifying Prospero's power over Caliban. The new point is that *The Tempest* is a political act.[35] □

She points out that an implication at least of 'revisionist' perspectives has been the downgrading of 'psychological' interests and even the rejection of the 'psychological' as a perspective, a rejection she connects with the project of Fredric Jameson (born 1934) in *The Political Unconscious* (1981).[36] Her summary is astute:

■ The emphasis now is on psychology as a product of culture, itself a political structure; the very concept of a psyche is seen to be a product of the cultural nexus evolved during the Renaissance, and indeed, psychoanalysis itself, rather than being a way of understanding the Renaissance psyche, is a marginal and belated creation of this same nexus.[37] □

She points out that an implication of this view is the invention of a ' "collective or associative" mind'. She credits the 'revisionist impulse' with making a significant contribution to 'correcting New Critical "blindness" to history and ideology' but suggests that the new movement has a blindness of its own, 'something more than the rhetorical excesses characteristic of any innovative critical movement'.

Skura suggests that a correction of emphasis might be required:

■ What is missing from the recent articles is the connection between the new insights about cultural phenomena like 'power' and 'fields of discourse' and the traditional insights about the text, its immediate sources, its individual author – and his individual psychology. There is little sense of how discourse is related to the individual who was creating, even as he was participating in, that discourse.[38] □

Skura efficiently summarizes much of the literature on the 'colonialist' *Tempest* and asks the important question: 'How do we know that *The Tempest* "enacts" colonialism rather than merely alluding to the New World?' if, indeed, it even does that. Skura points to, for example, Alden T. Vaughan's acerbic remark to the effect that if Shakespeare had intended to indicate the inhabitants of the New World encountered by the European explorers he signally failed.[39] She identifies the argumentative strategies employed by the proponents of the 'colonialist' *Tempest* and dismisses them: 'So long as there is a core of resemblance, the differences are irrelevant'.[40] Further, 'the differences, in fact, are themselves taken to be evidence of the colonialist ideology at work, rationalizing and euphemizing power – or else inadvertent slips'. The effect of this is quite sinister:

■ Thus the case for colonialism becomes stronger in so far as Prospero *is* good and in so far as Caliban *is* in some ways bad – he did try to rape Miranda – or is *himself* now caught trying to falsify the past by occluding the rape and presenting himself as an innocent victim of Prospero's tyranny. □

The case is of that unpleasant kind in which any protestations of innocence are taken as sure signs of guilt. This is not good reasoning. Nor is ignoring or belittling differences and Skura is effective on some of the differences to be noted, particularly on the complicating factor of Sycorax and Ariel in Caliban's claim 'This island's mine', and on many other ways in which the play will not quite match the stereotype. She describes the enumeration of differences *versus* resemblances as 'a counting contest' but this is dismissive: it is exactly in weighing similarities and differences that judgement consists and she is perhaps being (as she often seems to be in the course of this essay) tactically self-deprecatory.

Skura displays a similar combination of determined clear-sightedness and good scholarship in her account of the notion of 'colonialist discourse', which, upon examination, affords a variety of examples of views. This provides her with a background for making a very important point:

■ Shakespeare was the first to show one of *us* mistreating a native, the first to represent a native from the inside, the first to allow a native to

complain onstage, and the first to make that New World encounter problematic enough to generate the current attention to the play.[41] □

If he was so then subsuming the play within the generalization 'colonialist discourse' is to distort it considerably, and to do so by treating
differences as 'inadvertent slips' or as distortions revealing the operation of the discourse in question is to run the risk of circularity: one
finds what one is looking for by making the play conform to what one
is seeking within it.

Skura then sets out on a much more adventurous path: a search
for other 'Prosperos' and other 'Calibans' within Shakespeare's other
plays. She finds them as far afield as Vincentio in *Measure for Measure*,
the Duke of Navarre in *Love's Labours Lost*, and in Prince Hal in *Henry IV*,
parts 1 and 2. The respective 'Calibans' are Lucio, Costard and Falstaff.
These 'Calibans' Skura describes as representations of the Prospero-
figures' 'disowned passions'.[42]

These pairings represent the pairing of the Other, the figure comprising all that the mature adult has had to reject in order to achieve
maturity, with the mature adult. To make the case, Skura has to
gather together some characters whose resemblances to one another
may strike some observers as fleeting. It is essential to recall Skura's
own argument against the generalizing tendency of the 'revisionist'
party. At what point do resemblances become grounds for arguing
identity? What will really unite (not merely gather together loosely)
Falstaff and Shylock and Bakhtin's 'grotesque body'? Of course the
device that lies to hand is that other discourse so adept at gathering resemblances, Freud's. Skura starts by assembling suggestions
of 'primitive oral greed', such as Shylock's expressed desire to 'feed
fat' his revenge, Falstaff's characteristic self-indulgence in eating and
drinking, the often-expressed fancy that Caliban's name is an ana-
gram of 'cannibal'. Then sexual greed is identified in Falstaff, again,
in Jacques's confessions about his misspent past – Jacques, in *As You
Like It*, is conceived as Caliban to Duke Senior's Prospero – in Caliban.
Finally, an 'anal' dimension is identified:[43] Shylock is accused of
'Jonsonian "anal" virtues ("fast bind, fast find")', his gold is described
as 'fecal' and his outburst 'stop my house's ears, I mean my casements
(2.5.34)' is interpreted as a reference to 'his tightly locked orifices'.
The reference is to the comedies of Ben Jonson (dramatist; 1572–
1637) and their scathing satirization of the values of what he saw as
a society obsessed with money. Jonson did not regard these characteristics Skura describes as 'virtues' and his plays pour scorn on those
who do. Jacques is more convincingly associated with anality, or at
least with scatology, as there are punning references in the play to a
'jakes' (his name could be pronounced so in Elizabethan English), or

a privy. Caliban hiding under his cloak with Trinculo is mistaken by Stephano for a monster who 'vents' Trinculo: 'a Gargantuan act of defecation'.[44]

What Skura has done in the first part of her essay is to take the revisionists, as she has called them, to task for being cavalier about this sort of thing: what she is doing now is apparently falling into the same error herself. To make Duke Senior, Vincentio and Prince Hal 'Prosperos' and to make Falstaff, Lucio and Jacques 'Calibans', involves a high degree of abstraction as the unlikenesses between these characters are at least as striking as their likenesses. Without wanting to take issue with the notion of a 'counting contest' as advanced by Skura (I think in an overly self-deprecating gesture) it must be observed that for comparison to become compelling the likenesses must be both numerous and striking, at least as much so as the unlikenesses. Further, the unlikenesses must be shown to be scattered, disparate, and not themselves constituting a body of likeness with some third thing. If this is not the case then the likenesses must at least outnumber, or be very much more striking than, the unlikenesses to compel recognition. Otherwise we are in the case of Hamlet and Polonius:

> ■ *Hamlet*: Do you see yonder cloud that's almost in shape of a camel?
> *Polonius*: By th'mass, and 'tis: like a camel, indeed.
> *Hamlet*: Methinks it is like a weasel.
> *Polonius*: It is backed like a weasel.
> *Hamlet*: Or like a whale.
> *Polonius*: Very like a whale. □ (3.2.365–70)

Skura describes Caliban as the purest instance of the kind 'Calibans', and as child-like. He dreams of riches falling from the sky; he recalls his mother with fondness; he rebukes Prospero for stroking him then disciplining him. Such a picture is enticing, though hardly so specific as to identify, or to distinguish, minutely. Many of us will recognize at least aspects of it and if it will apply widely its use to distinguish is much diminished. If we all feel like that, then what is distinguished about Caliban or even about childhood?

What may be distinctive about Caliban is the innocence with which he feels these things, or we may want to call it naïvety. This leads Skura to a telling point: 'Prospero treats Caliban as he would treat the wilful child in himself'. This makes thought-provoking sense of 'this thing of darkness I acknowledge mine'. Skura makes an interesting comparison with Aaron's treatment of his son in *Titus Andronicus* and points out that Aaron's love for his child: 'this myself, The figure and the picture of my youth' (4.2.106) echoes Prospero's 'This thing of darkness I acknowledge mine'. Skura claims that what has been shown in the earlier play re-appears in the later, 'transformed'.

The reader should beware of the word 'transformed': that two things may be compared does not allow us to draw the conclusion that something has persisted from one play to another. Nor is there any need to: Aaron's love for his son illuminates by contrast Prospero's strained relationship with Caliban without there being any need to introduce any other connection between the two. However Skura does want to do more. In the spirit of Edward Dowden there is a theme to be pursued:

> ■ By merging his fantasy about a 'white' (but exiled and neurotically puritanical) duke with his fantasy about a villainous (but loving) 'black' father, Shakespeare for the first time shows, in Prospero, a paternal leader who comes back to power by admitting rather than denying the 'blackness' in himself.[45] □

When Prospero finally acknowledges Caliban he acknowledges the blackness within himself, the child within himself, and the contradictions at the heart of the colonialist position.

Skura concludes this section of her argument with an interesting insight into the relationship between Prospero and Antonio. She sees Prospero's life in his library as an Eden-like state, founded on his trust in his brother:

> ■ Only when Antonio's betrayal shattered that trust and Prospero was ousted from Eden – newly aware of both the brother as Other and of himself as wilful self in opposition – did he 'discover' the island and Caliban. In a sense, then, Caliban emerged from the rift between Prospero and Antonio, just as Ariel emerged from Sycorax's riven pine. Once the brother has shown that he is not identical to the self, reflecting back its own narcissistic desire, then he becomes the Other – and simultaneously rouses the vengeful Other in the self.[46] □

Thus Prospero's acknowledgement of Caliban 'partly defuses an entire dynamic that began long before he had ever seen the island'.

In a sort of *coda* to the main business of the essay Skura speculates on whether Shakespeare was deliberately musing on the end of things, as so many writers on the play have thought. She notes that John B. Bender has explored the significance of the play's presumed court debut as Hallowmas 1611, 'the feast of winter and the time of seasonal celebrations figuring the more final endings and death associated with winter'.[47] She points out in conclusion that Shakespeare was not 'merely reproducing a pre-existent discourse; he was also crossing it with other discourses, changing, enlarging, skewing, and questioning'.

Conclusion: Future Directions

The cultural distance that has developed in the course of the twentieth century can be measured by holding in the mind some of what Meredith Skura has been discussing and contrasting it with the following passage from Sir Arthur Quiller-Couch's lectures on *The Tempest* published in *Shakespeare's Workmanship* in 1918. Q imagines the aftermath of the performance:

> ■ The lights in the royal banqueting-house are out. Tomorrow the carpenters arrive to take down poles, rollers, joists – all the material structure of this play – and, a day after, comes the charwoman to sweep up sawdust with the odds and ends of tinsel. The lights are out; the company dispersed to go their bright ways and make, in the end, other dust. Ariel has nestled to the bat's back and slid away, following summer, following darkness like a dream. □

This rather beautiful vision of the insubstantial nature of play and performance, echoing, of course, Prospero's own reflections, leads Q to make a remarkable claim:

> ■ And I conclude by asseverating that were a greater than Ariel to wing down from Heaven and stand and offer me to choose which, of all the books written in the world, should be mine, I should choose – not the *Odyssey*, not the *Aeneid*, not the *Divine Comedy*, not *Paradise Lost*; not *Othello* nor *Hamlet* nor *Lear*; but this little matter of 2000 odd lines – *The Tempest*.[1] □

Q's peroration is a small masterpiece of a vanishing kind of critical discourse. He has imagined the opening night at the beginning of 1613, the performance of the play as part of the celebrations that marked the marriage of Princess Elizabeth and Frederic, the Prince Palatine Elector. Though Q discounts Dr Garnett's theory that the play was composed for the nuptials of Prince Frederic and Princess Elizabeth he acknowledges the appropriateness of the connection and of course the fact that the play was performed for those celebrations. The unfortunate brief reign of Frederic and Elizabeth over Bohemia (1619–20) earned him the nickname of 'the Winter King' and her that of 'the Winter Queen'. Q notes her cult in England: she was known also as 'the Queen of Hearts' as she was so popular abroad as well as in England.

This ill-fated couple, forced into exile, she so much loved, may seem a kind of emblem of doomed royalty, and that itself an emblem of doomed greatness of any kind. Certainly Q pulls out all the stops in his final remarks to convey the impression made on him by this play. This did not seem to modern critics to be criticism at all.

By the second half of the twentieth century a combination of psychoanalysis, linguistics and Marxism, recruited by feminists and others in the interests of a criticism dedicated to exposing the operations of ideology in sustaining a culture identified variously as capitalist, patriarchal, logocentric or all three (and more) had gone even further. To appeal to Francis Barker and Peter Hulme to recognize in *The Tempest* an emblem of doomed greatness of any kind would be to invite derision or worse.

However, as the brief survey of performances of *Pericles* and *Cymbeline* was intended to demonstrate, Shakespeare's late plays have a persistent charm that may have to do with what ingenious theatre companies can make them mean but that may also have to do with the endurance of certain images and of a poetry of theatrical action and of the words arranged for actors to speak which is what the critics of an earlier age were attempting to grapple with. The critics of the later age are ingenious at interpreting the meanings of this poetry but they are not perhaps as good at (because, at least, they are not as interested in) accounting for its power. For all Q's quaintness (and that may offend as easily as it may charm), he may be said to have caught something of the peculiar quality of *The Tempest*, its poignancy. All these late plays, however various the degrees to which they succeed in doing what their maker set out to do, share this sense of poignancy. It is certainly there in the earlier comedies, and markedly in the 'problem' plays, but it is the special concern of the late plays to take what in *The Merchant of Venice*, or in *As You Like It*, is an effect of the unreality of comedy, and extend it further towards extravagance to the point of exciting incredulity (as it did in Dr Johnson). It is the feeling of a dream deliberately sustained into waking in the full knowledge of its impossibility and the utter inability to resist its charm. Modern critics were suspicious of what Frank Kermode writing in 1954 called the 'hazardous and licentious enthusiasms'[2] of Romantic criticism because of a respect for 'reality' and an interest in being clear about it. Perhaps postmodern perspectives, suspicious as they are of 'reality', do not find the collision of dream and reality as powerful as Q did. There is nothing philosophical, though, about the notion of 'reality' considered here: the plays deal with a common enough phenomenon. The central characters in all these plays are people who lose things, through their own fault, through wickedness on occasion or neglect on others, through no fault of their own even, and who have those things miraculously restored to them. It is as though there is no such thing as remorse or regret except as temporary intrusions into a life that turns out well in the end. That this is not a common experience is a truth recognized by modernity, postmodernity, romanticism and many other perspectives as well.

Meredith Skura's essay offers a perspective on possible future directions in another sense as well in that she attempts to moderate what she sees as the excesses of Barker and Hulme and other 'revisionist' accounts. The development of critical discourse tends to resemble the model described by Thomas Kuhn (1922–96) in his essay *The Structure of Scientific Revolutions* (1962), in which he argued that what he called 'paradigm shifts' take place from time to time by means of which new areas of thought are opened up and between which thinking is occupied with cultivating the space opened up by the last 'paradigm shift'. We should expect any development in thought which follows such a pattern to be characterized by sudden intrusions into thought of new fundamental ideas that throw everything up in the air and which are followed by a period of consolidation in which the consequences of the new idea are followed through. The 1980s provide an example of such a 'paradigm shift': the work of Jacques Derrida (1930–2004) in particular had such an effect on the practice of literary criticism in the United States of America, ushering in an era of 'deconstruction'. The 'newer readings' to which Barker and Hulme refer resulted, however indirectly, from the new lease of life given to socio-historical and psychoanalytical literary studies by the new view of language opened up by Derrida's emphasis on the 'undecidability' of concepts and the texts that were developed around them. If there were excesses then critics such as Skura were not slow to address them. It seems likely that the overall change of direction, from a concern with works of art to a concern with texts as cultural phenomena, will continue, though there are signs, such as Suzanne Gossett's remark in passing that the lack of critical interest is 'based less on thoughtful aesthetic judgement than on immutable textual conditions',[3] that reports of the death of concern with works of art may have been exaggerated. It is true that what counts as art is judged according to criteria that change very much and not only between individuals: that Q disliked *The Winter's Tale* and liked *Cymbeline* while Leavis disliked *Cymbeline* and liked *The Winter's Tale* is not only a matter of personal preference but of changing criteria and perspectives. Postmodern preferences for jumbled narratives and an open display of artifice (what S L Bethell called the 'creaking of the dramatic machinery'[4]) will appear to tastes educated otherwise as uneducated, while the predilection of these audiences for unity will appear to postmodern tastes jejune.

We should also bear in mind Wordsworth's objection to the notion of 'taste' itself, as expressed in his 'Preface' to *Lyrical Ballads* (1801; 1802), and his contemptuous dismissal of the views of those:

■ Who talk of Poetry as of a matter of amusement and idle pleasure; who will converse with us as gravely about a *taste* for Poetry, as they express it, as if it were a thing as indifferent as a taste for rope-dancing, or Frontiniac or Sherry.[5] □

During the nineteenth century a view gathered strength of the serious-ness of poetry, of the contribution to our well-being that poetry, and the study of poetry, may make. The view is associated especially with the name of Matthew Arnold but its chief inheritor in the twentieth cen-tury is a person of decidedly different critical views, F R Leavis. Leavis was a student of Q's and the differences of opinion between these two may come to seem emblematic of a change in the twentieth century, or from the nineteenth to the twentieth, almost as far-reaching as the change from views characteristic of Leavis to those expressed by Barker and Hulme. It is not true of course that Leavis's views were universally accepted or even that they were representative but it is also not true that the views expressed by Barker and Hulme are universally accepted or even representative: criticism is a matter of individual views as well as it is a matter of broadly shaping consensus underlying individual views. It is the task of this Guide to try to indicate both.

As for the future it may well be that there will be a turning of the tide and a re-discovery of the 'high seriousness' of art: such essays as Kiernan Ryan's *Shakespeare* (Basingstoke: Palgrave, 3rd edition, 2002) and Andy Mousley's *Re-Humanising Shakespeare* (Edinburgh: Edinburgh University Press, 2007) show signs of seeking a *rapprochement* with liberal-humanist views without losing the gains of the discoveries made by historical and even historicist analyses; there will be no abatement in the flow of psychoanalytical studies, and some of them will show the same lack of embarrassment as Janet Adelman's study *Suffocating Mothers* (London: Routledge, 1992) at brushing off an approach that, in its biographical leanings at least, would not have surprised Edward Dowden, though its psychoanalytical method and some of its conclu-sions would have given him pause for thought. There will be further, and more detailed, forays into political references and resonances, such as those essayed by Simon Palfrey and David Bergeron with regard to *Cymbeline*; there will be socio-political studies of *The Winter's Tale* and *The Tempest* with a more anthropological bent (a direction indicated in respect of *Pericles* by some aspects of Suzanne Gossett's survey of opin-ion: see pages 133–46 on 'the family' and pages 146–51 on 'the gift'). It is not possible to guess what new paradigms will present themselves, but the presently operating paradigms are far from worked through in all their implications and consequences.

As this Guide has sought to show, these plays have been variously interpreted. Their author's intentions have been imagined in different ways and his own feelings speculatively adduced. The cultural work they did and have been doing has been variously analyzed and they have been judged feeble, powerful, threatening and subversive by turns. Their charm has survived and they continue to be performed. Only time will tell whether the future Q glimpsed will in fact take these last effusions of Shakespeare's genius to itself as cherished images of its best dreams, its yearnings and its hopes, or whether the future will in any way resemble the one he imagined, especially in its rather charmingly naïve astonishment that people really were as some others' plays presented them as being. Science-fiction often imagines a world like that, in which effortlessly civilized people live well-mannered and quiet lives. H G Wells (1866–1946) in 'the Time Machine' (1895) saw a more worrying prospect: an idle and childlike people, the Eloi, bred and eaten like cattle by an industrious subterranean race, the Morlocks. Something of that vision informed *Forbidden Planet*, the film version by Fred Wilcox of *The Tempest*, in which the technological advancement of the Krel is contrasted with the monsters they unleashed from their unconscious. They might have said, as Prospero says, 'This thing of darkness I acknowledge mine'. Visions of the future are an index of a kind of the age that forms them and of the people that form them: Q's was generous and hopeful, as his views of these plays were generous; Wilcox and Wells saw something else in their own time and their views are less hopeful. The extravagant promise offered by these late plays of unashamedly happy endings may be Shakespeare's own generous hopefulness, or it may be the flagrant wish-fulfilment demanded by his audience whether shared by him personally or not; it is now up to us to make our interpretations and our judgements and to work out the arguments by which we may stand by them.

Notes

INTRODUCTION

1   The term was first used by F S Boas in *Shakespeare and his Predecessors* (London: John Murray, 1896) with reference to Ibsen's tendency to create plays that addressed 'problems'. Boas referred to *All's Well that Ends Well, Measure for Measure* and *Troilus and Cressida* though others have included *The Merchant of Venice, Hamlet, The Winter's Tale, Julius Caesar* and *Antony and Cleopatra* at different times. As is the case with many generic distinctions this one has lost its elasticity due to over-exertion.
2   W K Wimsatt (ed.), *Dr Johnson on Shakespeare* (Harmondsworth: Penguin, 1969), p. 62.
3   Edward Bond, *Plays: One* (London: Eyre Methuen, 1977), p. 309.
4   Wimsatt (1969), p. 57.

1   THE LATE PLAYS: CRITICAL OPINION IN THE EIGHTEENTH AND NINETEENTH CENTURIES

1   W K Wimsatt (ed.), *Dr Johnson on Shakespeare* (Harmondsworth: Penguin, 1969), p. 72.
2   Wimsatt (1969), p. 101.
3   Wimsatt (1969), p. 100.
4   Wimsatt (1969), p. 100.
5   Wimsatt (1969), p. 101.
6   Wimsatt (1969), p. 101.
7   Wimsatt (1969), p. 109.
8   Wimsatt (1969), p. 136.
9   William Hazlitt, *The Characters of Shakespeare's Plays* (London: Dent, 1906), p. 262.
10   Hazlitt (1906), p. 1.
11   Hazlitt (1906), p. 2.
12   Hazlitt (1906), pp. 2–3.
13   Hazlitt (1906), p. 2.
14   Hazlitt (1906), p. 7.
15   Hazlitt (1906), pp. 7–8.
16   Hazlitt (1906), p. 90.
17   Hazlitt (1906), p. 92.
18   Hazlitt (1906), p. 94.
19   Hazlitt (1906), p. 95.
20   Hazlitt (1906), p. 214.
21   Hazlitt (1906), pp. 214–15.
22   Hazlitt (1906), p. 213.
23   Terence Hawkes (ed.), *Coleridge on Shakespeare* (Harmondsworth: Penguin, 1969), p. 114.
24   Hawkes (1969), p. 243.
25   Hawkes (1969), pp. 195–6.
26   Hawkes (1969), p. 222.
27   Hawkes (1969), pp. 222–3.
28   Hawkes (1969), p. 224.
29   Hawkes (1969), p. 225.

30 Hawkes (1969), p. 226.
31 Hawkes (1969), p. 226.
32 Hawkes (1969), pp. 229–30.
33 Hawkes (1969), p. 230.
34 Hawkes (1969), p. 230.
35 Hawkes (1969), pp. 230–1.
36 Hawkes (1969), p. 233.
37 Hawkes (1969), p. 231.
38 Hawkes (1969), p. 233.
39 Hawkes (1969), p. 234.
40 Kenneth Muir (ed.), *Shakespeare: The Winter's Tale* (Hampshire: Macmillan, 1968), p. 37.
41 Muir (1968), p. 56.
42 Giles Lytton Strachey, 'Shakespeare's Final Period', *Books and Characters* (London: Chatto & Windus, 1922), pp. 52–3.
43 Strachey (1922), p. 58.
44 Strachey (1922), pp. 59–60.
45 Strachey (1922), p. 60.
46 *Shakespeare's Workmanship* (Cambridge: Cambridge University Press, 1918; Pocket edition, 1931), pp. 179–80.
47 Quiller-Couch (1931), p. 183.
48 Quiller-Couch (1931), p. 184.
49 Quiller-Couch (1931), p. 190.
50 Quiller-Couch (1931), p. 214.

2   PERICLES

1 Suzanne Gossett (ed.), *Pericles* (London: Thomson, 2004), p. 8.
2 Gossett (2004), p. 54.
3 Gossett (2004), p. 54.
4 Gossett (2004), p. 97.
5 F D Hoeniger (ed.), *Pericles* (London: Methuen, 1963), p. lxxxvii.
6 Hoeniger (1963), p. lxxxviii.
7 Robert S Miola, *Shakespeare and Classical Comedy: The Influence of Plautus and Terence* (Oxford: Oxford University Press, 1994).
8 Richard Halpern, *Shakespeare Among the Moderns* (Ithaca, New York: Cornell University Press, 1997), p. 147.
9 Maurice Hunt, 'Shakespeare's *Pericles* and the Acts of the Apostles', *Christianity and Literature*, 49 (2000), pp. 295–309.
10 Jonathan Bate, *Shakespeare and Ovid* (Oxford: Oxford University Press, 1993), p. 221.
11 Gossett (2004), p. 117.
12 Gossett (2004), p. 117.
13 Caroline Bicks, 'Backsliding at Ephesus: Shakespeare's Diana and the Churching of Women', in David Skeele (ed.), *Pericles: Critical Essays* (New York and London: Routledge, 2000), pp. 205–27.
14 Gossett (2004), p. 118.
15 Gossett (2004), p. 119.
16 Bicks (2000), pp. 205–27.
17 F Elizabeth Hart, '"Great Is Diana" of Shakespeare's Ephesus', *Studies in English Literature*, 43 (2003), pp. 347–74.
18 Gossett (2004), pp. 120–1.
19 Gossett (2004), p. 122.
20 Simon Palfrey, *Late Shakespeare: A New World of Words* (Oxford: Oxford University Press, 1997), pp. 53 and 56.

21 Halpern (1997), p. 144.

22 Gossett (2004), pp. 122–3.

23 Steven Mullaney, *The Place of the Stage: License, Play and Power in Renaissance England* (Chicago: University of Chicago Press, 1988), pp. 143–8.

24 Gossett (2004), p. 124.

25 Gossett (2004), p. 124.

26 Gossett (2004), p. 124.

27 Gossett (2004), p. 124.

28 Constance Jordan, *Shakespeare's Monarchies: Ruler and Subject in the Romances* (Ithaca, New York and London: Cornell University Press, 1997).

29 Palfrey (1997), p. 65.

30 Halpern (1997), p. 150.

31 Linda McJannet, 'Genre and Geography: The Eastern Mediterranean in *Pericles* and *The Comedy of Errors*', in John Gillies and Virginia Mason Vaughan (eds), *Playing the Globe: Genre and Geography in English Renaissance Drama* (Newark, New Jersey, and London: Fairleigh Dickinson University Press, 1998), p. 88.

32 Constance Relihan, 'Liminal Geography: *Pericles* and the Politics of Place', *Philological Quarterly*, 71 (1992), pp. 281–302.

33 C L Barber, '"Thou that beget'st him that did thee beget": Transformation in *Pericles* and *The Winter's Tale*', *Shakespeare Survey*, 22 (1969), pp. 59–67.

34 Ruth Nevo, *Shakespeare's Other Language* (New York: Methuen, 1987), p. 42.

35 Gossett (2004), p. 135.

36 Gossett (2004), p. 137.

37 Gossett (2004), p. 137.

38 Gossett (2004), p. 138.

39 Gossett (2004), p. 138.

40 Gossett (2004), p. 147.

41 Gossett (2004), p. 147.

42 Gossett (2004), p. 149.

43 Gossett (2004), p. 150.

44 Palfrey (1997), pp. 230–1.

45 Gossett (2004), p. 157.

46 Coppélia Kahn, 'The Providential Tempest and the Shakespearean Family', in Murray Schwartz and Coppélia Kahn (eds), *Representing Shakespeare* (Baltimore, Maryland: Johns Hopkins University Press, 1980), pp. 217–43.

47 Nevo (1987), p. 42.

48 Barber (1969), pp. 59–67.

49 Richard P Wheeler, 'Deaths in the Family: The Loss of a Son and the Rise of Shakespearean Comedy', *Shakespeare Quarterly*, 51 (2000), pp. 127–53.

50 Gossett (2004), p. 159.

51 Hoeniger (1963), p. lxix.

52 *The Plays and Poems of Shakespeare*, eds, Boswell and Malone (London, 1821), vol. xxi, p. 228. Quoted in Hoeniger (1963), p. lxx.

53 Sir Walter Raleigh, *Shakespeare* (English Men of Letters) (Hampshire: Macmillan, 1928, first published 1907), p. 53. Hoeniger (1963), p. lxx.

54 *Modern Language Review*, 52, No. 4 (1957), p. 583 (Review of the *New Cambridge Shakespeare* edition of *Pericles*).

55 *Shakespeare Quarterly*, 4 (1953), pp. 257–70.

56 *Review of English Studies*, n.s. 3, 12 (1952), pp. 315–24.

57 Hoeniger (1963), p. lxxii.

58 Hoeniger (1963), p. lxxiii.

59 Hoeniger (1963), p. lxxiv.

60 G Wilson Knight, *The Crown of Life* (London: Methuen, 1947), pp. 32–75.

61 Kenneth Muir, *Shakespeare the Collaborator* (London: Methuen, 1960), pp. 80–1.

62 Knight (1947), p. 65.

63 Hoeniger (1963), p. lxxxv.

64 Hoeniger (1965), p. lxxxviii.

65 The Saint's plays have not survived in numbers though they seem to have been widely performed between 1100 and 1580 as Hoeniger notes (p. lxxxix). They and the tradition in which they sit are well described by Hoeniger's phrase 'vernacular religious drama (p. lxxxviii)'.

3 *CYMBELINE* (1)

1 William Hazlitt, *The Characters of Shakespeare's Plays* (London: Dent, 1906), p. 1.

2 Sir Arthur Quiller-Couch, *Shakespeare's Workmanship* (Cambridge: Cambridge University Press, 1918; Pocket edition, 1931)', p. 214.

3 Algernon Charles Swinburne, *A Study of Shakespeare* (London: Chatto & Windus, 1880), p. 225.

4 F R Leavis, 'The Criticism of Shakespeare's Late Plays: A Caveat', in Leavis, *The Common Pursuit* (London: Hogarth Press, 1984), pp. 173–81.

5 Leavis (1984), p. 174.

6 Leavis (1984), p. 174.

7 Leavis (1984), p. 174.

8 Leavis (1984), p. 176.

9 Leavis (1984), p. 177.

10 Leavis (1984), p. 178.

11 Leavis (1984), p. 178.

12 W K Wimsatt (ed.), *Dr Johnson on Shakespeare* (Harmondsworth: Penguin, 1969), p. 136.

13 Martin Butler (ed.), *Cymbeline* (Cambridge: Cambridge University Press, 2005), p. 1.

14 Butler (2005), p. 2.

15 Butler (2005), p. 7.

16 R Y Young, 'Slander in *Cymbeline* and Other Jacobean Tragicomedies', *ELR*, 13 (1983), 182–202; Robert Henke, *Pastoral Transformations: Italian Tragicomedies and Shakespeare's Late Plays* (Newark, Delaware: University of Delaware Press, Associated University Presses, 1997).

17 A C Kirsch, *Jacobean Dramatic Perspectives* (Charlottesville, Virginia: University of Virginia Press, 1972), pp. 1–6; G K Hunter, *English Drama 1586–1642: The Age of Shakespeare* (Oxford: Oxford University Press, 1996), p. 284 for example.

18 Butler (2005), p. 15.

19 Anne Barton, *Essays, Mainly Shakespearean* (Cambridge: Cambridge University Press, 1994), pp. 3–30.

20 Oxford (1988) says that the diary of the astrologer Simon Forman (1552–1611) records the heroine's name as 'Innogen' and comments 'and this name occurs in the sources; the form "Imogen", found only in the Folio, appears to be a misprint'. However the form 'Innogen' is, *pace* Forman and the sources, still relatively unfamiliar outside Butler and Oxford and so I have retained the traditional usage.

21 R A Foakes, *Shakespeare: The Dark Comedies to the Last Plays* (London: Routledge, 1971); see also Kirsch (1972).

22 Butler (2005), p. 22.

23 Butler (2005), p. 23.

24 Butler (2005), p. 24.

25 Stephen Orgel, '*Cymbeline* at Santa Cruz', *Shakespeare Quarterly*, 52 (2001), p. 284.

26 Butler (2005), p. 26.

27 Butler (2005), p. 26.

28 Butler (2005), p. 27.

29 Butler (2005), p. 28.

30 Butler (2005), p. 28.

31 See, for example, Nicholas Potter (ed.), *Shakespeare: Othello: A Reader's Guide to Essential Criticism* (Basingstoke: Palgrave Macmillan, 2000).

32 Siemon, J R, '"Perplexed beyond Self-explication": Cymbeline and early modern Postmodern Europe', in M Hattaway, B Sokolova and D Roper (eds), *Shakespeare in the New Europe* (Sheffield: Sheffield Academic Press, 1994), pp. 294–309.

33 Butler (2005), p. 30.

34 Butler (2005), p. 31.

35 Patricia Parker, *Literary Fat Ladies: Rhetoric, Gender, Property* (London: Methuen, 1988) and Catherine Belsey, *Shakespeare and the Loss of Eden: The Construction of Family Values in Early Modern Culture* (Basingstoke: Palgrave Macmillan, 1999).

36 Butler (2005), p. 32.

37 Butler (2005), p. 38. See F A Yates, *Shakespeare's Last Plays: A New Approach* (1975); G Wickham, 'Riddle and Emblem: A Study in the Dramatic Structure of *Cymbeline*', in J Carey (ed.) *English Renaissance Studies Presented to Dame Helen Gardner* (Oxford: Clarendon Press, 1980), pp. 94–113; Jonathan Goldberg, *Voice Terminal Echo: Postmodernism and English Renaissance Texts* (London: Routledge, 1986); W Maley, 'Postcolonial Shakespeare: British Identity Formation and *Cymbeline*', in J Richards and J Knowles (eds), *Shakespeare's Late Plays: New Readings* (Edinburgh: Edinburgh University Press, 1999), pp. 145–57.

38 Butler (2005), p. 50.

39 Butler (2005), p. 50.

40 Butler (2005), p. 50.

41 Janet Adelman, *Suffocating Mothers: Fantasies of Maternal Origin in Shakespeare's Plays* (London: Routledge, 1992).

42 See Peter A Parolin, 'Anachronistic Italy: Cultural Alliances and National Identity in *Cymbeline*', *Shakespeare Studies*, 30 (2002), pp. 188–215.

43 Butler (2005), p. 51.

44 L Woodbridge, 'Palisading the Body Politic', *Texas Studies in Language and Literature*, 33 (1991), pp. 327–54.

45 Butler (2005), p. 52.

46 Butler (2005), p. 52.

47 Butler (2005), p. 52.

48 Butler (2005), p. 54.

4 *CYMBELINE* (2)

1 J L Marsden, 'Pathos and Passivity: Thomas Durfey's Adaptation of Shakespeare's *Cymbeline*', *Restoration*, 14: 2 (1990), pp. 71–81 and Michael Dobson, *The Making of the National Poet: Shakespeare, Adaptation and Authorship, 1660–1790* (Oxford: Clarendon Press, 1992), pp. 85–90.

2 G W Stone, 'A Century of *Cymbeline*: Garrick's Magic Touch', *Studies in Philology*, 54 (1975), pp. 310–22.

3 Helen Faucit, *On Some of Shakespeare's Female Characters* (Edinburgh: Blackwood, 1885); Anna Jameson, *Characteristics of Women, Moral, Poetical and Historical* (London: Saunders and Otley, 1832). See also Judith Johnston, *Anna Jameson: Victorian, Feminist, Woman of Letters* (Aldershot: Scolar Press, 1997).

4 See Roger Warren, *Cymbeline (Shakespeare in Performance)* (Manchester: Manchester University Press, 1989) for the performances staged by Hall, Gaskill and Alexander.

5 Stephen Orgel, '*Cymbeline* at Santa Cruz', *Shakespeare Quarterly*, 52: 2 (2001), pp. 277–85.

6   Orgel (2001), pp. 277–85.
7   J M Nosworthy (ed.), *Cymbeline* (London: Methuen, 1995), p. xlii. Nosworthy's edition was first published in the Arden Shakespeare series in 1955.
8   Nosworthy (1995), p. xlvi.
9   Nosworthy (1995), p. xlvi.
10 Nosworthy (1995), p. lxxviii.
11 Nosworthy (1995), p. lxxix.
12 Nosworthy (1995), p. lxxx.
13 Roger L Green, 'The Phoenix and the Tree', *English* (1948), 7: 37, pp. 11–15.
14 Nosworthy (1995), p. lxxxii.
15 Nosworthy (1995), p. lxxxii.
16 Lena Orlin (ed.), *Othello* (Hampshire: Palgrave Macmillan, 2004), p. 2.
17 Orlin (2004), p. 1.
18 Jodi Mikalachki, 'The Masculine Romance of Roman Britain: Cymbeline and Early Modern English Nationalism', *Shakespeare Quarterly*, 46: 3 (Autumn, 1995), pp. 301–22.
19 Mikalachki (1995), p. 303.
20 'The placing of propositions or clauses one after another, without indicating by connecting words the relation (of coordination or subordination) between them, as in *tell me, how are you?' Oxford English Dictionary.*
21 Mikalachki (1995), pp. 303–4.
22 G Wilson Knight, *The Crown of Life* (London: Oxford University Press, 1947), p. 136.
23 Mikalachki (1995), pp. 321–2.
24 Friedrich Engels, *Dialectics of Nature*, trans. C P Dutt (New York: International Publishers, 1940). 'The second law of the dialectic asserts that everything has a self-contradictory character, containing within itself its own opposite. The bi-polar essence of all things manifests itself in change, which is a process of *alteration*, or transformation of something from its original state through a series of intermediate variations into its opposite' (Wm F Warde, 'Engels on Dialectics of Nature', *Fourth International*, 1: 17, December 1940, pp. 201–5).
25 Coppélia Kahn, *Roman Shakespeare: Warriors, Wounds and Women* (London: Routledge, 1997), p. 160; Robert S Miola, *Shakespeare's Rome* (Cambridge: Cambridge University Press, 1983). Kahn notes Wilson Knight's determination that the play be seen as historical because of its concern with the integrity of the island kingdom (*The Crown of Life*) and J P Brockbank in 'History and Histrionics in *Cymbeline*', *Shakespeare Survey* 11 (1958), pp. 42–9 stresses the historical aspect of the romance in that the account Holinshed gives of the descent and early life of Brute resembles the story of the lost princes in Wales. Resemblances are beguiling but must be more than merely striking to become convincing. Brockbank does not urge his case as strongly as Wilson Knight and that restraint, especially with a play that seems to sit so lightly to the claims of consistency as does *Cymbeline*, is a wise course.
26 Kahn (1983), p. 160.
27 Kahn (1983), p. 161; M Skura, 'Interpreting Posthumus' Dream from above and below: Families, Psychoanalysts and Literary Critics', in M M Schwartz and C Kahn (eds), *Representing Shakespeare: New Psychoanalytic Essays* (1980), pp. 203–16.
28 Frances A Yates, *Shakespeare's Last Plays: A New Approach* (London: Routledge, 1975).
29 Patricia Parker, 'Romance and Empire: Anachronistic *Cymbeline*', in G M Logan and G Teskey (eds), *Unfolded Tales: Essays on Renaissance Romance* (1989), pp. 189–207.
30 Kahn (1983), pp. 162–3; Mikalachki (1995), pp. 301–22.
31 Kahn (1983), p. 163.
32 Kahn (1983), p. 163; Janet Adelman, *Suffocating Mothers* (London: Routledge, 1992) p. 199.
33 Kahn (1983), p. 164; Linda Woodbridge, 'Palisading the Body Politic', *Texas Studies in Language and Literature*, 33: 3 (1991), pp. 327–54.

34   Kahn (1983), p. 168.
35   Kahn (1983), p. 168.
36   Kahn (1983), p. 168.

5   *THE WINTER'S TALE*: EARLY MODERNS

1   Sir Arthur Quiller-Couch, *Shakespeare's Workmanship* (Cambridge: Cambridge University Press, 1918; Pocket edition, 1931), pp. 241–2.
2   Quiller-Couch (1931), p. 242.
3   Kenneth Muir (ed.), *Shakespeare, The Winter's Tale: A Casebook* (Basingstoke: Macmillan, 1968), p. 80.
4   Muir (1968), p. 80.
5   Muir (1968), pp. 80–1.
6   Muir (1968), p. 81.
7   Muir (1968), p. 81.
8   Muir (1968), p. 82.
9   Muir (1968), p. 82.
10   Muir (1968), p. 82.
11   Muir (1968), p. 83.
12   Muir (1968), p. 83.
13   Muir (1968), p. 84.
14   Muir (1968), pp. 84–5.
15   Muir (1968), p. 85.
16   Muir (1968), p. 86.
17   Muir (1968), p. 116.
18   Muir (1968), p. 116.
19   Muir (1968), p. 118.
20   Theophrastus, 371 – *c.* 287 BCE, was the successor of Aristotle in the Peripatetic school. His work – if it is in fact his – *The Characters*, is a series of sketches of moral types. The work has much influence and many imitators: for example the Characters of *The Spectator* (1711–12) under Joseph Addison (1672–1719) and Richard Steele (1672–1729).
21   Muir (1968), p. 119.
22   Muir (1968), p. 119.
23   Muir (1968), p. 120.
24   Muir (1968), p. 120.
25   M R James (1862–1936) finishes it for him in 'There was a Man Dwelt by a Churchyard', *The Complete Ghost Stories of M R James* (London: Edward Arnold, 1931).
26   Muir (1968), p. 121.
27   Muir (1968), p. 122.
28   Muir (1968), p. 123.
29   Muir (1968), pp. 123–4.
30   Leavis (1984), p. 175.
31   Leavis (1984), p. 176.
32   Muir (1968), pp. 133–4.
33   Stephen Orgel, '*Cymbeline* at Santa Cruz', *Shakespeare Quarterly*, 52 (2001), p. 278.
34   Muir (1968), p. 118.
35   G Wilson Knight, *The Crown of Life* (London: Methuen, 1947), p. 9.
36   Leavis (1984), p. 174.
37   Knight (1947), p. 128.
38   Knight (1947), p. 76.
39   Knight (1947), p. 78.
40   Knight (1947), p. 78.

41   Knight (1947), p. 79.
42   Knight (1947), p. 80.
43   Knight (1947), p. 99.
44   Knight (1947), p. 97.
45   Knight (1947), p. 97.
46   See L C Knights, 'How Many Children Had Lady Macbeth? An Essay in the Theory and Practice of Shakespeare Criticism' (1933), in Knights, *Explorations: Essays in Criticism Mainly on the Literature of the Seventeenth Century* (Harmondsworth: Penguin Books in association with Chatto & Windus, 1964), pp. 11–30.
47   *The Tempest*, ed. Stephen Orgel (Oxford: Oxford University Press, 1987) pp. 32–5.
48   *Shakespeare's Workmanship* (Cambridge: Cambridge University Press, 1931) pp. 238–9.
49   G Wilson Knight, *The Crown of Life* (London: Methuen, 1947), p. 100.
50   See *The Burning Oracle: Studies in the Poetry of Action* (London, New York, and Toronto: Oxford University Press, 1939).
51   Wilson Knight (1947), p. 128.
52   *Nor Shall My Sword: Discourses on Pluralism, Compassion and Social Hope*, Chatto & Windus: London, 1972.
53   *Review of English Literature* 5 (April 1964), 72–82.

6 THE WINTER'S TALE: LATER MODERNS

1   Kenneth Muir (ed.), *Shakespeare, The Winter's Tale: A Casebook* (Basingstoke: Macmillan, 1968), p. 88.
2   Muir (1968), pp. 88–9.
3   Muir (1968), p. 89.
4   Study of magic and religion by the Scottish anthropologist Sir James Frazer (1854–1951) first published in two volumes in 1890, growing to twelve volumes by the time of the third edition of 1906–15. The work of the school of anthropology influenced by Frazer was itself a potent influence on Modernist writing.
5   Knight (1947), 989–9.
6   Nevill Coghill, 'Six Points of Stage-craft in *The Winter's Tale*', *Shakespeare Survey* 11 (1958), p. 35.
7   Muir (1968), p. 91.
8   Muir (1968), p. 93.
9   Muir (1968), p. 93.
10   Muir (1968), p. 94.
11   Muir (1968), p. 97.
12   Muir (1968), p. 99.
13   Muir (1968), p. 99.
14   S L Bethell, *The Winter's Tale, A Study* (London: Staples Press, 1947), p. 47 ff.
15   Muir (1968), p. 99.
16   Muir (1968), p. 99.
17   Muir (1968), p. 100.
18   Muir (1968), p. 103.
19   Muir (1968), p. 103.
20   Muir (1968), p. 105.
21   Muir (1968), p. 106.
22   Muir (1968), pp. 106–7.
23   See e.g. David Norbrook, *Poetry and Politics in the English Renaissance* (Oxford: Oxford University Press, 2002); David Moore Bergeron, *Textual Patronage in English Drama, 1570–1640* (Aldershot: Ashgate, 2006); Arthur F. Kinney, *A Companion to Renaissance Drama* (Oxford: Blackwell, 2002).
24   Muir (1968), pp. 108–9.

25   Muir (1968), p. 109.
26   Muir (1968), p. 109.
27   Muir (1968), p. 111.
28   Muir (1968), p. 111.
29   Muir (1968), p. 114.
30   Muir (1968), p. 197.
31   Muir (1968), p. 187.
32   Muir (1968), p. 184.
33   Muir (1968), p. 187.
34   Muir (1968), p. 188.
35   Muir (1968), p. 189.
36   Muir (1968), p. 189.
37   Muir (1968), p. 190.
38   Muir (1968), pp. 191–2.
39   G Wilson Knight, *The Crown of Life* (London: Methuen, 1947), p. 106.
40   Muir (1968), p. 192.
41   Muir (1968), pp. 192–3.
42   Muir (1968), p. 193.
43   Muir (1968), p. 195.
44   Muir (1968), p. 197.
45   Muir (1968), p. 198.
46   Muir (1968), p. 202.
47   Muir (1968), p. 203.
48   Muir (1968), p. 203.
49   Muir (1968), p. 204.
50   Muir (1968), p. 204.
51   John Dover Wilson and Sir Arthur Quiller-Couch (eds), *The Winter's Tale* (Cambridge: Cambridge University Press, 1931, reprinted 1950), p. xx.
52   Louise G Clubb, 'The Tragicomic Bear', *Comparative Literature Studies*, 9 (1972), pp. 17–30.
53   Muir (1968), pp. 205–6.
54   Muir (1968), p. 206.
55   Muir (1968), p. 208.
56   'I challenge anyone *to read the play through*, to seat himself at table, and write down what Autolycus does to further the plot (my italics)', Sir Arthur Quiller-Couch, *Shakespeare's Workmanship* (Cambridge: Cambridge University Press, 1931) pp. 238–9. It will be noted that Q assumes that the critic is a *reader*, not a member of the audience.
57   Muir (1968), p. 211.
58   Muir (1968), p. 210.
59   Muir (1968), p. 211.
60   Muir (1968), p. 212.
61   Muir (1968), pp. 191–2.
62   F R Leavis, *Nor Shall My Sword* (London: Chatto & Windus, 1972), p. 62.
63   Leavis (1972), p. 62.
64   Muir (1968), p. 212.
65   W K Wimsatt (ed.), *Dr Johnson on Shakespeare* (Harmondsworth: Penguin, 1969), p. 71.
66   Muir (1968), p. 219.
67   Muir (1968), p. 221.
68   Muir (1968), pp. 221–2.
69   J I M Stewart, *Character and Motive in Shakespeare* (London: Longman, 1949), pp. 30–7.
70   Muir (1968), p. 222.
71   Muir (1968), p. 222.
72   Muir (1968), p. 216.

73   Muir (1968), p. 224.
74   Muir (1968), p. 226.

7   *THE WINTER'S TALE*: POST-MODERNS

1   G Wilson Knight, *The Crown of Life* (London: Methuen, 1947), p. 9.
2   The reader should consult Dr Samuel Johnson's *Preface* to his edition of the plays of Shakespeare for an introduction to his theory of criticism, and Matthew Arnold's essays, 'The Function of Criticism at the Present Time' and 'The Study of Poetry' for Arnold's critical theory. Arnold's essay on Wordsworth is exemplary.
3   William Morse, 'Metacriticism and Materiality: The Case of Shakespeare's *The Winter's Tale*', *English Literary History* 58 (1991), 283–304.
4   Simon Palfrey, *Late Shakespeare: A New World of Words* (Oxford: Oxford University Press, 1997).
5   S Viswanathan, 'Theatricality and Mimesis in *The Winter's Tale*: The Instance of "Taking By The Hand"', in S Nagarajan and S Visnawathan (eds), *Shakespeare in India* (Oxford: Oxford University Press, 1987); James Edward Siemon, ' "But It Appears She Lives": Iteration in *The Winter's Tale*', *PMLA* 89 (1974), pp. 10–16; Richard Proudfoot, 'Verbal Reminiscence and the Two-part Structure of *The Winter's Tale*', *Shakespeare Survey* 29 (1976), pp. 67–78; see also Stephen Booth, 'Exit, Pursued by a Gentleman Born', in Wendell M Aycock (ed.), *Shakespeare's Art from a Comparative Perspective*, *Proceedings: Comparative Literature Symposium* (Lubbock, Texas: Texas Tech. Press, 1981).
6   *The Winter's Tale*, eds, Susan Snyder and Deborah T Curren-Aquino (Cambridge: Cambridge University Press, 2007) pp. 24–5; Murray M Schwartz, 'Leontes' Jealousy in *The Winter's Tale*', *American Imago*, 30: 3 (1973), pp. 250–73; C L Barber and Richard Wheeler, *The Whole Journey: Shakespeare's Power of Development* (Berkeley: University of California Press, 1986); Kay Stockholder, *Dream Works: Lovers and Families in Shakespeare's Plays* (London and Toronto: University of Toronto Press, 1987); Janet Adelman, *Suffocating Mothers* (London: Routledge, 1992); Peter B Erickson, 'Patriarchal Structures in *The Winter's Tale*', *PMLA*, 97 (1983), pp. 819–29; David Schalkwyk, ' "A Lady's 'Verily' is as Potent as a Lord's": Women, Word and Witchcraft in *The Winter's Tale*', *English Literary Renaissance*, 22 (1992), pp. 242–72; Marilyn Williamson, *The Patriarchy of Shakespeare's Comedies* (Detroit, Michigan: Wayne State University Press, 1986); Michael D Bristol, 'In Search of the Bear: Spatiotemporal Form and the Heterogeneity of Economies in *The Winter's Tale*', *Shakespeare Quarterly*, 42 (1991), pp. 145–67; Catherine Belsey, *Shakespeare and the Loss of Eden: The Construction of Family Values in Early Modern Culture* (Hampshire: Palgrave Macmillan, 1999).
7   Graham Holderness, Nick Potter and John Turner, *Shakespeare: Out of Court* (Basingstoke: Macmillan, 1990), pp. 239–40.
8   Lewis S Feuer (ed.), *Karl Marx and Friedrich Engels: Basic Writings on Politics and Philosophy* (Glasgow: Collins Fontana, 1969), p. 84.
9   Karl Marx, *The Poverty of Philosophy* (Moscow: Progress Publishers, 1955), p. 95.
10   Graham Holderness, Nick Potter and John Turner, *Shakespeare: Out of Court* (Basingstoke: Macmillan, 1990), pp. 239–40.
11   Holderness, Potter and Turner (1990), p. 240.
12   Holderness, Potter and Turner (1990), p. 240.
13   Cavell, Stanley, 'Recounting Gains, Showing Losses (A Reading of *The Winter's Tale*)', *Disowning Knowledge in Six Plays of Shakespeare* (Cambridge: Cambridge University Press, 1987), p. 1.
14   Cavell (1987), p. 3.
15   Cavell (1987), pp. 3–4.
16   Cavell (1987), p. 5.
17   Cavell (1987), p. 6.

18   Cavell (1987), p. 8.
19   Cavell (1987), p. 10.
20   Cavell (1987), p. 16.
21   Cavell (1987), p. 16.
22   Cavell (1987), p. 34.
23   Traub (1992), p. 42.
24   Valerie Traub, *Desire and Anxiety: Circulation of Sexuality in Shakespearean Drama* (London: Routledge, 1992), p. 41.
25   Cavell (1987), p. 193.
26   Cavell (1987), p. 193.
27   Cavell (1987), p. 194.
28   Cavell (1987), p. 195.
29   Cavell (1987), p. 195.
30   Cavell (1987), p. 196.
31   Cavell (1987), p. 199.
32   Cavell (1987), p. 200.
33   Cavell (1987), p. 203.
34   Cavell (1987), p. 204.
35   Cavell (1987), p. 204.
36   Cavell (1987), p. 198.
37   Cavell (1987), p. 126.
38   Cavell (1987), p. 127.
39   Cavell (1987), p. 202.
40   Cavell (1987), pp. 204–5.
41   Cavell (1987), p. 206.
42   Cavell (1987), p. 207.
43   Cavell (1987), p. 213.
44   Cavell (1987), p. 215.
45   Cavell (1987), p. 215.
46   Cavell (1987), pp. 217–18.
47   Valerie Traub, *Desire and Anxiety: Circulation of Sexuality in Shakespearean Drama* (London: Routledge, 1992), p. 41.
48   Traub (1992), p. 42.
49   Traub (1992), p. 43.
50   Traub (1992), p. 42.
51   Traub (1992), p. 44.
52   Traub (1992), p. 44.
53   Traub (1992), pp. 44–5.
54   Traub (1992), p. 45.
55   Traub (1992), p. 45.
56   Traub (1992), p. 45.
57   Traub (1992), p. 45.
58   Juliet Dusinberre, *Shakespeare and the Nature of Women* (New York: Barnes and Noble, 1975); Marilyn French, *Shakespeare's Division of Experience* (New York: Ballantine Books, 1981); Irene G Dash, *Wooing, Wedding and Power: Women in Shakespeare's Plays* (New York: Columbia University Press, 1981); Marianne L Novy, *Love's Argument: Gender Relations in Shakespeare* (Chapel Hill: University of North Carolina Press, 1984).
59   Coppélia Kahn, *Man's Estate: Masculine Identity in Shakespeare* (Berkeley: University of California Press, 1981); Carol Thomas Neely, *Broken Nuptials in Shakespeare's Plays* (New Haven, Connecticut: Yale University Press, 1985); Marilyn L Williamson, *The Patriarchy of Shakespeare's Comedies* (Detroit, Michigan: Wayne State University, 1986).
60   Carol Cook, ' "The Sign and Semblance of Her Honour": Reading Gender Difference in *Much Ado about Nothing*', *PMLA* 101: 2 (1986), p. 187. See also Linda Bamber, *Comic*

Women, Tragic Men: A Study of Gender and Genre in Shakespeare (Stanford, California: Stanford University Press, 1982).
61   Traub (1992), p. 47.
62   Traub (1992), p. 49.
63   Holderness, Potter, Turner (1990), p. 232.
64   Holderness, Potter, Turner (1990), p. 233.
65   Holderness, Potter, Turner (1990), p. 234.
66   Holderness, Potter, Turner (1990), p. 234.
67   Holderness, Potter, Turner (1990), p. 234.
68   Holderness, Potter, Turner (1990), pp. 234–5.

8   *THE TEMPEST*: MODERNS

1   F R Leavis, 'The Criticism of Shakespeare's Late Plays', *The Common Pursuit* (London: Hogarth, 1984), p. 179.
2   Leavis (1984), pp. 179–80.
3   D J Palmer (ed.), *Shakespeare, The Tempest: A Casebook* (Hampshire: Macmillan, 1968), p. 122.
4   Palmer (1968), p. 122.
5   Palmer (1968), p. 123.
6   Palmer (1968), p. 123.
7   Palmer (1968), p. 124.
8   Palmer (1968), pp. 128–9.
9   Palmer (1968), p. 129.
10   Palmer (1968), p. 131.
11   Palmer (1968), pp. 133–4.
12   Palmer (1968), p. 135.
13   Palmer (1968), p. 150.
14   Palmer (1968), p. 148.
15   Palmer (1968), p. 150.
16   G Wilson Knight, *The Crown of Life* (London: Methuen, 1948), p. 9.
17   Palmer (1968), p. 244.
18   Palmer (1968), p. 245. Kott reminds us of 'What cares these roarers for the name of king? (1.1.16)'.
19   Palmer (1968), p. 245.
20   Palmer (1968), p. 245.
21   Palmer (1968), pp. 246–7.
22   Palmer (1968), p. 244.
23   Palmer (1968), p. 247.
24   Palmer (1968), p. 247.
25   Palmer (1968), p. 250.
26   Palmer (1968), p. 251.
27   Palmer (1968), p. 251.
28   Palmer (1968), p. 251.
29   Palmer (1968), p. 252.
30   Not just the Fool in *Lear*: consider Feste in *Twelfth Night*.
31   Palmer (1968), p. 255.
32   Palmer (1968), p. 258.

9   *THE TEMPEST*: POST-MODERNS

1   Alden T Vaughan and Virginia Mason Vaughan, *Shakespeare's Caliban: A Cultural History* (Cambridge: Cambridge University Press, 1991).

2   Sexual ambiguities in *The Tempest* are explored by Kate Chedgzoy in *Shakespeare's Queer Children: Sexual Politics and Contemporary Culture* (Manchester: Manchester University Press, 1995) and by Jonathan Goldberg's 'Under the Covers with Caliban', in D C Greetham (ed.), *The Margins of the Text* (Ann Arbor, Michigan, 1997), 105–28.

3   'Nymphs and Reapers Heavily Vanish: The Discursive Con-Texts of *The Tempest*', in J Drakakis (ed.), *Alternative Shakespeares* (London: Methuen, 1985), pp. 191–205.

4   Barker and Hulme (1985), p. 191.

5   Barker and Hulme (1985), p. 192.

6   Barker and Hulme (1985), p. 193.

7   Barker and Hulme (1985), p. 194.

8   Barker and Hulme (1985), p. 194.

9   Perhaps the most succinct account of Marx's theory of the 'periods' into which history can be divided is to be found in his 'Preface' to the never-completed 'A Contribution to the Critique of Political Economy'.

10   Barker and Hulme (1985), p. 195.

11   Frank Kermode (ed.), *The Tempest* (London: Methuen, 1964), p. lxiii.

12   Kermode (1964), p. lxxv.

13   Kermode (1964), p. 103n.

14   Enid Welsford, *The Court Masque* (Cambridge: Cambridge University Press, 1927), pp. 335ff.

15   Barker and Hulme (1985), p. 199.

16   Kermode (1964), p. 67n.

17   Barker and Hulme (1985), p. 201.

18   Barker and Hulme (1985), p. 202; Kermode (1964), p. lxxv.

19   Barker and Hulme (1985), pp. 202–3.

20   Barker and Hulme (1985), p. 203.

21   Barker and Hulme (1985), p. 203.

22   Barker and Hulme, pp. 203–4.

23   Barker and Hulme, pp. 204–5.

24   Paul Brown, '"This Thing of Darkness I Acknowledge Mine": *The Tempest* and the discourse of colonialism', in Jonathan Dollimore and Alan Sinfield (eds), *Political Shakespeares* (Manchester: Manchester University Press, 1994), pp. 48–69.

25   Brown (1985), p. 48.

26   Brown (1985), p. 50.

27   Brown (1985), p. 58.

28   Brown (1985), p. 59.

29   Brown (1985), p. 54. The incident is recorded in John Nichols (ed.), *The Progresses and Public Processions of Elizabeth* (1823; rpt. New York: Burt Franklin, 1966), vol. I, pp. 436–8.

30   See Michel Foucault, *History of Sexuality: vol. I: An Introduction*, trans. Robert Hurley (Harmondsworth: Penguin, 1981).

31   A useful definition of this term, and of many other terms like it, can be found in David Macey (ed.), *The Penguin Dictionary of Critical Theory* (Harmondsworth: Penguin, 2000).

32   Brown (1985), p. 66.

33   Brown (1985), p. 66.

34   Brown (1985), p. 68.

35   Meredith Anne Skura, 'Discourse and the Individual: The Case of Colonialism in *The Tempest*', *Shakespeare Quarterly*, 40 (1989), pp. 42–69. Reprinted in *Shakespeare: An Anthology of Criticism and Theory, 1945–2000*, ed., Russ McDonald (Oxford: Blackwell, 2004), pp. 817–45: subsequent references to Skura are to this anthology.

36   Fredric Jameson, *The Political Unconscious: Narrative as a Socially Symbolic Act* (Ithaca, New York: Cornell University Press, 1981).

37   Skura (2004), p. 819.
38   Skura (2004), p. 820.
39   Alden T Vaughan, 'Shakespeare's Indian: The Americanisation of Caliban', *Shakespeare Quarterly*, 39 (1988), pp. 137–53.
40   Skura (2004), p. 822.
41   Skura (2004), p. 827.
42   Skura (2004), p. 831.
43   See Sigmund Freud, 'Character and Anal Erotism' (1908).
44   Skura (2004), p. 832.
45   Skura (2004), p. 833.
46   Skura (2004), p. 834.
47   Skura (2004), pp. 834–5; John B Bender, 'The Day of *The Tempest*', *English Literary History*, 47 (1980), pp. 235–58.

CONCLUSION: FUTURE DIRECTIONS

1   *Shakespeare's Workmanship* (Cambridge: Cambridge University Press, 1913; Pocket edition, 1931), pp. 298–99.
2   *The Tempest*, ed., Frank Kermode (London: Methuen, 1954), p. lxxxi.
3   *Pericles*, ed., Suzanne Gossett (London: Thomson, 2004), p. 8.
4   Kenneth Muir (ed.), *The Winter's Tale: A Casebook* (Basingstoke: Macmillan, 1968), p. 118.
5   William Wordsworth, *Poetical Works*, ed., Thomas Hutchinson, revised by Ernest de Selincourt (Oxford: Oxford University Press, 1950), p. 737.

Bibliography

GENERAL

Frye, Northrop, *A Natural Perspective: The Development of Shakespearean Comedy and Romance*. New York: Columbia University Press, 1965.

Hawkes, T (ed.). *Coleridge on Shakespeare*. Harmondsworth: Penguin, 1969.

Hazlitt, William, *The Characters of Shakespeare's Plays*. London: Dent, 1906.

Leavis, F R, 'The Criticism of Shakespeare's Late Plays: A Caveat', in *The Common Pursuit*. London: Hogarth Press, 1984.

Quiller-Couch, Sir Arthur, *Shakespeare's Workmanship*. Cambridge: Cambridge University Press, 1918; Pocket edition, 1931.

Strachey, Giles Lytton, 'Shakespeare's Final Period', *Books and Characters*. London: Chatto & Windus, 1922.

Tillyard, E M W, *Shakespeare's Last Plays*. London: Chatto & Windus, 1938.

Wilson Knight, G, *The Crown of Life*. London: Methuen, 1947.

Wimsatt, W K (ed.). *Dr Johnson on Shakespeare*. Harmondsworth: Penguin, 1969.

PERICLES

Gossett, Suzanne (ed.). *Pericles*. London: Thomson, 2004.

Hoeniger, F D (ed.). *Pericles*. London: Methuen, 1963.

CYMBELINE

Butler, Martin (ed.). *Cymbeline*. Cambridge: Cambridge University Press, 2005.

Kahn, Coppélia, *Roman Shakespeare: Warriors, Wounds and Women*. London: Routledge, 1997.

Mikalachki, Jodi, 'The Masculine Romance of Roman Britain: Cymbeline and Early Modern English Nationalism', *Shakespeare Quarterly*, vol. 46, no. 3, (Autumn, 1995), pp. 301–22.

Nosworthy, J M (ed.). *Cymbeline*. London: Methuen, 1955.

THE WINTER'S TALE

Bethell, S L, *The Winter's Tale, a Study*. London: Stapes Press, 1947. (An excerpt from this essay is reprinted in Muir, 1968).

Cavell, Stanley, 'Recounting Gains, Showing Losses (A Reading of *The Winter's Tale*)', in *Disowning Knowledge in Six Plays of Shakespeare*. Cambridge: Cambridge University Press, 1987.

Coghill, Nevill, 'Six Points of Stage-craft in *The Winter's Tale*', *Shakespeare Survey* 11 (1958), p. 35. An excerpt from this essay is reprinted in Muir, 1968.

Ewbank, Inga-Stina, 'The Triumph of Time in *The Winter's Tale*', *Review of English Literature* 5 (1964), pp. 83–100. An excerpt from this essay is reprinted in Muir, 1968.

Holderness, Graham, Nick Potter and John Turner, *Shakespeare: Out of Court*. Basingstoke: Macmillan, 1990.

Mahood, M M, *Shakespeare's Wordplay*. London: Routledge, 1968. An excerpt from this essay is reprinted in Muir, 1968.

Muir, K (ed.). *Shakespeare: The Winter's Tale*. Hampshire: Macmillan, 1968.

Schanzer, Ernest, 'The Structural Pattern of *The Winter's Tale*', *Review of English Literature* 5 (1964), pp. 79–82. An excerpt from this essay is reprinted in Muir, 1968.

Traub, Valerie, *Desire and Anxiety: Circulation of Sexuality in Shakespearean Drama*. London: Routledge, 1992.

THE TEMPEST

Barker, Francis and Peter Hulme, '*Nymphs and Reapers Heavily Vanish: The Discursive Contexts of* The Tempest', in J. Drakakis (ed.) *Alternative Shakespeares*. London: Methuen, 1985.

Brown, Paul, '*"This Thing of Darkness I Acknowledge Mine"*: The Tempest *and the Discourse of Colonialism*', in J. Dollimore (ed.) *Political Shakespeares*. Manchester: Manchester University Press, 1994.

Kott, Jan, *Shakespeare Our Contemporary*. trans. Boleslaw Taborski (2nd edition, London: Methuen, 1967). An excerpt from this essay is reprinted in Palmer, 1968.

Palmer, D J (ed.). *Shakespeare, The Tempest: A Casebook*. Hampshire: Macmillan, 1968.

Skura, Meredith Anne, 'Discourse and the Individual: The Case of Colonialism in *The Tempest*', *Shakespeare Quarterly*, 40, 1989, pp. 42–69.

WORKS BASED ON OR DERIVING FROM *THE TEMPEST*
Books

Césaire, Aimé, *Une Tempête*. Paris: Seuil, 1969; 1997.

Kirsch, Arthur C (ed.). *The Sea and the Mirror: A Commentary on Shakespeare's The Tempest by Wystan Hugh Auden*. Princeton, New Jersey: Princeton University Press, 2003.

Films (in chronological order)

Forbidden Planet, 1956, dir. Fred M Wilcox.
Prospero's Books, 1991, dir. Peter Greenaway.
The Tempest, 1979, dir. Derek Jarman.

Opera

Tippett, Michael, *The Knot Garden*: first performed at the Royal Opera House, Covent Garden, 2 December 1970.

FURTHER READING

All quotations from and references to the plays have been standardized to the Oxford edition of 1988 (Stanley Wells and Gary Taylor (eds), *William Shakespeare: The Complete Works*, Oxford: Oxford University Press, 1988). Where a quoted passage from a scholar or critic itself quotes from the plays and the quoted material does not conform to the Oxford (1988) text I have standardized and indicated that I have done so, using square brackets for act, scene and line references where those given by the author do not conform to Oxford (1988).

This guide to further reading is meant to supplement the bibliography. The following 'Casebook' and 'New Casebook' collections provide an excellent set of selections from many of the essays discussed in this Guide and offer a useful starting point:

Murphy, Patrick M (ed.). '*The Tempest*': *Critical Essays*. London: Routledge, 2001.

Thorne, Alison (ed.). *Shakespeare's Romances*. Hampshire: Palgrave Macmillan, 2002.

White, R S (ed.). *The Tempest*. Hampshire: Palgrave Macmillan, 1999.

The editions used and mentioned throughout this *Guide* also provide excellent bibliographies and guides to further reading. There follows a selection of the most recent studies.

GENERAL

Bishop, T G, *Shakespeare and the Theatre of Wonder*. Cambridge: Cambridge University Press, 1996.

Callaghan, Dympna, *Shakespeare without Women*. London: Routledge, 2000.

Eggert, Katherine, *Showing Like a Queen: Female Authority and Literary Experiment in Spenser, Shakespeare and Milton*. Philadelphia: University of Pennsylvania Press, 2000.

Foakes, R A, *Shakespeare: The Dark Comedies to the Last Plays*. London: Routledge, 1971.

James, Heather, *Shakespeare's Troy*. Cambridge: Cambridge University Press, 1997.

Mahood, M M, *Bit Parts in Shakespeare's Plays*. Cambridge: Cambridge University Press, 1992.

Marshall, Cynthia, *Last Things and Late Plays: Shakespearean Eschatology*. Carbondale: Southern Illinois University Press, 1991.

McCabe, Richard, *Incest, Drama and Nature's Law*. Cambridge: Cambridge University Press, 1993.

McDonald, Russ, *Shakespeare's Late Style*. Cambridge: Cambridge University Press, 2006.

McGuire, Philip, *Shakespeare: The Jacobean Plays*. Basingstoke: Macmillan, 1994.

McMullan, Gordon and Jonathan Hope (eds). *The Politics of Tragicomedy*. London: Routledge, 1992.

Miola, R S, *Shakespeare and Classical Tragedy*. Oxford: Clarendon Press, 1992.

Miola, Robert, ' "An Alien People Clutching Their Gods"? Shakespeare's Ancient Religions', *Shakespeare Survey*, vol. 54 (2001), pp. 31–45.

Orgel, Stephen, 'The Pornographic Ideal', in *Imagining Shakespeare: A History of the Texts and Visions*, Oregon Shakespeare Festival, 2003, pp. 112–44.

Paster, Gail Kern, *The Body Embarrassed: Drama and the Disciplines of Shame in Early Modern England*. Ithaca, New York: Cornell University Press, 1993.

Paster, Gail Kern, 'The Unbearable Coldness of Female Being: Women's Imperfection and the Humoral Economy', *English Literary Renaissance*, vol. 28 (1998), pp. 416–40.

Vickers, Brian, *Shakespeare: Co-author*. Oxford: Oxford University Press, 2002.

Warren, Roger, *Staging Shakespeare's Late Plays*. Oxford: Oxford University Press, 1990.

PERICLES

Skeele, David (ed.). *Pericles: Critical Essays*. New York and London: Routledge, 2000.

Skeele, David, *Thwarting the Wayward Seas: A Critical and Theatrical History of Shakespeare's Pericles in the Nineteenth and Twentieth Centuries*. Newark, New Jersey and London: University of Delaware Press, 1998.

CYMBELINE

Brockbank, J P, 'History and Histrionics in *Cymbeline*', *Shakespeare Survey*, vol. 11 (1958), 42–8.

Danson, Lisa, ' "The Catastrophe Is a Nuptial": The Space of Masculine Desire in *Othello, Cymbeline* and *The Winter's Tale*', *Shakespeare Survey*, vol. 46, (1993), pp. 69–79.

Hayles, Nancy K, 'Sexual Disguise in *Cymbeline*', *Modern Language Quarterly*, vol. 41 (1980), pp. 230–47.

Wayne, Valerie, 'The Career of Cymbeline's Manacle', *Early Modern Culture*, vol. 1 (2000), pp. 1–21.

THE WINTER'S TALE

Bennett, Kenneth, 'Reconstructing *The Winter's Tale*', *Shakespeare Survey*, vol. 46 (1994), pp. 81–90.

Danson, Lisa, ' "The Catastrophe Is a Nuptial": The Space of Masculine Desire in *Othello, Cymbeline* and *The Winter's Tale*', *Shakespeare Survey*, vol. 46 (1993), pp. 69–79.

Enterline, Lynn, '"You Speak a language That I Understand Not": The Rhetoric of Animation in *The Winter's Tale*', *Shakespeare Quarterly*, vol. 48 (1997), pp. 17–44.

Hamilton, Donna, '*The Winter's Tale* and the Language of Union, 1604–1610', *Shakespeare Studies*, vol. 21 (1993), pp. 228–52.

Hunt, Maurice (ed.). *The Winter's Tale: Critical Essays*. New York: Garland, 1995.

Hunt, Maurice, '"Bearing Hence": Shakespeare's *The Winter's Tale*', *Studies in English Literature*, vol. 44, no. 2 (2004), pp. 333–43.

Knapp, James A, 'Visual and Ethical Truth in *The Winter's Tale*', *Shakespeare Quarterly*, vol. 55 (2004), pp. 253–78.

Kurland, Stuart, '"We Need No More of Your Advice": Political Realism in *The Winter's Tale*', *Studies in English Literature 1500–1900*, vol. 31 (1991), pp. 365–86.

Lamb, Mary Ellen, 'Engendering the Narrative Act: Old Wives' Tales in *The Winter's Tale, Macbeth*, and *The Tempest*', *Criticism*, vol. 40 (1998), pp. 529–53.

Mowat, Barbara A, 'Rogues, Shepherds, and the Counterfeit Distressed: Texts and Infracontexts in *The Winter's Tale*', *Shakespeare Studies*, vol. 22 (1994), pp. 58–76.

Nuttall, A D, '*The Winter's Tale*: Ovid Transformed', in A B Taylor (ed.) *Shakespeare's Ovid: The Metamorphoses in the Plays and Poems*. Cambridge: Cambridge University Press, 2000, pp. 135–49.

Orgel, Stephen, '*The Winter's Tale*: A Modern Perspective', in Barbara Mowat and Paul Werstine (eds) *The Winter's Tale*. New York: Folger Shakespeare Library, 1998.

Parker, Patricia, 'Temporal Gestation, Legal Contracts, and the Promissory Economies of *The Winter's Tale*', in Nancy E Wright, Margaret W Ferguson and A R Buck (eds), *Women, Property, and the Letters of the Law in Early Modern England*. London and Toronto: University of Toronto Press, 2004, pp. 26–49.

Parker, Patricia, 'Sound Government, Polymorphic Bears: *The Winter's Tale* and Other Metamorphoses of Eye and Ear', in Helen Regueiro Elam and Frances Ferguson (eds) *The Wordsworthian Enlightenment: Romantic Poetry and the Ecology of Reading*, Baltimore, Maryland: Johns Hopkins University Press, 2005, pp. 172–90.

Richards, Jennifer, 'Social Decorum in *The Winter's Tale*', in Jennifer Richards and James Knowles (eds) *Shakespeare's Late Plays: New Readings*, Edinburgh: Edinburgh University Press, 1999, pp. 75–91.

Snyder, Susan, 'Mamillius and Gender Polarization in *The Winter's Tale*', *Shakespeare Quarterly*, vol. 50 (1999), pp. 1–8.

Sokol, B J, *Art and Illusion in The Winter's Tale*. Manchester: Manchester University Press, 1994.

THE TEMPEST

Goldberg, Jonathan, 'Under the Covers with Caliban', in D C Greetham (ed.) *The Margins of the Text*. Ann Arbor, Michigan: University of Michigan Press, 1997, pp. 105–28.

Hall, Kim F, *Things of Darkness: Economies of Race and Gender in Early Modern England*. Ithaca, New York: Cornell University Press, 1995.

Halpern, Richard, '"The Picture of Nobody": White Cannibalism in *The Tempest*', in David Lee Miller, Sharon O'Dair and Harold Weber (eds) *The Production of English Renaissance Culture*. Ithaca, New York: Cornell University Press, 1994, pp. 262–92.

Kastan, David Scott, '"The Duke of Milan and His Brave Son": Dynastic Politics in *The Tempest*', in Virginia Mason Vaughan and Alden T Vaughan (eds) *Critical Essays on Shakespeare's 'The Tempest'*, New York: G K Hall, 1998, pp. 91–103.

Lamb, Mary Ellen, 'Engendering the Narrative Act: Old Wives' Tales in *The Winter's Tale, Macbeth*, and *The Tempest*', *Criticism*, vol. 40 (1998), 529–53.

McDonald, Russ, 'Reading *The Tempest*', *Shakespeare Survey*, vol. 43 (1990), pp. 15–28.

Norbrook, David, '"What Cares These Roarers for the Name of King?": Language and Utopia in *The Tempest*', in McMullan, Gordon and Jonathan Hope (eds) *The Politics of Tragicomedy*. London: Routledge, 1992.

Paul, Brown, '"This Thing of Darkness I Acknowledge Mine": *The Tempest* and the Discourse of Colonialism', in Jonathan Dollimore (ed.) *Political Shakespeares*. Manchester: Manchester University Press, 1994, pp. 48–69.

Thomson, Ann, '"Miranda, Where's Your Sister?": Reading Shakespeare's *The Tempest*', in Susan Sellers (ed.) *Feminist Criticism: Theory and Practice*. Hemel Hempstead: Harvester, 1991, pp. 45–55.

Vaughan, Alden T and Virginia Mason Vaughan, *Shakespeare's Caliban: A Cultural History*. Cambridge: Cambridge University Press, 1991.

Index